MYTH AND IDEOLOGY
IN
AMERICAN CULTURE

Centre d'Etudes et de Recherches
Nord-Américaines et Canadiennes

Liliane Blary, Rachel Blau DuPlessis, Pierre Denain, Régis Durand,
Michel Fabre, Kathleen Hulley, Bernard Jacquin, Monique Lecomte,
Jean-Philippe Lecourt, Jean-Michel Rabaté, Catherine Rihoit,
Alain Solard, Roland Tissot.

edited by Régis Durand

MYTH AND IDEOLOGY

IN

AMERICAN CULTURE

PUBLICATIONS DE L'UNIVERSITE DE LILLE III
S.P. 18 — 59650 Villeneuve-d'Ascq

CONTENTS

Régis DURAND

Introduction

Le moutonnement indéfini des commen-
taires est travaillé de l'intérieur par le
rêve d'une répétition masquée : à son
horizon il n'y a peut-être rien d'autre
que ce qui était à son point de départ, la
simple récitation.

Michel Foucault,
L'ordre du discours

In the field of twentieth-century critical discourse (social and
literary) the two decisive interventions have been psychoanalysis
and the study of ideology. Although they are historically distinct,
recent developments show that far from being rival systems of
analysis, the internal dynamics of each carries over into the
other [1]. The emphasis of the essays collected here falls, however,
on the study of ideological problems — though several of them
show how closely related the two fields can be.

Men live in ideology, produce it, manipulate it and are
manipulated by it. This might be felt to be reason enough to devote
some energy to the study of ideological processes in a culture that
has often shunned the word itself but is in fact — like all others —
structured by deep, powerful and conflicting ideological currents.
Such a study, however, begs an almost discouraging number of
questions among which are : first, the inevitable problem of the
definition of ideology ; second, the nature of the conceptual and
methodological instruments required to deal with it. Fortunately, a
number of important contributions have appeared in the last few
years, here and in the U.S.A. That is not to say, of course, that they
provide all the answers. In fact, they probably raise more problems
than they solve, but they have at least paved the way for further
inquiry. Even a presentation limited to the latest developments in
the fields would be too long to be undertaken here and, besides,
would remain necessarily incomplete, for the object we are
concerned with is both controverted and fluctuating. It may be

preferable, then, to restrict ourselves to a few lines of force that seem to have emerged and that have direct relevance to the essays that follow.

Studies of ideology seem to fall, roughly speaking, into two types of approaches : the Marxist approach, and the communicational approach. Naturally, the distinction, like all such distinctions, is hardly more than a convenience, but it may help clarify a few points[2].

The Marxist approach is well known : ever since Marx and Engels, the analysis of ideology in society and in art has had a long and uninterrupted history, in which the works of Lukács and Brecht stand out prominently. Recently, however, in the wake of the considerable development of social sciences and related disciplines, a number of works, individual and collective, have begun to reconsider the traditional Marxist positions. One could take as an example two publications, one in France, the other in the U.S.A., that had considerable impact : the proceedings of a symposium held in 1970 at Cluny on «Littérature et ideologies» at the initiative of the Marxist journal *Nouvelle Critique*, and an issue of *New Literary History* on «Ideology and Literature» in 1973[3]. The first thing that strikes one is that the very notion of *a* Marxist theory of ideology has been superseded by that of a Marxist *typology of ideologies* and of their functions under a given mode of production and social relations. Another is that the classic restrictive concepts of ideology as «falsity» or «false consciousness», and as isomorphism (or «mirror-image», reflection of economic and social infrastructures) are now almost completely discarded, or at least severely qualified. For G.A. Huaco, for instance, a fresh look at Marx's theory shows that

> For him an ideology is not a new object or symbol, but a way of examining cultural creations along specific dimensions and an attempt to relate these creations to a specific social base. In principle, every cultural creation is ideological to some extent [4].

From there, Huaco goes on to suggest that the concept of ideology as falsity or distortion be replaced by a consideration of *mythical patterns* in works of fiction, and that this «modified version of Marx's model» can serve as «an adequate methodological tool for empirical investigations in the sociology of literature » [5]. Indeed several of the articles in this collection rely explicitly or implicitly on such a modified version of the sociological approach to literature. This model offers undoubtedly the advantage of being, as his author claims, compatible with other techniques of interpretation and analysis of myth (structuralist, Freudian, etc.). But as a theoretical model it cannot be considered quite satisfactory for it leaves out many important considerations. Among the first that come to mind is the problem of the relation between ideology and truth, a problem which remains essential even when the simplistic notion of ideology as distortion has been discarded. Jonathan Culler makes the point very aptly when he writes :

> An ideology is a theory which justified particular economic, political, and intellectual practices by concealing their historical origins and making them the natural components of an interpreted world. In this sense the notion of ideology is dependent on a conception of truth : one cannot recognize an ideology unless one understands the true nature of a particular situation, and one's task is to expose the reality which lies beneath the ideological superstructure [6].

This position, of course, has to be immediatly corrected if it is not to appear excessively dogmatic : the opposition between ideology as falsity, and «objectivity» or «fact» as truth, is far too simplistic and not dialectical. As Luis Prieto reminds us, «an ideological mode of knowledge is not necessarily false, nor is an objective mode of knowledge necessarily true» [7].

Ideology is a *process*, that of the subject-object dialectic, and a theory of ideology that does not take into account the intervention of a subject as well as the intervention of contradictions can be only of little use.

At this stage, there appear to be two ways of considering ideology, or rather the ideological process. Both ways see it as a cognitive process, but whereas the first sees it, very broadly, as the way the historical subject visualizes himself in the historical universe, makes himself the (mediate or immediate) object of his self-knowledge, the other, more restrictedly and critically, sees it as a degraded form of cognition.

Of the first wilhelm Girnus gives an excellent definition, which delineates both the inclusiveness and the looseness of the approach :

> As the hypothetical matrix in which the historical subject-object dialectic takes place, ideology is dependent, in respect to its truth-content, upon the particular stage this dialectic has reached. Its truth is therefore as subordinate to the law of development as every other truth. For this reason, we do not

share the view that ideology is the opposite of science. Economics, history, the social sciences, jurisprudence : all these, like religion, philosophy, art and poetry, are by definition ideological forms through which man as historical subject visualizes his position in the historical universe. These sciences are concerned primarily not with object-cognition, but with the laws of motion that govern a thinking, feeling, desiring, acting subject in different spheres, vis-à-vis a configuration of objects he himself has placed in the world. Statements made by these sciences are therefore essentially ideological events, independent of the theories and standpoints, interests and historical perspectives they express [8].

Most Marxists would probably find it difficult to agree with the concept of science Girnus uses, in as much as he makes no mention of its theoretical and critical functions [9].

The second definition is characteristic of a good many European theoreticians, among whom Roland Barthes, Luis Prieto, Umberto Eco to name only a few. It sees ideology at precisely the point where process «coagulates», where certain types of discourse appear whose aim is to conceal the historical nature of subject and object, to «naturalize» the cognitive process or the production of discourse and make it appear as the necessary consequence of its object [10]. An important body of criticism is geared at destroying the «naturalness» ideology imposes on historical processes, and R. Barthes has given masterful examples of what can be done to erase the gloss of ideological «innocence» from literature or social mythologies.

The communicational approach is implicit as soon as we are dealing with the relation between a subject, his cognitive process, and his production of discourse. That is why it shouldn't be seen in opposition to the first approach, but rather as an expansion or an exploration of certain aspects not explicitly developed in the Marxist theory. Of the different elements of the communication process (sender, receiver, channel, code, message), *sender, code,* and *connotation* are given particular attention. Eliseo Verón, for instance, insists, after R. Barthes, on the importance of connotation as a vehicle for ideology. For Verón, the connotative meaning of a message is what he calls its «metacommunicational dimension» : it is the part of the process of transmission of information «concerned not with the content of the messages, but with the

selective and combinatory operations made by the sender» [11].
At the societal level, connotation is a communicational dimension
through which «ideological metamessages» are transmitted, quite
apart from their referential — or denotative — functions.
Ideology, then, appears as a structural condition of messages
within a human language system (which also includes scientific
communication) :

> Just as in interpersonal relationships communicators transmit through
> metacommunication the 'image' they have with regard to the ongoing
> relationship and its norms, so the social mass-messages always meta-
> communicate a certain 'image' of society, a certain conception of social reality,
> the way of organizing it, and the way of understanding its different aspects.
> As this image and these ways of conceiving and understanding social reality
> are not the only possible ones, and as they are transmitted through meta-
> communication, *i.e.*, at an implicit level of meaning, the term *ideological
> communication* seems faily adequate [12].

Several of the essays in the second part of the book attempt a
pragmatic study of some aspects of this level of «communication»
in American society, with particular emphasis on minorities.

Verón's theory has far-reaching implications. First, it suggests
that an ideological system is not a set of values or propositions, but
rather «a set of semantic rules defining the constrictions to which
the production of a certain kind of proposition is subject», in other
words a system that generates messages, a *program* [13]. Second, if
it is true that ideology always exists as a level of meaning, it should
also be noted that it operates only when a particular message is
presented as «naturally» the only possible way of talking about its
subject. When that is not the case, the «ideological effect» can be
neutralized :

> The 'ideological effect' disappears when the selective and combinatory
> operations are denoted within the language, making explicit in this way the
> conditions under which the messages have been produced [14].

That the communicational analysis of ideology can — and does —
have a critical function is also underlined by Umberto Eco in his
attempt to study ideology on a semiotic basis. Ideology appears,
according to Eco [15] when a message becomes «coagulated»,
hardened, a formula with a fixed connotation which prevents its
having different significations in connection with different sub-
codes. Like Verón, Eco sees ideology as a matrix. It is indeed «the
very structure of the code», in as much as it is, according to him,
the *syntactic* structure of the code which generates the semantic

structure, and not the other way round. Ideology, then, becomes «the natural form that semantic systems take because of syntactic laws» 16. The semiotic formalization of ideology is interesting because it enables us to consider it in relation to rhetoric. It is manifest that rhetoric is always ideological, if only because a certain way of using language always identifies itself with a certain conception of society : rhetorical subversion never goes without ideological subversion, and *vice versa*. Eco's approach reminds us that the task of ideological analysis is always and perhaps foremost a study of *forms*, before being a study of «content» (values, myth, etc.). The importance of such a position, which is in the line of the Russian Formalists, will be immediatly perceptible if one thinks of poetry, painting architecture, and other artistic practices in which the ideological dimension cannot easily be apprehended at the level of «subject» or «theme», but becomes significant at the level of invention and transformation of forms. Eco's approach remains distinct from the Marxist approach on many points, but it is not unrelated to recent Marxist attempts at integrating semiotics and ideological studies, a good example of which is Charles Grivel 's study on the novel, already mentioned. It remains more limited than either the Marxists' or Verón's, if only because it does not concern itself specifically with the conditions of production of messages ; but it is a useful starting-point for the study of the critical functions of form, especially in periods of change and experimentation.

*

*   *

This rapid survey of some aspects of ideological studies does perhaps less than justice to the many stimulating works that have appeared in the last few years. But its purpose was essentially to sketch out the theoretical background against which the essays in this collection appear. In fact it is an «introduction» that should probably come as a postscript since it is being written after the essays have been collected. Which is to say that, as will be evident to the reader, no overall *a priori* theory was imposed upon the individual studies. What brought the different contributors to-gether, however, was the conviction that the ideological dimension is an essential component of a culture, and that it can and must be studied in fields as diverse as poetry, the novel, avant-garde painting, music, social relations, and many other fields that are not represented here.

The three essays on poetry included here exemplify three different ways of approaching the ideological dimension in a genre that is often studied from a strictly aesthetic point of view. Rabaté shows how a marxist approach can combine with semiotics to describe the complex interplay between truth and ideology, intertextuality and the various «voices» of Pound ; Lecourt explores Roethke's seeming rejection of ideology, of the «generalized other», and demonstrates the ideological nature of the poet's gesture as well as its psychic repercussions ; Blau DuPlessis examines three contemporary women poets and traces the dialectic between a critique of personal consciousness and a critique of political consciousness, and in particular of the long-held cultural ideologies dealing with women. The critique of personal consciousness, it appears, can only be successfully completed in poems that invent new myths to criticize the old, «myths historically specific rather than eternal». It is this new mode of the poems that combine lyric means of perception with a political and historical consciousness that Blau DuPlessis terms «lyric documents».

In her essay on James's novel *The Bostonians*, Rihoit, througha close reading of the structure of actants and of some linguistic features, studies the workings of one of those cultural ideologies. Her essay complements Blau DuPlessis's ; but it also provides the ground for a striking confrontation between ideological factors in two very different forms of the American novel : the intricate fiction of Henry James and the detective novels of Dashiell Hammett. Hulley's essay on Hammett demonstrates how his fiction is based on an ambivalent attitude to the ideological assumptions of American society, and the psychic patterns that accompany it. Tissot's study of Super-Realism is an investigation of the ideological connotations that lie behind certain artistic techniques and attitudes. It is a study of the kind that should be carried out in every area of artistic production. Jacquin's essay on Black Music in Part II, while paralleling Tissot's on painting, shows that problems require a different approach in the context of the Black American culture.

The essays in the second part deal precisely with such a context, and as they are introduced seperately 'by **Michel Fabre**, it is not necessary   to dwell on them at length. It is interesting to note, however, that the very *nature* of ideological problems appears to be different in the context of cultural minorities : problems tend to be of a much less theoretical nature, even in literature or in the arts. The issues are complicated, sometimes hopelessly so, but they always have direct relevance to immediate conditions of being in the community. This, in itself, is an observation of an ideological nature, since it evidences the pressures of the dominant ideology on cultural minorities and the urgent need it creates to define oneself over and against the «white» ideology.

Many important aspects and fields are not represented, if only because space did not allow it. But we believe that such studies are a necessary task, especially in contemporary American culture, because ideological studies, as W. Girnus reminds us, become particularly relevant in periods of change :

> Everyman produces ideology everyday, in more or less obvious ways. This is the reason for the enormous coagulative power of the images, thoughts and ideas that form the assemblage we term ideology, which then appears as a crystallized system of intellectual-moral coordinates, and the task of the specialists is to see to the filtration and purification of this coagulum for social purposes. The function and structure of ideological processes become especially noticeable when traditional forms reveal themselves as incapable of including new world-historical content and therefore have to be overturned and even destroyed [17].

No one will question that American culture — perhaps the whole of Western culture — is at such a juncture where traditional forms in literature and the arts, and traditional patterns in social relations are straining under the thrust of forces of change. This book, the first publication of the CENTRE D'ETUDES ET DE RECHERCHES NORD-AMERICAINES ET CANADIENNES at the University of Lille III is a modest contribution to the study of the ideological currents and foundations in contemporary American culture. We hope other studies will follow, here and elsewhere.

NOTES

1. As is demonstrated by the Lacanian or neo-Lacanian equation of ideology with «l'imaginaire». See for instance C.B. CLEMENT : **Le pouvoir des mots**, symbolique et idéologie, Paris, Mame, 1974.

2. Indeed a case can be made for an integrative conception in which all other approaches (communicational, semiotic, psychoanalytical) would eventually fit into the framework of the Marxist approach. On the compatibility of the communicational approach with the Marxist approach see Eliseo Verón, «Linguistique et sociologie, Vers une 'logique naturelle' des mondes sociaux», **Communications 20** (1973), 246-278, especially pp. 265-266.

3. **Littérature et idéologies**, Colloque de Cluny II, **Nouvelle Critique,** N° special 39 bis, 1970 ; **New Literary History (NLH)**, Vol. IV, N°3 (Spring 1973). See also **littérature 12** (Dec. 1973) («Codes littéraires et codes sociaux»), and 13 (Avril 1974) («Histoire/Sujet»). As for books : Tel Quel, **Théorie d'ensemble,** Paris, Le Seuil, 1968 ; Julia Krieteva, **Sémélotiké,** Le Seuil, 1969 ; and more recently Charles Grivel, **Production de l'intérêt romanesque,** The Hague : Mouton, 1973, a remarkably documented study of the ideology of the novel.

4. George A. Huaco, «Ideology and literature», **NLH,** IV, 3, 421-422.

5. **ibid.**, p. 436.

6. Johathan Culler, «Structure of ideology and ideology of structure», **NLH,** IV, 3, 471.

7. Luis Prieto, **Pertinence et pratique**, Paris : Editions de Minuit, 1975. (Ch. 5 : «Pertinence et idéologie», 159).

8 Wilhelm Girnus, «On the problem of ideology and literature», **NLH,** IV, 3, 485.

9. On the particular problem of the relations between science and ideology, Girnus's position is closer to the communicational approaches discussed below than it is to the Marxist definitions. See for instance L. Althusser : «...L'idéologie comme système de représentations se distingue de la science en ce que la fonction pratico-sociale l'emporte en elle sur la fonction théorique (ou fonction de connaissance)» **(Pour Marx,** Paris : Maspéro, 196, 238).

10. L. Prieto, **op. cit.**, 159-160.

11. Eliseo Verón, «Ideology and social sciences : a communicational approach», **Semiotica** III, i (1971), 65.

12. **ibid.**, 68.

13. **ibid.**

14. **ibid.**, 71.

15. Umberto Eco, **La structure absente**, Paris : Mercure de France, 1972 (for the French translation), 150.

16. **ibid.**, 151.

17. W.Girnus, **op. cit.,** 486.

PART I

Jean-Michel RABATE

«Sounds Pound» :

history and ideology in the China Cantos

Serious history revives, by bit, in our time. There
is no serious history without study of social texture
wherein IS the money factor. Book-fools (blessed be
the ideogram for that word), understanding nothing
of their present, naturally do NOT pick the live
details from past chronicle.

The LESSON of Chinese history ? As I can have
no pretence to «potting» it here, might nevertheless
be of two kinds. By implication, we might more
despise and suspect the kind of education we (my
generation) received, and we might acquire some
balance in NOT mistaking recurrence for innovation. [1]

1. THE VOICES IN THE SOCIAL TEXTURE

Pound's specific illegibility is perhaps more easily ascertainable
in the hundred pages he devoted to the history of China (Cantos
LII to LXI [2]) than in the later Cantos where obscurity is measured
by the forthcoming deciphering of personal allusions, of hidden
quotations, which would bring us back to an illusory future
plenitude. There is nothing of the kind in these Cantos, the project
is explicit enough, we know we are to read a detailed exposition of
the evolution of China from the origins to the eighteenth century :
at that point, China is replaced in the economy of the Cantos by
the America of John Adams. The source is almost one single book,
and we can follow step by step the notes Pound took from de
Mailla's history [3]. In various prose writings of that time we find
the gist of the double «lesson» to be drawn from Chinese history : a
mistrust of official scholarship, a sense of balance afforded by
historical relativization.

But the rather simple aim, pointing towards a real reading of
the texts of Confucian China, becomes increasingly complicated as
we shift from the abrupt statements of the *Guide to Kulchur* to the
layered chronicle constituted by the dynastic Cantos. These Cantos
do little to inform the lay reader about the history of China :
the bluntness of transitions, the lack of elementary explanations
would frustrate his desire for knowledge ; on the other hand,
sinologists would no doubt be horrified by such bold vistas over
vast and heterogeneous periods.

How can we refer the tangle of «details», of anecdotes, of
changing and confusing names, to the totalizing insight into a
study of «social texture», itself determined by the monetary level ?

Let us recall that for Pound only fools deal with history without including economy, an economy hinged to the concept of usury, i.e. the process by which an undue interest is levied on natural and agricultural production, thus undermining it. How can we connect the highly individual style and its off-hand imitations of spoken dialect with the will to have writers play a social role in a state which must needs be totalitarian ? And finally, how is it possible to appreciate the faceted interplay of varied styles which handle five or six different historical references, while tracing out a series of ideological instances which are at times contradictory ?

This paper proposes to outline a marxist approach that could account for the stylistic play and insert it between the ideological dominants and reality as defined by history. It should try to build up a model capable of posing, if not solving, the problem of the musical voices in Pound's text, assigning them less to real history or real economy than to the way the reading-writing subject is involved in ideological discourses, so as to keep — or to restore — its radicality to the creative gesture of *The Cantos*.

2. TRUTH, KNOWLEDGE. IDEOLOGY

> Napoleon has invented a word, Ideology,
> which expresses my opinion. (C.33, p.164)

> and they had an ideological war (C.LV, p.312)

Pound notably displaces the problem of truth in history towards the introduction of some kind of knowledge that must be afforded obliquely to the reader. He does not aim at a «historical truth», he does not, for example, try to multiply the sources ; one source is enough as soon as it is of Confucian inspiration and can admit certain graftings (such as the *Chi King* in Canto LIX, or other quotations from Confucius) and certain ellipses :

> Wars,
> > wars without interest
> boredom of an hundred years' wars. (C.LIII, p.282)

And above all, when he follows de Mailla, Pound is careful to erase the introductory presentation of the historian's chief concern, that is truth. De Mailla sees in the Chinese historiographers the perfect model of the work he achieves while writing his own book. The Chinese historians feel a responsibility to truth, they prefer to «lose their lives rather than to betray the truth.» Here is an example of their typical scrupulous accuracy : «These historiographers, impelled by the sole desire to tell the truth, carefully observe all the things as they happen, which they write down on a loose leaf, each one for himself, without communicating anything to anybody...» (BK I, iii). Thus the dynastic records are accumulated, and only collected when the reigning family loses the throne or disappears. De Mailla also quotes this statement from the judge presiding the Court of the Empire Historians : «This impartial severity must be history's main attribute, if it is to check the Princes and to prevent them from committing mistakes.» Pound echoes this in : «History a school-book for Princes» (C.LIV, p.292, between quotation marks), but he for his own part neglects the asceticism implied by the constitution of real records, and invokes the authority of Confucius to condense his own material : «He (Confucius) had 2000 years of documented history behind him which he condensed so as to render it useful to men in high position, not making a mere collection of anecdotes as did Herodotus» [4]. Pound enhances the practical usefulness of such teachings for the creation of a social order, appealing to enlightened Princes : «The proponents of a world order will neglect at their peril the study of the only process that has repeatedly proved its efficiency as social coordinate» [5].

Far from cultivating the neutral tone of self-effacement, Pound chooses to be partial, and subordinates the historian's disinterested pursuit to his will to rationalize and introduce order into history. This is the point where the discourses generated by ideology will come into full play. Let us try to analyse for example the beginning of the «China Cantos». The Cantos have up to now brought some fragments of truth about economics, which are summed up at the opening of Canto LII, the first of this new section :

> And I have told you of how things were under Duke Leopold in Siena
> And of the *true* base of credit, that is the abundance of Nature
> with the whole folk behind it.
> (p.267, italics mine)

All the world's misfortunes stem from ignorance : «IGNORANCE, sheer ignorance ov the natr ov money / sheer ignorance of credit and circulation» (id.). But in order to fight against that ignorance — which is an active force, the omnipresent usury — the mere disclosing of economic mechanisms proves itself inadequate. Pound whishes to convince, but also to persuade, and he is fond of repeating Griffith's statement : «Can't move 'em with a cold thing like economics» [6]. This sequence of Cantos will then provide a new rhetorical strategy, for this new «knowledge» offers us a translation of the *Yueh Ling* (monthly command) of the *LI KI*, the book of rites, with a solemn overture :

> Know then :
> Toward summer when the sun is in Hyades
> Sovran is Lord of the Fire   (C.LII, p.268)

What does this knowledge consist of ? The cyclic return of seasons, each marked by a peculiar rite, weaves a net of correspondences between colours, foods, activities, thus pointing to an ordered and centered cosmos. The shift toward the ritual introduces at the same time a new tone, a new scansion, spacing out our hearing. The only previous example of this dimension was in Canto 49 :

> Sun up ; work
> sundown ; to rest
> (.....)
> The fourth ; the dimension of stillness.
> And the power over wild beasts.   (p.256)

Here, rites are not only a codified ceremony, they organize a «know-how», adapted to every moment. In that case, truth is implicit : Nature creates riches, one must respect Time's natural rhythms, otherwise Usura will proliferate. There is no meta-language about truth, truth speaks from itself :

> Call things by the names. Good sovereign by distribution
> Evil king is known by his imposts.
> Begin where you are said Lord Palmerston.   (p.271)

This is the conclusion of Canto LII. But in order to give the reader a sound insight into good and evil (aiming at telling a good government from a bad one) Pound has brought into play a whole rhetorical form which has formed our ears, providing this musical «sense of proportion» [7], this desire for stillness which must arise from the contemplation of the natural order :

> Month of the longest days
> Life and death are now equal
> Strife is between light and darkness
> Wise man stays in his house   (p.269)

Now this new knowledge constitutes only one of the «voices» which are united to exhibit the history of China : this voice comes up irregularly and entwines itself with the others. Here, the truth of order seems to be dominant. Is the same pattern repeated in the whole section ?

3. STYLISTICS OF THE VOICES.

> We have not even heard of Tai Tsoung
> or of Tchin Tsoung. The America of
> our immediate forebears considered
> ideogram as a laundry check.   (*Kulchur*, p.274)

> And Tchang-tsong wrote of music, its principles
>   Sun-ton made record of rites
> And this was written all in red-character, countersigned by the assembly
> sealed with the Imperial Seal
>   and put in the hall of the forebears
> as check on successors.   (Canto LIV, p.288)

The main difference between the *Guide to Kulchur* and these Cantos resides in the musical possibility of articulating different voices in a poetical text ; the *Cantos* re-utilize the system of the *personae* (masks, voices) scattered in the first poems, while joining them together in a fugal pattern («Rather like, or unlike subject and response and counter subject in fugue» 8). This difference is primarily stylistic, and we just need to give ear to the first two dynastic Cantos to perceive how the voices fan out.

Canto LII began, we have seen, with a very strong assertion of the author apostrophizing us :«And I have told you...» This voice coming from the author soon manifests its spoken character, and respects the distortions of an American accent ; in its sometimes caricatural excesses («sojer», p.321, «millyum», p.314, «iggurunce», p.433, «proppergander», p.353) it is supposed to be Pound's own accent, that twang taking possession of his letters and prose texts : «...ov the natr ov money» (p.267). Against this, the hieratic music of the «record of rites» offers a brutal contrast in the second half of the Canto :

> To this month is SEVEN
>   with bitter smell, with odour of burning
> Offer to gods of the hearth
>   the lungs of the victims   (p.269)

The -th endings («winter ruleth», «cricket bideth») stress the aspect of ritual psalmody in this sacrificial calendar.

Between these two extreme and opposed voices, a third voice appears mid-way in the next Canto, the middle voice of the Chronicle itself : «Yeou taught men to break branches...» (p.272). This is the voice reciting deeds and actions of ancient empires, and it hesitates between the dry technique of shorthand notes from the French text :

28

Fou Hi taught men to grow barley
2837 ante Christum
and they know still where his tomb is   (p.272)

and the vocal dramatization of some episodes :

Hia ! Hia is fallen
for offence to the spirits
for sweats of the people   (p.275)

This recitation which seems about to dominate the following Cantos is soon interrupted by a series of puns, plays on different languages : Greek, French, and Chinese characters. And this is not only the irruption of written signs into the vocal chronicle : the opposition between written and spoken elements also cuts through that new level : for it is at this point that intertextuality [9] disperses the writing and tightens the web of allusions. The Chinese sacred herb Tsing-mo' calls up μῶλυ (p.273), the magic plant through which Odysseus can free himself from Circe's drugs. The French quotation : ·

que vos vers expriment vos intentions et que la musique conforme (p.273)

looks like a «literal» quotation from de Mailla's book, since it is in the «original» language, but we must not forget that Pound very often re-writes his quotations (or just distorts them by quoting from memory only). In the *History* we read : «Que vos vers expriment votre intention et que la musique y soit analogue : qu'elle soit simple et naturelle.» (I, p.93) Pound has chosen, at the cost of a mistake in French, to condense the sentence, in order to bring this nearer to the definitions given by the troubadours («motz el son») : thus he really appropriates the phrase. This last stylistic level is that of the «foreign words and ideograms» which «enforce the text but seldom if ever add anything not stated in the english» (note page 446) ; these «underlinings» help to build the system of echoes, self-quotations and cross-references of the Cantos.

Beside the four stylistic level sketched here, the ritual, the Chronicle, the «Poundisms» and the insertions in foreign tongues, we can distinguish four levels of spatial and temporal references :
—   the essential reference is China and occasionally Japan, from «2837 ante Christum» to the Mandchu dynasty. The chronicle stops in 1735.
—   France and Enlightened Europe are perceived through the Jesuits and de Mailla : a key-period, since it brought about the discovery of Confucius in Europe. The Jesuits play an important

part in China itself (Cantos LVIII to LXI).
— the history of China tends towards the history of the U.S.A.,
that takes the lead in 1735 : «new style John Adams» (p.357).
— Italy, as contemporary with the time of the writing («anno
seidici», p.267) and re-discovering trends forgotten since the
Malatestas, brutally appears in Canto LIV, by an allusion to a
historical submarine manoeuvre :

(Pretty manoeuvre but the technicians watched with their hair standing on end
anno sixteen, Bay of Naples)   (p.291)

Main references	Historical models
Chinese dynasties and Japan....Confucius	
Enlightened Europe...........The Jesuits	
The U.S.A..................Jefferson / Adams	
Contemporary Italy ....Mussolini	

4. A TENTATIVE CLASSIFICATION OF THE VOICES, REFERENCES AND SOCIAL INSTANCES.

Facing the subtle interplay of voices and references, we should
set the problem of the precise interaction of these instances. On
the one hand, we need a theory of ideology that would be supple
enough to account for the complex character of Pound's
discourses ; on the other, we have to be aware that their interaction
allows for a relative autonomy of each instance. Marxist theory too
often reduces art to ideology, which is, in its turn, understood as a
compact machinery. If we succeed in giving a more diversified
layering to ideology, we can then arrive at a concept of different
discursive practices according to different functions of the social
determination of the writer. In Mao Tse-tung's *Lectures about
literature and art*, Badiou [10] distinguishes four categories which
might help us to define our aims and methods : the class-being, a
function of the social origin of the author ; the class-position, that
is the locus of his general outlook and set of problems ; the
class-attitude, or the application of the class-position to precise
problems ; and finally, the class-study, i.e. the theoretical or
cultural tools evolved by the writer to legitimatize his

class-position. As for Pound, we can say that his class-being is American petty-bourgeoisie, whose prejudices he shares (such as anti-semitism, which he condemned at the end of his life, as «a stupid, suburban prejudice» [11]). His class-position includes his peculiar status as poet and impresario, «producer» of poetical movements and discoverer of new talents, and his concern for a rigorous verbal production, his wish to become a «craftsman» (as W. Lewis said [12]) of the verse, «il miglior fabbro» (T.S. Eliot) curing the diseases of language by a careful re-examination of the relation between words and money. His class-attitude covers his specific choices deriving from his position, his decision to extol Confucius, using him as a guide to faith and behaviour («I believe in the Ta Hio») and to expose the evils of usury. Pound's class-study is his activity as translator, as philologist playing on the registers of several languages and civilisations, as well as his quest through universal history in order to reach the origins of Usura.

Such a classification in levels will only prove its usefulness when it works with the texts ; it is operative first if we define the modalities of the transitions from one stratum to the other : in the logical as well as in the historical order, aestheticism takes us from (1) to (2), Confucianism from (2) to (3), practical and theoretical totalitarianism from the total state (3) to universal culture (4).

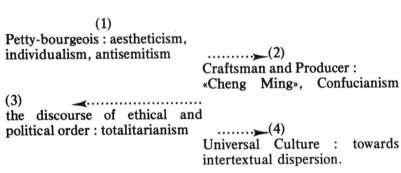

(1)
Petty-bourgeois : aestheticism,
individualism, antisemitism ....➤(2)
Craftsman and Producer :
«Cheng Ming», Confucianism

(3) ◄........................
the discourse of ethical and
political order : totalitarianism ....➤(4)
Universal Culture : towards
intertextual dispersion.

A		B	
Voices	Stylistic markers	Produced discourses	Sociological instances producing discourses
(1)		(1)	
American idiolect	Spoken style	Antisemitism, individualism	class-being : American petty-bourgeoisie
(2)		(2)	
Historical Chronicle	Elliptical style	Poet as crafstman : the integrity of the word	class-position : the writer concerned with the health of language
(3)		(3)	
Impersonal ritual	High, hieratic style	Ethical and political call to order	class-attitude : extolling Confucius attacking Usury
(4)		(4)	
Intertextuality	Quotational style (in original languages)	The literato re-enacting universal culture	class-study : languages, universal history

This tabulation should account for the multiple interactions between the different levels. It is obvious, for example, that passages in French do not only connote the Europe of Enlightenment, and that, even in this case, other instances interfere, as in the following lines :

    TÇIN HIAO told a girl she was 30
       and the strangled him
    (piquée de ce badinage) he drunk at the time (Canto LIV, p.294)

Here, the France of the Jesuits is evoked on the level of the historical chronicle by the introduction of French (quotation, fourth level) and at the same time the chronicle shows its limits as translation, implying the impossibility of rendering this apt expression.

Finally, such a chart is not merely limited to pigeonholing, classifying, but should also be able to throw some light on the dynamic tension between «voices» (inside A) and on the tension between the writing of voices and the subject's involvement in some ideological discourses (between A and B). To test it out, let us come back to the sequence of the Cantos.

5. FUNCTIONS OF «POUND'S VOICE».

> But beautiful as the sentences of the liberati in love with splendour may be, or prestigious as the expressions they use in their chronicles, «the rise of Han», «the age of Han expansion», «the age of Han renaissance» may be, we cannot help feeling that their phrasings are too ambiguous, while appreciating the merits of their case. A more direct way of expressing oneself would be :
> 1) the periods during which we vainly aspired to be slaves ;
> 2) the periods during which we momentarily succeeded in being slaves. These periods constitute a cycle qualified by the former literati of «periods of order» and of «periods of disorder».
>
> *Notes under the lamp*, LUXUN [13]

> «great works by oppression,
> by splendid oppression»   (Canto LIV, p.297)

The style of the Chronicle dominates Canto LII, which is devoted to covering the period going from the mythical Emperors to Confucius. There is an echo of the ritual with the foundation rite of Sié, page 281 :

> RITE IS :
> Nine days before the first moon of spring time,
> that he fast...

If we except usual abbreviations (wd/, shd/, yr., &..), we must wait until Canto LIV to see plays on Pound's voice, on intertextual references and on graphical signs. The names of some Emperors begin to get blurred and they are a pretext for visual echoes :

> The Prince of Ouei put out hochangs *
> put out the shamen and Taotssé
> a.d. 444, putt' em OUT
> in the time of OUEN TI   (p.294)   (* hochangs &c.. = buddhists)

The pun on OUT and OUEN TI, and OU TI next page, calls up puns on OΥ TIΣ (page 457 and 532 for instance) in the Pisan Cantos, which develop the persona of Odysseus. In addition, these pages reveal such expressions as : «Emp'r'r huntin' and the Crown Prince full of saki» (p.295), «...allus droppin' 'em and restorin' 'em» (p.296), «jobs for two millyum men» (p.296). The progressive introduction of this American voice, which would have been completely discordant some pages earlier, follows close upon the enigmatic allusion to the writer's present situation : «(Pretty manoeuvre...)» (p.291). These bracketed lines have no relation whatsoever with their context : no similar date or action are there to echo. The interpolation is deliberate and must create surprise, working as another theme. Here, then, as in other Cantos preceding this «decade», the play of voices begins to be effective through a system of displacements, of abrupt shiftings. It is precisely when this voice — the personal idiom — comes into play, that history undergoes modifications, is «cut» in a more arbitrary and conspicuous way. We ought to follow the text in details, but, to summarize, we will state briefly that this «Pound's voice» has three main functions bearing on :

1) historical selection and temporal rhythms ;
2) the role of Confucius and of Buddhism ;
3) the parallels with the U.S.A. and fascist Italy.

1) From this Canto (LIV) onward, Pound shows that periods follow each other in cycles, that (Chinese) history has a tempo of its own, different from the mere succession of the dynasties. The American idiom stresses the chronicle so as to give it a rhythm it could not acquire by itself, and this rhythm is marked in effects of acceleration or deceleration. We have an example of this page 296 : «halls were set to Kung-fu-tseu / yet again, allus droppin' 'em and restorin' 'em», or again in the next Canto : «The hen sang in MOU'S time, racin', jazz dancin' / and play-actors, Tartars still raidin' «(p.303) and : «Y TSONG his son brought a jazz age HI-TSONG» (p.304). Only this singular idiom could hint to a jazz rhythm, insisting on the decadence of the Empire confronted with the Tartars.

On the other hand, in Cantos LX and LXI, Pound wants to enhance some aspects of the relations between the Jesuits and the Chinese, and his specific voice intervenes to slow down the action, to show Captain Tching Mao's distrust of the Europeans :

and the Dutch are the worst of the lot of them, poifik tigurs (p.347)

or to convey the warning of a mandarin :

You Christers wanna have foot on two boats
    and when boats pulls apart
you will d/n well git a wettin' 'said a court mandarin tellin' 'em.　(p.353)

or to comment on the Portuguese : «...for the Portagoose boss who had sent him / i,e. he wuz honoured but cdn's spill proppergander» (ibid.).

2) The specific voice of Pound also helps to emphasize the role of Confucius in the history of China. First Confucius is opposed quite systematically to Buddhism from the moment that Buddhists prevail in the administration : «And now was seepage of bhuddists...» (p.291) ; this is the point where the Italian sub-marine is mentioned. The Buddhists become all that Pound execrates : «last TÇIN down in a Bhud mess» (p.294) and : «(Foé's, that is / goddam bhuddists.)» (p.296). When everything goes wrong, Buddhists are not far, or the Confucianists have been perverted by them :

> Students went bhud rather than take Kung via Ngan,
> Flood relief, due to Ngan ?
>   joker somewhere ? (p.311)
>
> HOEÏ went *Taozer*, an' I suppose
> Tsaï ran to state usury. (p.311)

Here, Pound deliberately refutes a Chinese legend because it contradicts his starting-point : a Ngan cannot actually have stopped a flood, since he distorts Kung's teachings to suit his private interests ; as for Tsaï King, who is like Ngan a Confucianist tempted by Buddhist interpretations, he must be involved in usurious practices.

But this very voice knows how to sum up the essential principles of a just government (according to Confucius) ; thus, when we read the last of Emperor TAÏ TSONG'S precepts :

> and the last on keepin' up kulchur
>   Saying 'I have spent money on palaces
>   too much on 'osses, dogs, falcons
> but I have united the Hempire (and you 'aven't)   (p.299)

3) Lastly, the third function of this popular as well as individual voice is more evasive but perhaps more effective than that of the former two. It makes us draw continuous parallels with the history of the U.S.A. The most characteristic example is in Canto LX, where we learn about the embargo decreed by Lord Kang : «so our lor KANG layed an embargo / (a bit before Tommy Juffusun's)» (p.346). The leading voice animates the chronicle, enlivens the details and shows their contemporaneity.China and the U.S.A. get superimposed, acclimatized. And the mentions of working men : «an' woikinmen thought of...» (p.352), or the fight against foreign corruption : «And they druv out Lon Coto fer graftin'» (p.352), or the praise of honest peasants who are rewarded only for their

merits : «Chiyeou didn't do it on book readin' / nor by muggin' up history» (p.354), conjure up the first American settlers who are recurrently lurking there, as in filigree : they are these «original» Americans whom Pound protects against monopolies and banks. That is the very theme of the following Cantos («Came Kien, 40 years before 'our revolution'», p.355) which arises from elements disseminated throughout Chinese history :

    patriots need legal advisor
        measures involvin' pro-fessional knowl-edge
    (...)
    Encourage arts commerce an' farmin'   (Canto LXII, p.358)

At that moment, two pages after the last Canto about China, Pound's voice has taken such a rhythmical momentum that its importance is multiplied : Pound, like a ventriloquist, speaks through the personae of Adams and Jefferson, without our perceiving any hiatus.

    common men like the rest of us
    subjekk to   passions   (C. LXII, p.359)

The authority of the «I» who compresses, selects, restrains, speeds up, beats different rhythms, interprets and mimes all the voices becomes then overwhelming :

    and as for Hamilton
    we may take it (my authority, ego scriptor cantilenae)
    that he was the Prime snot in ALL American history
                                            (Canto LXIII, p.367)

Indeed the temptation is already plain in the China Cantos property, since Captain Tching Mao (Canto LX) or Emperor Taï Tsong (Canto LIV) were partly speaking Pound's idiom. But it played against a very layered context : «Died TAÏ TSONG in the 23rd of his reign / And left not more than fifty men in all jails of the empire» (p.299). The «empire» in the voice of the chronicle sounds here against the «hempire» of the «Notes of Conduct» quoted above.

6. MODALITIES OF IDEOLOGY IN THE CHINA CANTOS.

    «Urbanity in external, virtu in internals
        some in high style for the rites
    some in humble ;
    for Emperors ; for the people
    all things are here brought to precisions»   (Canto LIX, p.339)

«IF moral analysis
be not the purpose of historical writing»   (Canto LXII, p.362)

In these Cantos, ideology is more clearly revealed through the strategic domination of one of the voices — this specific American twang — than by the presence of formed ideological blocks which would intrude upon historical narration in order to orientate it : we do not find universal statements that could appear as «truths» without their being backed by some voice situated in the chronicle. Chinese wisdom is for instance undertaken by authentic Chinese characters who replace it in the historical context :
«Zinkwa observed that gold is inedible» (p.316), «Said Tai-Tsou : Kung is the master of emperors» (p.306) or :

> Ruled SIUEN with his mind on the 'Gold Mirror' of TAI TSONG
>   Wherein is written : In time of disturbance
>   make use of all men, even scoundrels.
>   In time of peace reject no man who is wise.   (p.304)

Thus we see Chun Tchi commenting the CHI-KING (Canto LIX) or Lieu-yu-y setting up a system of *Ammassi* approved by the Emperor. The only great exception to this is to be found on page 299 with TAÏ TSONG'S «Notes on Conduct» : «...keepin' up kulchur» for example proves they are presented through Pound's unmistakable voice, not through the chronicle. The fact is yet that, at that point, the selection is more obvious : from a whole series of rules, we only retain rules number 3,5,7,10 and 11 ; and even then, all the expressions concerning the maintenance of unity in the Empire are brought to the fore.

This «wisdom» accumulates in a different way throughout the rest of the chronicle, it is part of it, and words of wisdom are added surreptitiously by Pound's voice, when it comments upon the chronicle or applies this knowledge to facts. The petty-bourgeois ideology of these Cantos then works in a manner quite opposed to that of the nineteenth century bourgeois ideology that could be located for example in Balzac or Austen, it would be nearer to what a Céline achieves.

	1) It does not question the status of its language nor its stylistic levels.
Bourgeois ideology :	2) We notice the presence of ideological blocks, which are hidden in descriptions, analyses, thus transmitting an unavowed reactionary wisdom.

A cultural universality is taken for granted and camouflaged under various statements and maxims.

Petty-bourgeois ideology :

1) It brings into question the status of its language insofar as it is stated in its inter-relation with other instances (such as universal culture, economics...)

2) A strong assertion of an «I-voice» inserts a gesture tending toward order, into the disorder, into the chaos of the languages.

Nature's universality is given at the outset, it is also to be brought back at the end ; it guarantees the universality of a political order that an individual gesture can inaugurate through certain precise discourses.

This is why the wish to go beyond the opposition between knowledge and ignorance by the introduction of a ritual can only be achieved through the «I-voice», which carries out this project, stresses the record that would otherwise be too neutral or too uninterpretative, gives it a scansion defining cycles of order and disorder. Thus, but on the last page only, the style of the chronicle is devoured by that of the individual voice :

```
and condensed the Ming histories
     literary kuss, and wuz Emperor
fer at least 40 years        (p.356, italics mine)
```

The road of history has to curve back to its spring, periodically exhuming Confucius who himself restores the mythical origins of the great Emperors :

```
«Yao and Chun have returned»
     sang the farmers
Peace and abundance bring virtue. «I am
    'pro-Tcheou'» said Confucius five centuries later.
With his mind on this age.        (p.278-279)
```

There is a stylistic hint suggesting that these ten Cantos have a circular structure : the first two and the last two are the only ones to be headed as «Canto n°..», while the remaining eight are only numbered. Now a rapid examination shows that the first two lead to Confucius who sums up the lessons to be drawn musically from the rest. The four intermediate Cantos oppose Confucius to Buddhists (LIV to LVII) and the last four, Confucius to Christians (LVIII to LXI).

	2		4		4
LII	*LIII*	/	LIV LV LVI LVII	/	LVIII LIX *LX LXI*

(In the 2nd cycle of 4, the last 2 (Jesuits) answer the first 2). This reduces a real linear, or dialectical, history to a retrospective and regressive *utopia* moving in cycles. And while history is solved in returns and restorations, economics are dissolved in ritual and ethics.

Pound gains in poetic density, since this movement creates his aesthetics based on recurrent rhythms and patterns which give unity to the Chinese chronicle ; but he loses in accuracy on the level of historical analysis. Instead of an interpretation of history, we have exempla confirming a pre-given agrarian utopia. In the place of a historical methodology or of a «guide» to China, the only truth yielded by the text is of a «socio-logical» kind : Chinese history revisited through Confucius shows that all order begins at home, in one's family, and spreads thereafter to the state, by an exact homology of structure. From the patient inquiry into the causes and effects of usury in various economies, we only retain a moral affirmation or «eternal» constants in human nature, such as filial respect, a sense of responsibility tending to define the social realm — and this ethical assertion itself must then confront usury. Moral analysis indeed becomes the purpose of historical writing, but this historical re-writing ideologically masks a «sociology» which is to be realized in the praxis by its very integration to a totalitarian order.

We have to trust Pound's own voice to give us a sense of historical reading, for no method can be derived from his «ideogrammatic» writing, since it subordinates the scattered fragments to the gesture unifying them. The only traces of a more «historical» method are to be found on the level of the intertextual cross-references ; thus Hanno's periplum evoked in : «periplum not as land looks on map / but as sea bord by men sailing» (p.339) provides a figure for our own progress toward truth. Greek refers to Aristotle's monetary theories :

And King Wang thought to vary the currency

$$\mu \epsilon \tau \alpha \theta \epsilon \mu \acute{\epsilon} \nu \omega \nu \ \tau \epsilon \ \tau \tilde{\omega} \nu \ \chi \rho \omega \mu \acute{\epsilon} \nu \omega \nu$$

against council's opinion.   (p.283)

Italian words (Ammassi, Fondego) allude to modern economy, French curiously introduces the «Cheng Ming» (dénominations correctes). But the chronicle fails to present one characteristic and important feature of Chinese economics, the creation of state — — not bank — notes ; these T'ang notes are mentioned often in Pound's prose-writings[14], but not in Canto LV which deals with this period.

Against these scattered and centrifugal fragments in foreign tongues that have no other centre than the whole array of references to other Cantos and that really show us how a text reads history and is to be read as historical, ritual is there to re-assemble, as a «great bass» underlying Pound's voice ; this voice in turn brings focus and coherence, animates the protagonists, and handles them one after another. Thus in Canto LXI, the recurrent hint to the LI-KI of the beginning :

> and the peasants in gt / mass sang the hymns
> befitting this field work
> as writ in LI KI in the old days   (p.352)

is followed by the typical voice : «You Christers wanna have...» In a paradoxical way, this increasing ritualisation of history, which ends by being only the assertion of a recurring order (of order as recurrence and recurrence as order) very uncritically mimes the (historical) movement through which Confucius has been sanctified, promoted to the rank of official sage and invoked to conceal or initiate all the dynastic restorations in China : «And HIEUN TSONG decreed Kung posthumous honours / That he shd / be henceforth called prince not mere 'maistre' *in all rites*» (p.300, C. LIV, italics mine). Pound does not attempt to dissociate Kung's teachings from more «legalist» applications of his views by tyrannical Emperors [15]. Kung, now the master of rites, organizes and consecrates the ritual of his history which only respects order. History opens on nothing but the assertion of a total, religious and agrarian order.

The legalist overthrows the literato, or rather annexes him, reducing the implications that could be drawn from the intertextual play — fundamentally refractory to an ideology of order — to a few traces from other texts already written, not translated yet. «All order comes into such a norm» (p.339) : it is the ethical norm of Confucian morals, written for Princes and from their point of view :`«History is a school-book for Princes...»

The tension we can notice between truth and ideology, between intertextuality and other voices, comes from the fact that the discourse of order compels the disseminated texts to serve order, at the expense of the polyphonic play, since the other voices are shattered, reduced to partial quotations, and finally completely dependant on some ideological practices.

We have to wait until the Pisan Cantos to hear that polyphony again. The actual trauma of the incarceration brings about not a redistribution of ideological positions, but a layering on the level of

Pound's voice itself. The rapid shifts of tone, the discovery of a new kind of «truth» through the dialogue with oneself and one's past, disentangle the tight net of codified discourses and restart the craftsman's main study, a study of the relations between words and money. At that moment, the whole discourse about Confucius and China, passing to the level of intertextual references — being part of the «past» of *The Cantos* — and conveyed by a discontinuous and «exploded» texture of multiple allusions, functions in a richer and more economical way.

> ...it is for this reason
> that the great gentleman
> must find the precise
> verbal expression for his
> inarticulate thoughts. [16]

NOTES

1. Ezra POUND : **Guide to Kulchur**, (1938), New Directions Paperbooks, 1970, p.277 and p.274. Both quotations come from the chapter : KUNG. «Sounds Pound» comes from James Joyce's **Finnegans Wake**, (1939), third ed., Faber, page 309, line 23.

2. Ezra POUND : **The Cantos**, Faber, 1968 (first ed. Cantos 1-109 : 1964). I use roman figures for the «China Cantos», LII-LXXI. Critics call «China Cantos» the section dealing with China (LII to LXI) and with America («John Adams» : LXII-LXXI). For all other references to **The Cantos** I shall use arabic numerals.

3. Joseph Anne-Marie de Moyriac de MAILLA : **Histoire générale de la Chine**, 12 vols, Paris, 1783.

4. Ezra POUND, **Confucius (The Unwobbling Pivot, The Great Digest, The Analects)**, New Directions Paperbooks, 1969, p.19.

5. Ibid. This comes from the Note preceding : **Ta Hsio, The Great Digest.**

6. **Guide to Kulchur**, p.105. Also in Canto 19.

7. **Guide to Kulchur**, p.283 : «The magic of music is in its effect on volition. A sudden clearing of the mind of rubbish and the re-establishment of a sense of proportion.»

8. Ezra POUND, **Selected letters 1907-1941**, ed. Paige, New Dir. Paperbooks, 1971, p.210. Letter to Homer L. Pound, 11/4/1927.

9. Julia Kristeva used this term after Bakhtin's analysis of Dostoievsky and Rabelais to replace «intersubjectivity» and trace the movement in which a text «reads» others texts, is implicitly or explicitly constituted by other texts. See Julia KRISTEVA, **Sêméîôtikê. Recherches pour une sémanalyse**, Seuil, 1969.

10. Mao Tse-tung's text was written in May 1942, opening and closing a meeting in Yenan. A. BADIOU comments on it in : «L'autonomie du processus esthétique», **Cahiers Marxistes-léninistes**, 12-13, 1966, p.77-89.

11. Interview with Allen Ginsberg, June 1968, publ. M. Reck. Quoted in Sullivan's **Penguin Critical Anthology**, p. 354.

12. Wyndham LEWIS, in **Time and Western Man**, (1927) Beacon Press, 1957, Book I, «The Revolutionary Simpleton» thus characterizes Joyce, Pound and Gertrude Stein.

13. LUXUN (Lou Sin), **Un combattant comme ça**, selected texts ed. by M. Loi, Editions du Centenaire, 1973, p.86.

14. Ezra POUND, **Selected Prose 1909-1965**, ed. Cookson, Faber, 1973, p.260 («What is money for ?» (1939)) and p.313 («Gold and Work» (1944)). The first reference places the event in «A.D. 840», the second in «856».

15. See Etiemble, **Confucius**, Gallimard, Idées, 1970, Introduction and passim.

16. **Confucius, Ta Hsio : The Great Digest**, p. 51.

Jean-Philippe LECOURT

Theodore Roethke :

the inner wilderness and the barrier of ideology

In an article entitled «The Case Against Robert Frost» [1], Malcom Cowley opposes two distinct traditions in American Letters. The one, starting from Charles Brockden Brown, «our first professional novelist», was continued by Poe, Melville and Henri James, and extends into the late work of Hemingway and Faulkner. It consists in «striking far inward into the depths of the self and, if a label were needed, might be called the tradition of the Inner Wilderness». The other, extending from Whitman through Dos Passos, consists on the contrary in «standing on a height to observe the panorama of nature and society». The difference between the two traditions is much more than an opposition between two artistic viewpoints : it goes far beyond the realm of aesthetics to reveal two opposed attitudes towards ideology. Indeed, being inward-looking, the tradition of the Inner Wilderness implies a refusal to deal with the concerns of the social group and even to reflect any system of political, social and moral values commonly referred to as «ideology». On the surface at least, in its desire to probe the mysteries of the self, it would refuse to be the vehicle of ideology, whereas the other tradition would accept to be involved in it.

To say that Roethke belongs to this first tradition enables us to underline a few basic features of his poetry : that it is clearly a poetry of the self from which society is virtually absent, that his world is to a large extent a self-generated world, and that his sensibility is non-historical in so far as it is unrelated with the preoccupations, experiences and modes of feeling of his time. Going one step further, one might repeat the view often expressed by critics that Roethke's lack of interest in ideology contributes to limit his stature as a poet. This view however fails to provide us with an answer to a central question : How can we explain Roethke's refusal of ideology and what is the impact of this refusal on the process of poetic creation ?

If we are not satisfied with the mere realization that ideology is absent in Roethke's poetry, if we think that an artist cannot totally abstract himself from the environment he is steeped in, then we must take the paradoxical view that Roethke's refusal of ideology is itself the product of an age which is surfeited with it. In other words, that this stand against ideology is indeed ideological. This is precisely what M.L. Rosenthal suggests after re-asserting the common opinion that Roethke's poetry is exclusively inward-looking and totally unrelated to his time :

We have no other modern American poet of comparable reputation who has absorbed so little of the concerns of his times into his nerve-ends, in whom there is so little reference to the character and experiences of the age-*unless the damaged psyche out of which he spoke be taken as its very embodiment.*(italics are mine) [2]

Thus, taking this paradoxical view, we shall attempt to define the ideological content of Roethke's refusal of ideology, while showing how his poetic impulse finds its origin in his «damaged psyche» ; how his ideological isolationism, so to speak, determines the nature of his poetic world, of his poetic sensibility, and even of his poetic mode of expression.

Roethe's refusal of ideology, first of all, explains the very composition of his poetic world, a world which, in the words of Denis Donoghue, is «distinctly underpopulated» [3]. Indeed, apart from the omnipresent «I», the only characters to be found in his poetry are the Mother, the Father, the Lover and a few persons drawn directly from his childhood. His refusal of ideology may be taken as sheer misanthropy ; but more interestingly, it also represents a deliberate attempt to isolate the self from the pressures of society. The self is not defined by any social influence, but by all the natural objects - flowers, birds, darkness, fish, mould, light, insects, moss, etc — that make up a kind of primeval garden. This deliberate exclusion of society as a basis for self-definition means that Roethe's refusal of ideology is not passive but active ; that it is at the root of the poetic impulse, giving it its original impetus.

Roethke's non-ideological isolationism has nothing to do with indifference or lack of interest, but is of a militant nature. It should be understood as the dynamic opposition against the intrusion of society into the realm of the self, an opposition which determines the creation of his poetic world. His refusal of ideology is far more radical that a simple quarrel with the various «isms» that compete for the possession of the mind of modern man in the sense that it tries to reject even the social basis of the self for being destructive of the soul.

At this stage it seems that the term «ideology» ought to be extended far beyond its common usage, if one wants to get a better understanding of the nature of Roethke's quarrel with it. Ideology can be identified with the concept of the «generalized other» defined by G.H. Mead in *Mind, Self, and Society* as «the form in which the social process or community enters as a determining factor into the individual thinking» :

> It is in the form of the «generalized other», Mead writes , «that the social process influences the behavior of the individuals involved in it and carrying it on, i.e., that the community exercises control over the conduct of the individual members ; for it is in this form that the social process or community enters as a determining factor into the individual thinking. In abstract thought the individual takes the attitude of the generalized other toward himself, without reference to its expression in any particular other individuals ; and in concrete thought he takes that attitude in so far as it is expressed in the attitudes toward his behavior of those other individuals with whom he is involved in the given situation or act [4].

Seen from this angle, ideology is not only a collective structure of meaning and reference by which the categories of thought and the axioms of logic become self-evident ; it is not only the vehicle for concepts and representations developed in society which thus offers a sure basis for communication between individuals, but it is also part of the individual consciousness as a kind of barrier, as a sort of watchdog against the vagaries of the individual thinking.

Roethke's poetic impulse can be seen as a reaction against the repressive character of the generalized other and all that limits the possibilities of the individual man. Like the body, ideology is perceived as an unbearable burden which the self must lay down at all cost if it is to find its freedom and its true identity. After all, poetry for Roethke was an act of defiance. As Alan Seager put it,

> Roethke suspected that poetry, having no voice in the community where he lived, was anti-social. It was even subversive because the poet tore down all kinds of carefully erected façades, went right into the house, and cut up rough. Poetry was akin to crime [5].

Thus the intention to «keep open house» which he proclaims right at the beginning of his poetic career coincides with this reaction against ideology. Not only is it at the root of his poetic impulse, but it is also the starting point of the development of his poetry. «To keep open house» means tearing down all the ideological walls so as to get rid of what he called the «dreck»of contemporary life, of «the multiplicity, the chaos of modern life» so as to find «the way of establishing a personal identity in the face of that chaos» [6]. It also means a tremendous effort, which often goes as far as rage or fury, to destroy that generalized other which is part of himself, to return to bare essentials and rediscover a state of naked simplicity and absolute innocence :

My truths are all foreknown,
This anguish self-revealed,
I'm naked to the bone,
With nakedness my shield.
Myself is what I wear :
I keep the spirit spare.   «Open House»   *CP*. p.3.

This explains why what W.D. Snodgrass calls «a perilous rage against the forms of the world» 7 does not find an outlet into a picture of alienation in contemporary society. His aim is not to depict the modern waste land or to show the destructive effects of ideology for the self, but to find a way *out* of alienation, a new nakedness which will enable him to find his personal identity : the *Son* must be *lost* so that he may later find himself.

The real purpose of the few representations of society in Roethke is not to dramatize the ideological void of the contemporary world, as in T.S. Eliot for instance, but rather to represent the self submitted to the generalized other and bogged down in a state of spiritual emptiness. A poem like «The Longing» (*CP*. p.187) can be taken as a perfect example of this mode of representation. What appears to be a direct picture of contemporary society is in fact the description of «a bleak time» in which the self has been so corrupted by the generalized other as to be totally unable to «transcend this sensual emptiness». Yet the evocation of the horrors of modern life has the important effect of rousing the rage of the poet, which will give him the courage to deny his ideological self, confront nothingness, and later be reborn. It is precisely this ideological self that Roethke destroys in the opening lines of the poem with a pent-up fury which appears in the cumulative rhythm and the sybillant quality of the lines, until finally :

...The spirit fails to move forward,
But shrinks into a half-life, less than itself,
Falls back, a slug, a loose worm
Ready for any crevice
An eyeless starer.

This self-destructive rage is necessary for him to recover his essential nakedness, to become «bare as a bud, and naked as a worm», to become part of the Garden through the identification with the lower forms of life — for him to be granted his new identity through the confrontation with nothingness :

Out of these nothings
—All beginnings come.

Thus, Roethke's creative energy finds its origins in the destruction of his ideological self, a destruction which leads to a confrontation with nothingness, to a regression which is necessary for the poet to re-establish his personal identity in a self-generated world — the world of the Garden.

Roethke's refusal of ideology determines the creation of a mythic world which is essentially pastoral since the Garden replaces the generalized other as the basis of personal identity. This is the world of his childhood ; the cold landscape of Michigan where «the marsh, the mire, the void is always there, immediate and terrifying»[8] ; and the more familiar landscape surrounding his father's famous greenhouses, the woods, the field, the river, etc... Being based on intimate memories of childhood, this world is a highly personal one. This essential feature of Roethke's world is not only due to the ideological emptiness of our modern age which has deprived the modern poet of any common myth, thus forcing him back upon his own experience and imagination, but to his rejection of ideology which in any case would have turned him away from ready-made modes of thought. Roethke could not accept fo follow T.S. Eliot

> Down the passage which we did not take
> Toward the door we never opened
> Into the rose-garden [9].

His could not be the Garden of any Utopian Tradition : it had to be private, and therefore rely mainly on what Louis L. Marz called «the inner force of memory» [10].

In the tradition of the Inner Wilderness, as in *Walden, Moby Dick*, or *Huckleberry Finn*, the hero withdraws from society toward nature. The Garden which is created is far more that a mere decor : it is somehow a metaphor of the mind being reconstructed on a non-ideological basis. Roethke's Garden thus develops against the generalized other, against the background of spiritual stasis and «sensual emptiness» which characterizes the mind of modern man. It counterbalances the destructive influence of ideology and restores the creative energy of the poet by providing him with a key metaphor for the growth of a new personal identity :

> And soon a branch, part of a hidden scene,
> The leafy mind, that long was tightly furled,

Will turn its private substance into green,
And young shoots spread upon our inner world.

«The Light Comes Brighter» *CP*. p.II

The Garden thus operates the necessary transformation of negation into affirmation, of sterile violence into creative power, of stasis into growth, of alienation into identification.

As in «The Far Field» for instance, once the ideological self has been abolished, along with its horrible chaos of complexities and artificialities, the hero finds himself «naked to the bone», he can return to first things, and identify himself throuth sheer contact with essentials :

—Or to lie naked in the sand,
In the silted shallows of a slow river,
Fingering a shell,
Thinking :
Once I was something like this, mindless,
Or perhaps with another mind, less peculiar ;
Or to sink down to the hips in a mossy quagmire ;
Or, with skinny knees, to sit astride a wet log,
Believing :
I'll return again,
As a snake or a raucous bird,
Or, with luck, as a lion.

CP. p. 200

The way identity is reached is shown by the general pattern of this piece which is clearly one of regression followed by progression. This Jungian pattern is fundamental in Roethke since it becomes structural both in the poem, and in the overall development of his poetry. Indeed, after «keeping open house», Roethke explores the regressive metaphor of the Garden in the «Greenhouse Poems», so as later to use it as a basis for the development of the self in the long experimental poems of *The Lost Son*.

Jung's theory of regression and progression has been described in these terms by Karl Malkoff who first applied it to Roethke's poetry :

> According to Jung, when a man encounters an obstacle with which he cannot cope, he regresses to childhood, or even to the time before childhood — that is, to the collective unconscious — to find a new way of dealing with his current situation [11].

Unfortunately Karl Malkoff remains somewhat vague as to the nature of an obstacle which to us is largely ideological. From this angle, the regressive quality of Roethke's Garden is caused by his realization that ideology is indeed a formidable barrier which cannot be overcome by a direct assault on alienation, that to avoid frantic but sterile agitation, he must work his way round it, as it were, by projecting himself into the Garden of his childhood.

The representation of the world of childhood is thus part of the general pattern of regression-progression which dominates Roethke's poetry. The child image — like so many of his images — is essentially dynamic for it is both the symbol of a return to pre-ideological simplicity and the symbol of Becoming and spiritual growth. Yet, contrary to what happens in the Romantic tradition, the impression which is conveyed most of the time is one of suffering and guilt. Roethke's is not always a Garden of happiness and innocence for, as is made clear in the *Lost Son* sequence, if the experience of growing up can be a painful one, that of regressing also corresponds to a «bleak time» for the soul, especially when carried to such extremes of primitivism. Indeed, in this regressive scheme, the child is a «lost» child, one who is deprived of all his cultural connections and tries, desperately at times, to strike new roots into the natural world.

But Roethke's regression is so radical that it goes even beyond the world of childhood, or as in «The Longing», beyond the identification with the Indians. In his attempt to get round the barrier of ideology, in his search for the most elementary roots of the self, Roethke goes back to the utmost simplicity — or, to put it in Freudian terms, he returns to the pre-conscious stage of existence and to the collective past. Such is the case in «Where Knock is Open Wide» for instance —

What's the time, papa-seed ?
Everything has been twice.
My father is a fish.   *CP*. p. 72

— where the protagonist relives all the different stages of life («Everything has been twice») to go back to the moment of conception («What's the time, papa-seed ?») and to the primeval past of the human race («My father is a fish.»)

The use of such Freudian imagery however is only one way of regressing beyond the world of childhood. A constant identification with the small is another. Whether animal or vegetal, the «minimals», the «lovely diminutives» that people his Garden also become mediators that help him in his enterprise to find a state of «mindlessness» and re-establish the existential links with the world of nature that have been severed by the modern world. By using his microscopic eye, Roethke constantly underlines the correspondence between the small, primitive forms of life and the depths of the human mind, and thereby gives it back its deepest roots. Finally, far from being negative, the identification with the lower forms of life in the Garden can be said to have a curative effect :

I study the lives on a leaf : the little
Sleepers, numb nudgers in cold dimensions,
Beetles in caves, newts, stone-deaf fishes,
Lice tethered to long limp subterranean weeds,
Squirmers in bogs,
And bacterial creepers
Wriggling through wounds
Like elvers in ponds,
Their wan mouths kissing the warm sutures,
Cleaning and caressing,
Creeping and healing.   «The Minimal», *CP*. p. 50

But the most regressive aspect of Roethke's Garden seems to lie elsewhere, in the constant reduction of what might have been a landscape to its simplest components — the elements and the cosmic forces that work through them. The most convincing example of this reduction can be found in the «Greenhouse Poems». Surely this series of poems conjures up a precise image of the greenhouse of his childhood, with its soil, its flowers, and the work that was effected there, and gradually one realizes that the greenhouse emerges as a sort of microcosm — in the words of Roethke, as «a symbol for the whole of life, a womb, a heaven on earth» [12]. And yet, the lasting impression one retains from these poems is the extraordinary, and sometimes frightening power of the forces at work in it — forces of corruption and death, yet forces of life and growth. Instead of merely describing this world, Roethke explores the elements of earth, water, fire, and air that conspire to make it an essentially dynamic world, a world animated by the dialectic of life and death: he plunges us into its sickening earth (in «Root Cellar», *CP*. p. 38), makes us follow in microscopic details the way «the delicate slips keep coaxing up water» (in «Cuttings»,*CP*. p.37), shows us how «the live heat billows from the pipes and pots» (in «Forcing House», *CP*. p. 38), and makes us smell its warm air and the «musky» smell of orchids (in «Orchids»,*CP*. p. 39), or the «congress of stinks» of the root cellar.

At this ultimate stage in Roethke's «long journey out of the self» («Journey to the Interior», *CP*. p. 193), away from the generalized other, and back to elemental simplicity, it looks as though his own world were about to be reduced to a single point, the point where the forces of death turn into forces of life, the meeting-point between being and non-being. Although in a sense Roethke's Garden could not be more concrete, its regressive features make it look strangely abstract at times : intimate and personal as it is, it finally transcends its individual character to become universal.

In the face of such an attempt to get round the barrier of ideology, there remains one central question to be asked about the nature of Roethke's poetic world : since it has cast off the moorings that tied it to the generalized other, has Roethke's self become a sort of «Bateau Ivre» roaming the rough seas of primitivism ? Or, to put it differently, is his world the realm of personal anarchy and chaos ? Here again, the image of the greenhouse which is at the heart of the Garden provides an answer, even though it is an ambiguous one.

Although Roethke deliberately turns to the chaos of the soils of the greenhouse and to its vegetal anarchy, he always finally refrains from total mergence with them and looks for some new kind of order. A poem like «Weed Puller» (*CP.* p. 39) is characteristic of this attitude and helps define the kind of order Roethke is striving for :

Under the concrete benches,
Hacking at black hairy roots, —
Those lewd monkey-tails hanging from drainholes,—
Digging into the soft rubble underneath,
Webs and weeds,
Grubs and snails and sharp sticks,
Or yanking tough fern-shapes,
Coiled green and thick, like dripping smilax,
Tugging all day at perverse life :
The indignity of it !—
With everything blooming above me,
Lilies, pale-pink cyclamen, roses,
Whole fields lovely and inviolate,—
Me down in that fetor of weeds,
Crawling on all fours,
Alive in a slippery grave.

In his study of Roethke's «Minimals», William Heyen notices that this poem «suggests a hierarchy of minimals and illustrates the horror of confrontation with the lower forms of life» [13]. Indeed, one can distinguish clearly two levels in the vegetation of the poem : «*under* the concrete benches», close to the soil or in the decaying compost, he sees the «fetor of weeds» and more generally the obscene, «perverse» life of origins. But *above* him there are also the «lovely» and «inviolate» fields of lilies, pale-pink cyclamen and roses, symbols of perfection aṅd purity. The poem thus presents us with a delicate balance between two worlds, the obscure, chaotic and terrifying world of origins, a world in genesis from which one must emerge ; and the perfect world of Beauty, the world of order and purity for which he yearns. The vegetal hierarchy on which the poem is based finally expresses a desire to be born, to leave the womb of chaos so as to reach the eternal world of ordered Beauty.

Instead of being a social norm, instead of being enforced from the outside by the generalized other, the order Roethke looks for is the direct, spontaneous expression of the chaos that lies deep at the core of the self. Following the dialectic pattern of regression and progression, Roethke needs to court chaos so as to establish order. Such spontaneous ordering of chaos finally is the basic function and meaning of the act of poetic creation ; such is the essential purpose of his art [14].

Yet this type of spontaneous order is often nothing more than a wish or a dream. In fact, if through the image of the greenhouse Roethke does strike a perfect balance between the two worlds of feminine chaos and paternal order, this order is often imposed from the outside. In his gardening activities the father clearly embodies a germanic kind of order :

Scurry of warm over small plants.
Ordnung ! ordnung ! Papa is coming !   «The Lost Son» *CP*. p. 57

—an order which, being founded on property, organization and hierarchy, is of a social nature. Thus the father-figure can be equated with the generalized other imposing its discipline upon the world, and forcing its standards of behavior upon the Son.

The image of the greenhouse which provides the poet with those two contradictory ideas of order is in itself extremely ambiguous. The very choice of the greenhouse as a key symbol is meaningful and reflects the fundamental ambiguity underlined by Leo Marx in the design of such American fables as *Walden, Moby Dick* or *Huckleberry Finn*. Indeed, in the «Greenhouse Poems» as in those works, «the superfluities and defenses of everyday life are stripped away, and men regain contact with essentials» ; yet this ideological nudity is not final and constitutes merely «a temporary return to first things» [15]. The greenhouse thus appears as «a landscape of reconciliation» [16] combining chaos and order, the natural and the artificial. In Freudian terms, it could be said to establish a perfect balance between a high level of instinctual gratification and a degree of repression ; in sociological terms, it could be presented as a compromise between the demands of purely individual thinking and those of the generalized other.

Later in his career, Roethke was to become increasingly aware of this ambiguity and critical of the artificial order implied by the metaphor of the greenhouse. So much so that he began to perceive that if the greenhouses of his childhood were «a heaven on earth», they could be hell as well : «They were to me, I realize now», he wrote in *An American Poet Introduces Himself*, «both heaven and hell, a kind of tropics created in the savage climate of Michigan where austere German-Americans turned their love of order and their terrifying efficiency into something truly beautiful» [17]. And yet, the hold of the greenhouse upon his imagination always remained intact. All he could do in *The Far Field* was to turn more and more toward the chaos of the Michican landscape so as to discover a purely spontaneous order emerging from it. But the choice remained open to the end, between the wild rose of Michigan,

> A single wild rose, struggling out of the white embrace of the morning glory,
> Out of the briary hedge, the tangle of matted underbrush,
> Beyond the clover, the ragged hay,
> Beyond the sea pine, the oak, the wind-tipped madrona,
> Moving with the waves, the undulating driftwood,
> Where the slow creek winds down to the black sand of the shore
> With its thick grassy scum and crabs scuttling back into their glistening
>   craters...   «The Rose» *CP*. p. 203

and the hybrids of the greenhouse, the symbols of artificial order and «terrifying efficiency» :

> And I think of roses, roses,
> White and red, in the wide six-hundred-foot greenhouses,
> And my father standing astride the cement benches,
> Lifting me high over the four-foot stems, the Mrs Russels, and his own
>   elaborate hybrids,
> And how those flowerheads seemed to flow toward me, to beckon me, only
>   a child, out of myself.
> What need of heaven, then,
> With that man, and those roses ?...   «The Rose» *CP*. p. 203

Thus the tension between an artificial order and a spontaneous one was only transferred to an opposition between the landscape of the greenhouse and that of Michigan, without ever being resolved. The same ambiguity appears in «Otto», the beautiful poem dedicated to his father. In this piece we see his father producing beautiful flowers out of sheer work and violence, and protecting his property against the intrusion of poachers. Roethke defines clearly, and surely not without a mild irony, a kind of order which is basically social in nature ; and yet, despite his misgivings, he eventually returns to his father's world and the ideological values it embodies :

O world so far away ! O my lost world !   «Otto», *CP.* p. 224

This ambiguity means that if Roethke somehow could get round the barrier of ideology, he could not, or would not, destroy it altogether. Although he kept longing for a spontaneous principle of order which, like Wallace Stevens's «Jar in Tennessee», would «take dominion everywhere» and control «the slovenly wilderness» within, he kept coming back to the ideological principle of order that prevails in the greenhouse.

In spite of the ambiguities about the ultimate aim of Roethke's journey, the regression from the generalized other into the chaos of the Inner Wilderness remains the decisive element in his creative impulse. At the same time as this regression defines the very nature of his poetic world, it determines the adoption of a certain type of aesthetics, ie. both a certain sensibility and a certain mode of expression.

An essential part of Roethke's aesthetics of regression is his cultivation of a sensibility which is radically subjective and non-ideological in the sense that it tries to remove the influences, controls, and limits imposed by society upon individual ways of thinking and feeling. Roethke's sensibility rests upon the rejection of reason in favor of intuition — of the direct, immediate and concrete experience of a fusion with the world. In other words, his aim is to recreate the mentality of the child or the primitive.

Roethke's attitude to reason is clearly expressed on several occasions in his poetry, often in exclamations of disapproval, not to say of disgust. For instance, the old woman of the «Meditations» sighs :

O to be delivered from the rational into the realm of pure song...
«What Can I Tell My Bones»,*CP.* p. 172

whereas in another often-quoted line the poet exclaims :

Reason ? That dreary shed, that hutch for grubby schoolboys
«I Cry, Love ! Love !»,*CP.* p. 92

Reason is thus felt by the poet as something constricting, a «shed», a «hutch», an ideological barrier that must be broken through so as to escape to the freedom of a totally individual mode of thinking and feeling.

This attitude explains the apology for madness to be found in his poetry, and more particularly in a poem like «In a Dark Time» :

> What's madness but nobility of soul
> At odds with circumstance ?   *CP*. p. 239

This poem which Roethke himself presented as «an effort to break through the barrier of rational experience» [18], reveals a primitive sensibility in which identification is the only mode of knowing. It is a kind of madness which can be interpreted in sociological terms as the sign of the poet's attempt to destroy the barrier of ideology in order to recover the essential «nakedness» of a child or a primitive. «Madness», Roethke said in his commentary on this poem, «is a sociological term a good deal of the time : what is madness in the North West is normal conduct in Italy, and a hero's privilege in Western Ireland», by which he meant that it is a departure from the norms imposed by the generalized other, from norms that often vary from one culture to another [19].

Charles Blondel, who under the influence of Durkheim developed a sociological theory of madness, presented it as such a departure. To him, insanity is essentially a desocialization of the mental structure of the individual who finds himself incapable of operating within the collective frame of reference. Thus refusing the discipline imposed by his ideological self and rejecting the collective structures of thought, he becomes incapable of rationality and is rejected into a purely private mode of thinking and feeling [20].

It is this type of madness which determined the nature of Roethke's poetic sensibility and ranked him among the visionary poets, along with Blake, Christopher Smart and John Clare, who turned their madness into great art. A poem like «Heard in a Violent Ward» shows that Roethke cultivated this kind of madness :

> In heaven, too,
> You'd be institutionalized.
> But that's all right,—
> If they let you eat and swear
> With the likes of Blake,
> And Christopher Smart,
> And that sweet man, John Clare.   *CP*. p. 228

Indeed, the only possible knowledge which is left after this refusal to be «institutionalized» is of an intensely personal nature. It is an ecstasy, a «blaze of being» («A Walk in Late Summer», *CP*. p.149), a burning fusion with the world which is hardly communicable. Roethke's reliance upon this kind of intuitive knowledge is at the root of his symbolic vision, a vision which is based on the assumption that there are deep, instinctive and sympathetic affinities between man and his natural surroundings. That is why his poetry can be described as «a steady storm of correspondences» («In a Dark Time», *CP*. P; 239) in which the poet is one with the world.

If Roethke's sensibility is regressive it is therefore not only because of the nature of his poetic world, but also, and perhaps mostly, because of this intuitive mode of perception which restores the essential unity of the poet and the world. Being freed from the restrictions of ideology, Roethke's sensibility is able to break down all the barriers between subject and object, and even between the objects themselves. As R.J. Mills, Jr. put it,

> The world, from the new point of view Roethke provides, is transformed into a densely populated, because animistic, place where the normal distinctions of object and subject, conscious and unconscious, will and instinct are abolished and synesthesia is an accepted mode of perception [21].

This mode of perception re-establishes the vital links between man and nature that have been severed by the imposition of ideology upon the individual consciousness, which implies that the poet strips things of their ideological coat of abstraction in order to see them directly in their essential nakedness. In this attempt to return to the state of primeval innocence which precedes the intrusion of rationality, the world is no longer defined by social representations and no longer lives under the reign of ideas. Moreover, by refusing to dissociate the normally separate factors of objective perception and subjective feeling, the poet is able to participate in the life of things and perceive them in their essential concreteness. Indeed, like a child or a primitive, Roethke suffers from «that anguish of concreteness» («I Cry, Love ! Love !», *CP*.p. 92) ; in him, as in the primitive mentality, things become intensely themselves in an act of total participation. In a way they become even more that themselves for they cease to be merely objective to become instinct with Being, charged with some sort of presence which transcends their individual existence. The poet's perception of the world, finally, is a dialogue with that presence hidden in the concreteness of things, with the eternal that lives in the heart of reality, with God :

> I could say hello to things ;
> I could talk to a snail ;
> I see what sings !
> What sings ! «O Lull Me»,*CP*. p. 83.

> God's in that stone, or I am not a man» «A Walk in Late Summer»,*CP*. p. 149

Roethke's poetic sensibility was not static but dynamic ; it was the result of an effort, not to say a fight, to break through the barrier of ideology so as to re-establish such an existential relationship with the world. Beyond the sufferings and despair involved in this effort, his aim was to regain a pre-ideological mode of perception which would enable him to feel the very presence of things and transmute it into song.

> I am that final thing
> A man learning to sing

he said in «The Dying Man» (*CP*. p. 153) : his aim was to build up a new sensibility which would eventually give him the power to write the kind of poetry he was longing for. In a sense the work was never done and he was learning every day.

Real poetry for him had to describe the poet's dialogue with things, rather than the things themselves ; it had to be a song or a dance which reproduced the very rhythm of reality, even more than reality itself. As is made clear by his recurrent habit of breaking into song and listening to the voices and echoes of the universe, it should be a celebration of reality going even beyond the concreteness of things to capture in their presence the pure rhythm of Being, a spontaneous ordering of experience ; it should be an incantation of reality, pure music, a pure dance of words, a «wordless song». («Four for Sir John Davies», *CP*. p. 105)

Roethke's attempt to free his sensibility entirely from the grip of ideology to put it exclusively under the law of participation constitutes his answer to the problem of alienation in the modern world. In this sense it hits one of the central questions of our time. Intensely personal as it may be, this reaction is part of what Nathan A. Scott, Jr. called «the remarkable rebirth of savage thought which begins to be a central development in cultural life to day». For him, Roethke is indeed part of a general movement in the arts and politics which is «searching for ways of reconceiving the human universe as a world which offers the promise and possibility of life under the law of participation» 22. But this search raises a fundamental problem of expression, for the artist who tries to «reconceive» his relationship with the world on such terms must reject any conventional manipulation of language which bears the stamp of ideology, and therefore denies even the possibility of participation. In a sense,what is needed is a mode of expression entirely free from the collective structures of meaning and reference, one that conveys the direct and immediate nature of the links that are woven between the artist and the world in the act of participation. It is this ideal language Roethke would like to create, a language which would exclude totally the generalized other in order to be purely personal, even at the risk of moving entirely beyond the limits of communicability.

This dream explains Roethke's impatience with language, an impatience which was to last throughout his career. He thought that he should experiment with language, and that each new book of his ought to be written in a new style. But this was not experimentation for the sake of novelty : what he wanted in fact was to «blow up» the language, in order to divest it of ideology and make it the vehicle of his regressive sensibility 23. In a way, regression in language was a subversive enterprise, and Roethke was fully aware of this ; yet its aims was positive for it was an attempt to restore the fundamental unity between the word and the thing.

To put it clearly, although perhaps a little schematically, one could say that Roethke's regression in language runs along two lines, that of simplification and that of intuition.

Simplification appears in the choice of a vocabulary and an imagery which are predominantly concrete, limited and almost obsessive. It appears also in his use of primordial images —either archetypes or elemental images — which enable the poet to appeal directly to the deeper layers of his reader's consciousness and to his most basic experiences, thus ignoring the more recent acquisitions of ideology. It appears finally in the use of a poetic style characterized by the mere juxtaposition of very short clauses or sentences whose concentration can go as far as ellipsis or aphorism to suggest a rudimentary mode of perception as opposed to the false sophistication of ideology, and by a marked preference for free forms and a free use of rhythm in which the length of the lines is gradually reduced to one final word, as if to show that the ultimate form of simplicity is silence.

Roethke's second way to reach naïveté in language is through the rejection of logic and abstraction, a rejection which explains his intrusion into the realm of nonsense and his reliance upon an associational method or upon pun-logic. Indeed, to create an intuitive language, he had first to break up all the conventional structures that normally provide language with a «meaning». The absence of rhetoric and a free use of grammar are among the main devices he uses to blow up conventional logic. The end product of all this is a language which consists of small, simple units that are merely brought together in a kind of pointillist technique :

> At Woodlawn I heard the dead cry :
> I was lulled by the slamming of iron,
> A slow drip over stones,
> Toads brooding wells.
> All the leaves stuck out their tongues ;
> I shook the softening chalk of my bones,
> Saying,
> Snail, snail, glisten me forward,
> Bird, soft-sigh me home
> Worm, be with me.
> This is my hard time...   «The Lost Son»,*CP*. p.53

It is a technique which merely associates broken sensations or reminiscences, fragmentary experiences of reality that come long before ideas and concepts distort things, long before reason and logic impose upon them any kind of interpretation or order. It is a technique in which the experiences of reality offer themselves line by line, punctually as it were, to represent the return to a pre-ideological contact with the world which, beyond the present «hard time», should eventually lead to a new synthesis and to the proclamation of «a condition of joy» («I Cry, Love ! Love !», *CP*. p. 92).

The underlying principle which animates Roethke's regression in language is the same law of participation which governs his sensibility. His language is the language of intuition, a non-ideological language in which the words do not refer to abstractions or socially-imposed representations, but exclusively to the experience of a direct participation with things. If, as Karl Malkoff put it, Roethke is «recharging language with experience» [24], it is because in his poetry the word is nothing but the experience itself — ie. the relationship between the perceiver and the perceived, without the outside intervention of the generalized other.

Thus trying to break through the barrier of ideology to explore the Inner Wilderness was a dangerous enterprise. Regression brought Roethke close to nihilism and the assertion of disorder at its most extreme, while progression remained problematic. It meant courting chaos, and could lead to total mergence with the world and total incommunicability in language ; and yet Roethke avoided such dangers for he always remained possessed by a rage for order which finally saved him. His poetic world, his sensibility, and his aesthetics are dominated by such a tension between personal chaos and ideological order — a tension which reflects the ambivalence of his feelings toward the paternal order that prevails in the greenhouse. His journey away from ideology into the Garden is one which ends in ambiguity.

NOTES

1. In **Robert Frost, A Collection of Critical Essays**, edited by James Cox, Prentice Hall Inc., Englewood Cliffs, N.J., 1962 p. 36

2. M.L. Rosenthal, ‹The Couch and Poetic Insight›, **Reporter,** March 25, 1965 p. 52.

3. Denis Donoghue, **Connoisseurs of Chaos - Ideas of Order in Modern American Poetry**, N.Y., Macmillan, 1965, p. 228.

4. G.H. Mead, **Mind, Self and Society**, the University of Chicago Press, 1934, p. 155.

5. Alan Seager, **The Glass House, The Life of Theodore Roethke,** MacGraw-Hill, N.Y., 1968, p. 60.

6. These are two of the four principal themes with which, according to Roethke, the poet is faced :
    1)‹the multiplicity, the chaos of modern life›
    2)‹the way, the means of establishing a personal identity, a self in the face of that chaos›
    3)‹the nature of creation, that faculty for producing order out of disorder in the arts, particularly in poetry›.
    4) ‹the nature of God Himself›.
    cf.‹On Identity›, **Selected Prose of Theodore Roethke**, edited by R.J. Mills Jr., University of Washington Press, Seattle, 1965, p. 19.

7. W.D. Snodgrass, ‹That Anguish of Concreteness›, in **T. Roethke-Essays on the Poetry,** Arnold Stein, editor, University of Washington Press, Seattle and London, pp. 78-94.

8. quoted by Gerald Meyer in ‹Logic of the North›, **Saturday Review**, XXXVII, Jan. 16, 1954, pp. 18-19.

9. T.S. Eliot, ‹Burnt Norton›, **Four Quartets**, Faber Edition p. 13.

10. Louis L. Marz, ‹A Greenhouse Eden›, T. Roethke., **Essays on the Poetry**, Arnold Stein, editor, op. cit. p. 21.

11. Karl Malkoff, `T. Roethke,` **An Introduction to the Poetry**, Columbia U.P., N.Y., London, 1966, p. 60.

12. ‹Open Letter›, in **On the Poet and His Craft, Selected Prose of T. Roethke,** op. cit. p. 39.

13. William Heyen, ‹T. Roethke's Minimals›, **Minnesota Review**, 8-4-68, p. 362.

14. This constitutes the third of the four principal themes facing the poet according to Roethke. Cf. note 6.

15. Leo Marx, **The Machine in the Garden - Technology and the Pastoral Ideal in America**, Oxford U.P., N.Y., 1964, p. 69.

16. id., p. 70.

17. in **On the Poet and His Craft, Selected Prose of T. Roethke,** op. cit. p. 8.

18. 19. T. Roethke, ‹On 'In a Dark Time'›, in **The Contemporary Poet as Artist and Critic,** Anthony Ostroff, editor, Boston, Little, Brown and Co, 1964, p. 49.

20. Cf. Charles Blondel, **La Conscience Morbide, Essai de Psycho-pathologie Générale**, Paris, Alcan, 1913.

21. Ralph, J. Mills, Jr., ‹The Lyric of the Self›, in **Poets in Progress**, Edward Hungerford, editor, Northwestern U.P., 1967, p. II.

22. Nathan A. Scott, Jr., **The Wild Prayer of Longing, Poetry and the Sacred**, Yale U.P., New Haven and London, 1971, p. 31

23. Alan Seager tells us that Roethke admired e.e. cummings because ‹he blew up the language›. Cf. **The Glass House, the Life of T. Roethke**, op. cit. p. 186.

24. Karl Malkoff, **T. Roethke, An Introduction to the Poetry,** op. cit. p. 108.

Rachel BLAU DUPLESSIS

Lyric Documents :

*the critique of personal consciousness
in Levertov, Rich and Rukeyser*

«There is no private life which is not determined by a wider public life.» This statement of George Eliot is one of two epigraphs Adrienne Rich chose for her book *Diving Into the Wreck* ; it announces a complex of concerns that Rich shares with two other contemporary poets, Muriel Rukeyser and Denise Levertov. In the last decade and a half, these poets have posited the relations of self and society as a primary poetic situation and have explored these relations in several ways. It is not simply that they speak to public issues (such as the war in Vietnam), but rather that within lyric poetry, they enact a personal awakening to political and social life, and that they situate their consciousness and its formation at a specific historical moment [1].

The summary statement from George Eliot, epitomizing these poets'concern for the relationships of consciousness and society, is joined, on that first page of Rich's book, by a citation from André Breton's *Nadja*, which approaches the self in another fashion. «Perhaps my life is nothing but an image of this kind ; perhaps I am doomed to try and learn what I should simply recognize, learning a mere fraction of what I have forgotten». Fluid, self-dramatizing, and self-questioning, this book, which begins «Who am I ?» and which concerns a man who imagines or encounters a woman in order to imagine and encounter himself, evokes another major aspect of the work of these three poets. For Breton here announces a self-exploration which doubles back on its own questions and which incorporates a critical, self-questioning posture into the very mythic and formative journey he takes. The citation Rich has selected indicates that the invention of self-exploratory myths is crucial to her ; this is true of the other two poets also.

The discussion that follows comes from a longer paper about consciousness and myth in Levertov, Rich and Rukeyser. The excerpt deals with the critique of personal consciousness found as a motif in contemporary writing by women. Let me, however, offer an overview of the issues treated in the essay as a whole, so that the reader can set this excerpt in its context. The essay shows how the women poets began with a critique of personal consciousness and tried to extend this approach to the political realities of the 1960's, particularly the war in Vietnam, in poems which are only partially successful. The true completion of the critique of personal consciousness is found in poems which invent new myths, myths which are critical of prior mythic thought. They are historically

specific rather than eternal and replace archetypes by proto-
types [2].

The mode of the poems of personal and political consciousness
and of the new myths can be summed up in the term «lyric
documents». The poems in this mode combine lyric and imagistic
means of perception with tactics of analysis and critique, and,
unlike traditional lyrics, they do not disengage themselves from the
time, place and situation in which they were written.

In the material that follows, we see the poets using their poems
to analyze women's assumptions and patterns of action (as in
Levertov's «Hypocrite Women»). They investigate their old and
new consciousness in, for example, its linguistic patterns
(Rukeyser, «Despisals»), and they reveal the cultural values that
uphold the old consciousness of women and try to destroy the new
before it is formed (Rich, «Snapshots of a Daughter-in-Law»). The
poems, taken as a group, constitute a poetic attack on long-held
and complex cultural ideologies dealing with women.

*

*　　*

Denise Levertov wavers between defining herself in terms of
general personhood or specific womanhood. In either case, the
creation and re-creation of the self is one of her most important
themes. Her richest poems are epiphanies of self discovery and
moments of sacramental rededication to the self. Levertov has
written that these Romantic themes of «soul-making», to borrow
Keats' term as Levertov herself does, are naturally integrated with

what, woman

and who, myself,
I am...

(citing «Stepping Westward»). For her, discovering womanhood
and discovering personhood are one seamless quest. Yet in fact,
the question of women does sometimes emerge as a specific critical
problem in Levertov's work. Certain of the conflicts she writes
about can be analyzed as classic conflicts for women, which appear
in many works by women because they reflect conditions of their
lives and the demands of the culture. The conflict between the
claims of the self and the claims of others appears so often that it
can be considered one thematic motif of women's writing.

Poems such as «An Embroidery (I) », «In Mind » and «About Marriage» do show the conflicting pull between nurturing others and self-absortion, between marriage and pilgrimage. Lervertov works within the tacit assumption that a resolution to these conflicts will be found. Yet that resolution is often unstable. Even for the woman who takes an interior journey, like Rose White in «An Embroidery», a bridegroom is expected, but this bridegroom has an ambiguous status. The bridegroom may be truly another, or he may represent an awakened aspect of the self. Thus at the very resolution of the poem the original tension between marriage and selfhood is preserved.

It seems to me that the story of Psyche: and Amor, in general so suggestive a myth in its quest motifs and a prime myth of soul-making, structures Levertov's attitudes to women, because in this myth marriage and pilgrimage are not, finally, in conflict. The soul's quest and its tasks are provoked first by a question about love, symbolized by Psyche's desire to see Cupid, and then by the question where — and thus who — she is. After her long trials and her journey, including a trip to the underworld, Psyche is reunited with her transformed bridegroom, whom, in part, she has altered in her search for self-knowledge, and yet who, conversely, has always had the power of a god — to elevate her as his bride in a sacrament of joy. A balance between striving and passivity in the female personality is achieved in this myth ; this is why Erich Neumann uses the myth as a model of «the psychic development of the feminine» [3]. It is precisely this balance that Levertov seeks. The marriage will be strengthened and enriched by her pilgrimage ; the claims of the self and the claims of others will not be in conflict. In «Relearning the Alphabet», a major pilgrimage poem, this balance or poise after conflict is shown in several ways. Her impulse to journey forward to perception is combined with a desire to be visited by the illumination she seeks (as Psyche was by Cupid) ; the poem's pilgrimage brings her «home» to the loved one and their marriage.

«Hypocrite Women» (in *O Taste and See*, 1964) is a poem in which Levertov does discuss the special burdens and pressures which set the fact of womanhood as a barrier to the achievement of personhood. The poem inserts the «woman question» into the larger context of the soul's journey, asking what can prevent or inhibit the choice to make one's life a prilgrimage to selfhood. In answering this question, Levertov studies self-repression in women.

Hypocrite women, how seldom we speak
of our own doubts, while dubiously
we mother man in his doubt !

And if at Mill Valley perched in the trees
the sweet rain drifting through western air
a white sweating bull of a poet told us

our cunts are ugly — why didn't we
admit we have thought so too ? (And
what shame ? They are not for the eye !)

No, they are dark and wrinkled and hairy,
caves of the Moon...   And when a
dark humming fills us, a

coldness towards life,
we are too much women to
own to such unwomanliness.

Whorishly with the psychopomp
we play and plead — and say
nothing of this later.   And our dreams,

with what frivolity we have pared them
like toenails, clipped them like ends of   (p. 70)
split hair.

In this poem, the «hypocrite women» repress whatever they feel
—even their own self-doubt— to preserve a generous, unruffled
surface, while they «mother man in his doubt», encouraging the
nuances and moods necessary for his self-expression. They act
unthinkingly the nurturing role the culture prescribes for women
in their relations with men. The poet is outraged by the women's
bland acquiescence in the rather pompous male attack on their
integrity, but her poem does not ask why men belittle women, but
rather asks, in an archly bitter tone, why women continue
unquestioningly to defer to men. She traces this deference to a
conflict between what the women really feel, and what the culture
suggests they should feel.The women really feel cold, moon-struck,
self-absorbed ; in a word, «unwomanly». To hide the paradox they
are ashamed of — the interplay between a woman and
«unwomanliness» — they put on the mask the culture has long
made available to them : flirtation used as self-repression.

The women mask their hardness with an excessive display of
flirtatiousness ; by so doing they also hide the intensity of the
conflict from themselves. Hence they are doubly hypocrites in their
behavior — with men and with themselves — and prevent
themselves from seeing or telling truths about themselves.

Whorishly with the psychopomp
we play and plead—   (p. 70)

The term psychopomp alerts us to what is at stake. This guide of souls, possibly Hermes, the traditional psychopomp of Greek mythology, is waiting to lead the women forward to mystery or to transformation. The god, of great importance to spiritual development, and who plays a key role in the myth of Psyche, is assailed by a teasing display of charm, which the women use as a deliberate strategy of refusal. They refuse to acknowledge their own capacity for growth, and they refuse to be faithful to their deepest selves. Key words such as «to mother», «whorishly», and, the phrase which concludes the poem, cutting dreams «like ends of split hair» are linguistic allegories criticizing the roles which the women play. The poem closes with a sharply etched portrait of women concerned simply with pleasing men, tailoring their responses to ignore messages of myth and dream, always so vital in Levertov. By their self-censorship, women deny themselves the challenge of soul-making.

The emphasis of «Hypocrite Women» falls on the women's strategies for self-denigration, not on the nuances and meanings of the acts of the man. The women have agreed with the man that they —that their cunts— are ugly. In this poem, the word *cunt* has been used openly and carefully as a counter-strategy of affirmation. The poem is valuable in part because it argues for the positive association of woman and cunt ; as a synecdoche, *cunt* has, of course, long been a term of opprobrium. The explicit naming of sexual organs and bodily functions in this and other recent poems by women is, I think, an attempt to reappropriate so-called «dirty» or «clinical» words, and by so doing, to construct a critique of the cultural values that have kept these words taboo and unspeakable. In Levertov's poem, the word *cunt* is another linguistic allegory. As cunt is a hidden fact and a hidden word, so other truths about women have been hidden, and, the poem implies, women should begin to speak them. It is as if women, by the act of writing, see themselves contributing to the undermining of cultural structures repressive of women by re-evaluating canons of proper language and canons of proper subject.

Another example of this use of taboo words will clarify its intention. A recent poem of Muriel Rukeyser, «Despisals» (*Breaking Open*, 1973), likewise consciously and programmatically uses forbidden words, here in a poem exploring the social implications of self-denigration and self-hatred.

> In the body's ghetto
> never to go despising the asshole
> nor the useful shit that is our clean clue
> to what we need. Never to despise the
> clitoris in her least speech.   (p. 5)

Rukeyser suggests that first self-hatred and then the hatred of others come about through the repression of one's childhood anal and sexual interest in the name of cleanliness. The ghettos of the body precede and, in some way, have caused the ghettos of the city. Through the creation of individual consciousness, reproduced in the up-bringing of every child, an intolerant, destructive society is also created. The poem is a study in the continuity of repression from the individual psyche to the collective city.

And through the flat, bold words of «Despisals», Rukeyser has also dramatized the power of the reader's assumptions. For at first the reader is likely to be startled at the forbidden words, and shocked that the poet did not exclude such terms and locutions. Since the theme of the poem is rejection of all forms of shame and contempt, readers are taught that their normative expectations for the poem's tone or diction are a version of the «despisals» the poem criticizes. The poet causes the reader to examine the repressive function of canons of right language.

With their deliberate use of certain words, and with the thematic purpose these words symbolize in the poems, the poets provide unwitting support for Virginia Woolf's argument in the essay «Professions for Women». (*Collected Essays*, volume II) Woolf predicts that women writers — and all women who wish to achieve professional status in other areas — will be faced with two major tasks. First, they must «kill the angel in the house», that self-sacrificing, charming, flirtatious phantom who always pleases others, never herself. Levertov's poem «Hypocrite Women» can be viewed as one more invitation to that murder, which, Woolf states, takes place only after a long struggle. And the verdict on this «murder» must be self-defense. The death of the angel of self-repression, in fact, the death of the old consciousness, insures that there will be no sex-linked taboos on women's self-exploration.

The second task of the woman writer will then be the aggressive act of truth-telling from a woman's experiences. Appropriately, and poignantly Woolf has no amusing summary phrase for this problem which she states she has not succeeded in solving. She says it has to do with expressing feelings about woman's sexuality, about passion, about the body. Talking about these matters has been inhibited by conventions, long traditions of self-censorship, and fear of male disapproval. Although Woolf notes these taboos about sexual matters exclusively, we can extend her argument to include all aspects of womens's lives. And what inhibits this investigation ? Precisely those configurations of consciousness that these poets confront : women's internalization of repressive patterns, women's self-hatred, women's role as «the angel in the house», all necessarily ignoring their buried authenticity. Indeed the two parts of woman's task now appear to be dialectically related. The real expression of a woman's feelings can only be accomplished by including and absorbing the recurrent «murder» of the old consciousness of women. These women poets have therefore chosen to attack precisely their own patterns of consciousness and the social and cultural structures that uphold them, all of which prevent them from telling the truth about themselves. Adrienne Rich's «Snapshots of a Daughter-in-Law», dated 1958-1960, is an outstanding poem of this critique of consciousness, analyzing the mental and cultural structures that have formed women and inspecting the meaning and function of their strategies of response. As Rukeyser and Levertov have confronted canons of acceptable language in their concern for women, so Rich, beginning the poem, had to pit herself against canons of subject : «I had been taught that poetry should be 'universal', which meant, of course, non-female» [4]. In an act of self-defense she excluded the pronoun «I» from the work (although she ends with «we»), she used extensive allusions, which constitute one of the important features of the poem, and she chose a title with a somewhat ironic reference to the «feminine» sources of her authority in writing the poem : her marital status and her family relationships.

The poem alludes to many texts, references and cultural figures, lifts them into view, examines them, and sets them in the new context formed by this «re-vision». A critique of assumptions about women's roles and behavior takes shape in three sections of three poems each ; finally, a coda projects a new woman, beginning to liberate herself from the cultural constraints the poem details [5].

The three poems of the first section discuss the intricate but limited patterns of behavior of actual women in her own family. They have few options. The mother lives through memories of past elegance ; yet because she does not think, but only feels, all her experience is «useless». Although the daughter-in-law almost churlishly tries to differentiate herself from the older woman, both are, in fact, disintegrating. The younger woman hears, and, with a deep self-denying perversity, represses unseen voices that call on her to rebel or to be selfish, demands she cannot begin to follow. The third poem of the first section exposes sisters without sisterhood, who express the monstrous dimensions of their self-hatred through hostility to each other. Such a bleak sketch of the limited «personal» options available to women — frustration taking shape as vagueness, madness, bitchiness — demands some causal explanation, which the poet discovers by referring to and analyzing classic, often literary, texts that evoke the history of women's condition and the fate of their gifts.

When a woman as gifted as Emily Dickinson appears, as she does suddenly in the next poem, as an image of Rich herself, she is compelled, as a woman, to pursue her ideas and images in the interstices of domestic life, a life that exists in diffuse, interruptible contrast to Dickinson's explosive power [6]. Alternately, endless domestic tasks will give shape to a women's life. She will put all her energy into the upkeep of a life, not into the living of it, «dusting everything on the whatnot every day of life».

If domesticity is one social expectation which shapes a woman's personality, and to which her gifts must conform, the demands of beauty (set forth in the next poems) are another. The clear, grotesque lines

> she shaves her legs until they gleam
> like petrified mammoth-tusk   (p. 22)

present the woman as idol, objectified by the necessity to preserve a sleek and beautiful surface, besides suggesting that the woman is an extinct animal, once powerful, now powerless because of that beauty.

The poem that follows, with its oblique citation from Campion, argues that the traditions of courtship (presented in traditional love lyrics) immobilize women. The accomplished woman bending over a lute is not truly immersed in art for its sake of for hers ; art is one of the ornaments of her beauty ; art enhances her as an image to be worshipped. Love, along with domesticity and beauty, is the third term, creating the traditional boundaries, which mold and define the woman. The woman takes shape as an individual drastically limited by social norms. And in each of these three terms, women's condition creates typical traits : the combination of repressed power and actual powerlessness ; the bitterness of a person prevented from full fruition ; a «keenness» about Nature and human relationships that comes from a woman's utter dependence on love.

Having summed up three centuries-old social expectations, and having shown how these create the individual, Rich turns to three more modern touchstones of cultural attitudes to women, showing in each case, with condensation and subtlety, the complex psychological paralysis and kinds of failure that have been the lot of women who themselves appropriate and are controlled by male opinion of their possibilities. She recalls (in section 7) how Mary Wollstonecraft was reviled by men for her analyses of the status of women. To attack the publicist and not recognize the problem, to blame the victim are both ways of confusing the issues and blurring one's perception of the real problem. But Diderot's praise of the lush flowering of women, cited in section 8, is no less a mystification, for as a result of attitudes like his, women are aroused to self-pity and infinite regrets for their past potential ; they are tacitly forgiven for their lack of actual accomplishments.

In the poem's most brilliant section, Rich caustically challenges both majority opinion about women and women's acceptance of it.

Our blight has been our sinecure :
mere talent was enough for us—
glitter in fragments and rough drafts.

Sigh no more, ladies.
            Time is male
and in his cups drinks to the fair.
Bemused by gallantry, we hear
our mediocrites over-praised,
indolence read as abnegation,
slattern thought styled intuition,
Every lapse forgiven, our crime
only to cast too bold a shadow
or smash the mould straight off.

> For that, solitary confinement,
> tear gas, attrition shelling.
> Few applicants for that honor.   (p. 24)

(The imagery of a sexual war, already present, grows more intense in Rich's recent work). Women are praised precisely when their work has not called male «superiority» and male analysis into question. Women are safe and childlike, mental «invalids», as she says just before the section cited, and they may be patronized generously because of their failure to grow and to persevere. Rich exposes the double face of the major culture — its paternal protection of female mediocrity and its destructive attack on female boldness or innovation.

Given what the poem says, a woman must literally re-invent herself ; hence, at the end of the poem, she is compared to a new invention — the helicopter. To construct her new consciousness, the woman must at once move beyond the destructive ideologies of the past, while also transcending the presence of the destructive ideologies in herself.

> Her mind full to the wind, I see her plunge
> breasted and glancing through the currents,
> taking the light upon her
> at least as beautiful as any boy
> or helicopter...   (p. 24)

So she must be like a «helicopter», like a «boy», open to ways of behaving and perceiving not limited by former ideas of what a «woman» should be. Rich suggests power, striving, strength — and integration between body and mind [7].

«Snapshots of a Daughter-in-Law» traces a critique of culture by re-examining the key texts from the past, noting their assumptions and showing the way a woman is molded within these cultural and social constraints. Rich's aim is «not to pass on a tradition but to break its hold over us», by analyzing the controlling paradigms of consciousness [8].

All three poets found some evidence of a double consciousness —whether in their own views of themselves, in women generally, or in society's views about women. One consciousness is traditional and does correspond in roles, attitudes and language to Woolf's «angel in the house» ; the other consciousness is critical, trying to analyze — and change — what the traditional consciousness would simply accept. The above group of poems by Levertov, Rich and Rukeyser share a concern for individual mental structures and their cultural roots. The poems examine the consciousness of women and the sets of expectations in society and culture about women's feelings, acts, possibilities. They see that the contents of consciousness inhibit the work of the imagination and of perception itself. In this set of poems, they mount critical attacks on accepted patterns of perception and behavior, as these are enshrined in cultural ideologies.

NOTES

1.   Prior to this fifteen years' work (1958-1973), none of the poets were unaware of the relations of consciousness and society. On this one issue, Rukeyser merits a separate study ; I will not here discuss the nuances of her poetic career. Yet the War in Vietnam forced the poets to rediscover the way that the public world impinges on the self, affecting hidden parts of consciousness. The war evoked for them fundamental questions about the qualities of power and the necessity for change.

2.   Levertov's myths are an apparent exception to some of these summary statements.

3.   For the whole myth of Psyche, and for an interpretation of significance to women, see Erich Neumann, **Amor and Psyche : The Psychic Development of the Feminine. A commentary on The Tale by Apuleius** (New York : Pantheon Books, 1956).

4.   Adrienne Rich, «When We Dead Awaken : Writing as Re-Vision», **College English** 34, 1 (October 1972), p. 24.

5.   The function of myths about women, and their destructiveness, particularly for women writers, are themes touched on in the important essay in **College English**, from which I have taken the term «re-vision». In this essay, Rich speaks about exploring a «new psychic geography» with little to guide women, and talks of the terror and promise of that quest. The implication for her poems is clear. She also speaks of the «drive to self-knowledge» which is necessarily accompanied by a «radical critique of literature» and of cultural ideologies.

6.   Two versions of the poem exist, in the first edition of **Snapshots** and in a later reprinting of the book, each with different lines from Dickinson. One line emphasizes the sapping of energy by diffusion ; the other suggests Emily Dickinson's explosive, pent-up power. The respective lines are, «This is the gnat that mangles men» and «My life had stood — a loaded gun...»

7.   As we see in her note, **Snapshots of a Daughter-in-Law**, p. 64, Rich has borrowed from the peroration of Simone de Beauvoir's **The Second Sex**, a work that clearly had a great impact on her and on this poem. Curiously, Rich has reversed de Beauvoir's intention, which was to argue against the expensive, costly charm of women which comes, in the citation Rich selected, from the depths of the jungle, from the most modern technological artifice (helicopter) and from fertile nature (bird). But the primitive depths and modern brilliance united in women are quite suggestive for the invention of the new woman — the turn Rich gives de Beauvoir's images at the end of her poem. I give the full context from de Beauvoir, somewhat more than Rich cites. «...adorned with the most modern artifices, beautified according to the newest techniques, (the 'charming woman') comes down from the remoteness of the ages, from Thebes, from Crete, from Chichen-Itza ; and she is also the totem set up deep in the African jungle ; she is a helicopter and she is a bird ; and there is this, the greatest wonder of all : under her tinted hair the forest murmur becomes a thought and words issue from her breasts. ...Does such a fugitive miracle — and one so rare— justify us in perpetuating a situation that is baneful for both sexes ? One can appreciate the beauty of flowers, the charm of women, and appreciate them at their true value ; if these treasures cost blood or misery, they must be sacrificed». Simone de Beauvoir, **The Second Sex**, translated by H.M. Parshley (New York : Bantam Books, 1961), p. 687. **The Second Sex** was originally published in 1949.

8.   Rich, **College English**, p. 19.

BIBLIOGRAPHY

Denise LEVERTOV.
With Eyes at the Back of Our Heads, 1959.
The Jacob's Ladder, 1961.
O Taste and See, 1964.
The Sorrow Dance, 1967.
Relearning the Alphabet, 1970.
To Stay Alive, 1971.
Footprints, 1972
The Poet in the World, 1973. (Selected Essays)

All the works are published by New Directions.

Adrienne Rich.
Snapshots of a Daughter-in-Law, 1963.
Necessities of Life, 1966.
Leaflets, Poems 1965-1968, 1969.
The Will to Change, Poems 1968-1970, 1971.
Diving into the Wreck, Poems 1971-1972, 1973.

All the works are published by W. W. Norton and Company.

Muriel Rukeyser.
The Life of Poetry, New York : Current Books, Inc., 1949.
Selected Poems, New York : New Directions, 1951.
Waterlily Fire, Poems 1935-1962, New York : Macmillan Company, 1963.
The Speed of Darkness, New York : Random House, 1968.
Breaking Open, New York : Random House, 1973.

Other Sources

Charles ALTIERI, «From Symbolist Thought to Immanence : The Ground of Postmodern American Poetics», *Boundary 2,* I, 3 (Spring 1973), pp. 605-637.

Barbara DEMING, «Two Perspectives on Women's Struggle», *Liberation 17,* 10, (June 1973), pp. 30-37.

Florence HOWE and Ellen BASS, ed., *No More Masks ! An Anthology of Poems By Women* (Garden City, N.Y. : Doubleday Anchor Books, 1973). Introduction by Florence Howe.

James MOORE, «American Poetry in & Out of the Cave ; Part II: Becoming an Adult», *The Lamp in the Spine,* Number 4 (Spring 1972), pp. 18-31. (On Levertov's «Staying Alive»).

Tillie OLSEN, «Women Who Are Writers in Our Century : One Out of Twelve», *College English* 34, 1 (October 1972), pp. 6-17.

Adrienne RICH, «When We Dead Awaken : Writing as Re-Vision», *College English* 34, 1 (October 1972), pp. 18-30.

«Talking with Adrienne Rich», *Ohio University Review* 13, 1 (1971), pp. 29-46.

Catherine RIHOIT

The Bostonians :

*an investigation of the female feature
in James's cosmogony*

1. THE FEMININE FEATURE IN THE LANGUAGE OF JAMES'S FICTION

The importance of woman actants [1] in the Jamesian fictional world is such that one tends instinctively to think in terms of the Jamesian heroine, not hero. This is not unusual in fiction, though perhaps more so in the case of an author who is known not through one or two heroines whose impact overwhelms the rest of his work, but through a considerable number of novels [2], each of them brimming with a considerable number of characters. Other prolific writers such as Balzac or Dickens do not strike one as so woman-orientated, however great the importance of the feminine element in their fiction may statistically be.

One should embark on the study of women written about by men with particular care. It seems that the additional distanciation brought about by this situation has not been sufficiently stressed, even when the analysis of actants is no longer conducted as though these had an independent life of their own, a «psychology». Although few people seem to contest that, in Barthes's words, «il n'y a pas d'art qui ne désigne son masque du doigt» [3], the additional opacity of the mask in the situation we have just outlined has, it seems, attracted little notice in a man's world where even women find it natural to be represented by men when they themselves would find it a stress to do the reverse : one knows that as a rule women writers have heroines. And even when the importance of verisimilitude as a literary criterion was emphasized and a novel was judged by the degree to which it was deemed «true to life», the artificiality of woman actants — especially the heroines of course —, the fact that what was depicted under that denomination was not a woman, but a man's phantasm of one, attracted singularly little notice.

On this last point precisely James would appear to be an exception. To the female reader, his women seem to live more than his men [4]. One may wonder whether James is not one of the rare successful instances — Stephen Crane being another — of a writer choosing his actants in a section of society — here the section of upper middle-class women — to which he himself did not belong ; with an aim to sociological analysis combined with a desire for exoticism.

James's procedure, however, seems precisely opposite. He apparently did not feel the attraction of sections of society foreign to him as writers with naturalistic leanings did. On the contrary, he took as his stock of materials the world he knew, that he had been bred in and showed no signs of ever trying to escape, that of the transatlantic fraternity of the end of the 19th century upper classes. Yet we have tried to show elsewhere how, starting with familiar elements of this world, he proceeded to treat them as if they were strange, remote and never to be taken for granted [5]. One may wonder whether in that well-known world he did not pick out women precisely because they both appeared familiar and were in fact the «black continent». That this reason if valid can only have been secondary to the more likely one that the destiny of women in James's time afforded the best adequation to the basic structural pattern of his novels, is what we shall here try to develop.

In order to delimitate the field of investigation in such a way as to make it suitable for a short study based on a close scrutiny of James's writing, we have selected the novel *The Bostonians* as a specific target, both because its obvious theme is feminism, and because in the huge quantity of criticism on James it has attracted relatively little notice, although F.R. Leavis writes of James, with some reason, that :

> *The Portrait of a Lady* is a great novel, and we can't ask for a finer exhibition of James's peculiar fights as we get there and in *The Bostonians* (they seem to me the two most brilliant novels in the language) [6].

Lastly, the relative obscurity of *The Bostonians* in the Anglo-Saxon world has not deprived it of a certain notoriety in France, since a recent paperback edition ensured that it was one of the first novels by James to be read by a wide French public.

In a previous study quoted above, we had noticed the occurence of a shift between the value of the feature (+ feminine) in the language at large and in that of Henry James in the opening paragraph of *The Portrait of a Lady*. It seemed interesting to enquire whether this also proved true in another novel dealing specifically with the problem of women. It must be recalled that we had believed such semantic shifts to be favoured by James's conception of the world of his fiction as a microcosm operated not by the laws of the world at large but by specific laws. This specificity may be thought to stem from the importance for James of authorial responsibility in his creation of a world, resulting in a sharpening of the individual vision such that the world of appearances is pried into and another world appears, hitherto secret, now revealed and revelatory :

Anything in short, I now reflect, must always have seemed to me better — better for the process and the effect of representation, my irrepressible ideal — than the mere muffled majesty of irresponsible «authorship». Beset constantly with the sense that the painter of the picture or the chanter of the Ballad (whatever we may call him) can never be responsible *enough*, and for every inch of his surface and note of his song, I track my uncontrollable footsteps, right and left, after the fact, while they take their quick turn, even on the stealthiest tiptoe, toward the point of view that, within the compass, will give me most instead of least to answer for [7].

In *The Portrait of a Lady*, we had concluded that the feature (+ fem) designated not so much the sex as the marked term in the opposition «distinguished or not distinguished by the author's approval», so that the feature could be, in the realization of feminine attributes, given to actants of the male sex, the result being that they appeared not effeminate but good, interesting, morally to be approved of ; all terms which could be entered under the heading (+ positive).

The feature (+ fem) is thus made to endorse, over and above its general meaning when necessary — that is the designation of sex by such formal means as gender and appellations — the designation of a degree of excellence through the endowment of masculine actants with attributes which are contextual variants participating of the semantic feature (+ fem).

*
* *

2. *THE BOSTONIANS*, A TITLE

Jamesian titles are noticeable for their symbolic content. As a result they are both mysterious and — for this last reason partly — alluring to the reader before reading ; and after reading, their full implications appear. They are thus particularly revelatory, the loss in weight of mystery being compensated by the weight of evidence — by the weight alone : such *The Golden Bowl, The Wings of the Dove, The Ambassadors*.

Compared with the other titles *The Bostonians* appears as perhaps the most neutral. Its form easily fits into the paradigm of

many Jamesian titles, the basic structure of which is as follows :
(art) + (qualifier) + substantive + (NP complement)

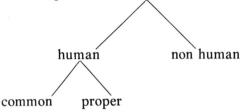

human   non human

common   proper

In this particular case the substantive has no qualifier or
complement ; the information conveyed is at first glance of merely
spatial character ; it may be included in a smaller paradigm :
> *The American*
> *The Europeans*
> *The Bostonians*

But this last title has a particularly restricted scope. Boston,
though by no means without connotative value (tradition, English
influence, snobbishness) cannot compare in symbolic richness with
the America/Europe opposition.

Another neutralizing factor is the plural. If one tries to define
the import of the plural as a morphosemantic element in the
paradigm above, one finds it delimitates the type of novel
concerned : the focus will be not on the plight of an individual, not
even on the interrelationship between two or three individuals, but
on the sociological analysis of a category of people, the plural
acting as a signal for : «members of a class». Thus the use of the
(+ plur) feature means more than (+ human) multiplied by two,
three, four ; it indicates the passing from one type of novel to
another. This confirms our postulate that *The Bostonians* is
concerned with a sociological problem, that of the place of women
in the society of the time and their relation to it : one can never be
too careful with a priori assertions of what a novel is about.

In *The Ambassadors*, the structural feature «suspense» is
heralded in the title by the combination of the grammatical features
(+ subst)
(+ definite)
(+ plural)
together with the semantic feature (+ occupation) which produces
ambiguity — does the term «ambassador» denote a job or a

temporary mission of a friendly or family nature ?

While in *The Bostonians* the sociological nature of the novel is announced by the features (+ place name)
(+ plural)
the presence of the grammatical feature (+ def) still contributes, in terms of structural features, to the constitution not of the «genre» feature (+ sociological) but to the structural feature (+ suspense) prevalent in all titles containing the grammatical feature (+ def) independently of other extant features, through the «in medias res» effect produced by the anaphoric article. The definite article prevails in titles of mystery stories : *The Italian, The Castle of Otranto*. This last feature thus appears as the only element so far which does not orientate the title toward neutrality.

We do not, however, believe the title «The Bostonians» to be insignificant. The apparent insignificance is — here as so often with James — functional. The constellation of features making for neutrality sets off the marked feature, which is the ambiguity of gender.

Gender in English is generally said to be «natural», that is, corresponding to reality by denoting human/non-human, male/female features. However, the elements which are brought to bear the mark of gender in English being pronouns, the presence of gender by suffixation in substantives being less frequent than in French, and in the articles non-existent, ambiguity is bound to thrive in the absence of a larger linguistic context. The covers of two paperback editions of the novel — one in English, one in French, (*Penguin* and *Folio*), are striking. Since paperback covers generally bear an illustration destined to attract the reader by emphasizing the advertisement of the contents already present in the title, cover illustrations provide an indication of the impact of the title on several supposedly competent persons such as the publisher, the illustrator and the author if alive.

The English edition reproduces a «detail from *A Cup of Tea* by Mary Cassatt, in the Museum of Fine Arts, Boston» (quote from the cover). The painting chosen is the work of a woman, and the occasion, that singled out as conveying the marked feature (+ fem), that is : (+ fem) = (+ pos), in *The Portrait of a Lady*. The picture furthermore gives an impression of worldly intimacy and conventionality alien to the atmosphere of the novel. The only relevant element is a slight intimation of lesbianism. As to the composition of the title, on the upper righthandside of the cover, the name of the author appears on a white ground ; just underneath, the title, printed this time on the reproduction of the picture. The publisher's intention appears to have been above all to emphasize that those «Bostonians» are women.

The French paperback edition is also inadequate but for different reasons. It reproduces a cartoon by Searle representing two women, ugly, naked, chained and altogether ridiculous in the way particular to Searle victims. The point is obviously that the women are frustrated, the element «women» being taken for granted. The cartoon is also alien to the spirit of the novel, but this does not concern us here. The interesting fact is that the feature (+ fem) may be taken for granted because in the translation the mark of gender is expressed by the suffix : *Les Bostoniennes.*

In the case of an unillustrated edition, when knowledge depends entirely upon the text, the title is truly ambiguous. The impression received is that the novel is about Boston society in general, male and female, which is in fact not the case since the most emphasized feature about Basil Ranson, the only major male actant, is that he is a Southerner. A picture of society at large is indeed to be found, but only as a background and New York is given as much attention as Boston : witness the descriptions of the Dutch grocery, p.160, the German beer-cellar, p. 165. On the other hand, the author might easily have suppressed the ambiguity with a title such as «Women in Boston», for instance. That he did not, considering what a careful stylist James was, must attract attention.

This ambiguity in the title may profitably be compared to the sentence introducing actants in *The Portrait* :

> The persons concerned in it were taking their pleasure quietly, and they were not of the sex which is supposed to furnish the regular votaries of the ceremony I have just mentioned [8].

The first two data given about human beings in *The Portrait* are that they are concerned in *taking pleasure*, — we shall not discuss the emphasis on hedonism in *The Portrait* here — and that they are of the male sex. This last point is expressed by *the negation of its opposite* (the «ceremony» in question being tea). In *The Portrait* negation is expressed through litotes ; in *The Bostonians* femaleness is expressed by non-expression of gender and one knows that in that case «male» is understood and concord if need be is masculine. This preoccupation with linguistic indications of sexual classification, far from being futile, is still as we know among the preoccupations of today's feminists who, though no longer like Mrs Pankhurst preoccupied with the use of the masculine gender when referring to God, are exasperated by the predominance of the male gender in the language and also, for instance, try to erase the outdated distinction between matron and virgin by the use of the term «Ms» : knowing very well that linguistic usage reflects and prolongs cultural stereotypes. We can hardly imagine that Henry James was inspired by exactly the same preoccupations ; but we may wonder what the implications of this apparent desire to erase the linguistic expression of sex category can be in a work which is concerned with the female sex.

*

* *

3. MALE VERSUS FEMALE ? THE PATTERN OF HUMAN RELATIONSHIPS IN *THE BOSTONIANS*

An investigation of the part played by male actants may first of all help us to circumscribe that played by the women.

There are only four male actants of any standing : the heroine's father, Selah Tarrant ; an officious young man, Mr Matthias Pardon ; and the heroine's two suitors, Robert Burrage and Basil Ranson, of whom the latter is the only major male actant ; this results in his being the only one which can be observed independently of his relation to the heroine, according to the Jamesian theory of «organic centre» : secondary actants gravitate round the heroine to the point of having virtually no existence outside this relation, and at the same time do not enter the privileged relation central to the plot :

Each of these persons is but wheels to the coach ; neither belongs to the body of that vehicle, or is for a moment accomodated with a seat inside. There the subject alone is ensconced, in the form of its «hero and heroine», and of the privileged high officials, say, who ride with the king and queen [9].

James writes of Ransom :

This lean, pale, shallow, striking young man is, as a representative of his sex, the most important personage in my narrative [10].

Ransom appears in the novel before the heroine Verena, according to the essential Jamesian device of the observer :

> The Prince, in the first half of the book, virtually sees and knows and makes out, virtually represents to himself everything that concerns us — very nearly (though he doesn't speak in the first person) after the fashion of the other reporters and critics of other situations. Having a consciousness highly susceptible of registration, he thus makes us see the things that may most interest us reflected in it as in the clean glass held up to so many of the «short stories» of our long list ; and yet after all never a whit to the prejudice of his being just as consistently a foredoomed, entangled, embarrassed agent in the general imbroglio, actor in the offered play [11].

This part of the involved observer is played by Ransom in *The Bostonians*, though not as consistently as by the Prince in *The Golden Bowl*. So, Ransom both «makes us see» and is «entangled».

In the coach of *The Bostonians* is the central figure, the heroine Verena ; in with her, at the structural core, but accessory to the heroine, the hero, Basil Ransom, but also another woman, Olive Chancellor.

The relational conflict which will motivate the development of the novel then appears not as a two-term relation, but as a triangle :

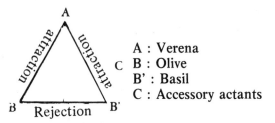

A : Verena
B : Olive
B' : Basil
C : Accessory actants

Around Verena, Olive and Basil, outside the coach, gravitate secondary actants, related to the members of the triangle by fugitive, multiple occasional relationships.

The pattern of relations between the three main actants develops according to the opposition attraction/rejection, the two poles of amorous relationships. The schema above represents the pattern of relations at the point before the crisis, that is at the most complex ; in terms of development, the genesis of the relations between the members of the triangle is as follows, in the right order :

1. Basil attracts Olive [12]
2. Verena attracts Basil
3. Verena attracts Olive
4. Olive attracts Verena
5. Basil attracts Verena

As a consequence, Verena being the object of both Olive and Basil's desire :

6. Olive rejects Basil
7. Basil rejects Olive.

As a result the pattern of relationships is upset and for a time we have a fluctuation between 4 and 5, the one receding temporarily for the benefit of the other, and vice versa :

8. Verena rejects Basil (this occurs several times).

The situation cannot for ever remain in this state of unbalance. Order is reestablished through Basil's use of force ; this acts as a catalyser and as a result :

9. Verena rejects Olive.

But one should bear in mind that the direct cause of the way the dilemma is solved is Basil's use of force : Verena is *forced to reject* Olive [13].

As we know, the pattern outlined above only concerns the relationships between the central actants. But the relations affecting secondary actants have also for their substance attraction and rejection ; though this time Verena is not the only goal ; rather, they gravitate around the triangle diversely and temporarily linked, in either a positive or a negative way, to each other. Thus Mrs Luna's relation to Ransom alternates between attraction and rejection, with the predominance of attraction, while her relation to Olive shifts from negative to positive depending upon the state of her relation to Basil ; and her relation to Verena is negative owing to the predominance of the positive in her relation to Basil. So we can see that in the last resort everything does revolve around Verena who is indeed the organic centre dear to James in this novel, the other two characters «in the coach» only acting as intermediaries.

The background actants, however, do not have this only function : they also help to develop the sociological analysis which in fact underlies the triangular conflict. In this the structure of *The Bostonians* differs from that of *The Portrait of a Lady* :

Trying to recover here, for recognition, the germ of my idea, I see that it must have consisted not at all in any conceit of a «plot», nefarious name, in any flash, upon the fancy of a set of relations, or in any of those situations that by a logic of their own, immediately fall, for the fabulist, into movement, into a march or a rush, a patter of quick steps ; but altogether in the sense of a single character, the character and aspect of a particular engaging young woman, to which all the usual elements of a «subject», certainly of a setting, were to need to be superadded [14].

Here James exposes the different possible structures and it appears that although *The Bostonians* is indeed dominated by «a particular engaging young woman», the subject and setting seem to have been anterior to that conception : or at least, more important. The «set of relations», the modulation of the triangular pattern, is also meant to serve the sociological analysis further.

What is particular in *The Bostonians* is the presence of Olive. The triangle appears in other Jamesian novels such as *The Golden Bowl, The Wings of the Dove* : but here we have not two women in conflict over a man or even two men in conflict over a woman, but a man and a woman in conflict over a woman ; in this way, not only does woman acquire the position of strength, through being present both as object of the conquest and as conqueror ; but, given that this position of strength is usually that of a man, she appears as equal to man through her assumption of the same roles so that the difference between the sexes, the strong and the weak, is abolished, and the traditional pattern of the novel fulfills the promise of the title : until the crisis occurs at the very end, and Verena is taken away from this equalitarian world.

*

*   *

4. MALE VERSUS FEMALE ? AN INQUIRY INTO THE CONSTITUENT FEATURES OF MALE AND FEMALE ACTANTS

We founded the analysis of the pattern of relationships undertaken above upon the play of two antithetic types of relations : one positive, a relation of attraction, the other negative, a relation of rejection. Attraction and rejection being considered as an underlying oppositional pattern in all relationships, we shall now try to establish what factors direct the relation towards one or the other pole : and also exactly what factors prompted the final victory of male over female since the tug of war between Olive and Basil over Verena ended in Ransom's victory which resulted in the destruction of the triangle and the establishment instead of a one-to-one relation between himself and Verena at the dénouement.

Here we shall not focus merely on the three central characters, since this would offer too little scope for the comparison of the structural pattern of actants, especially as regards the male element. Here is a list of the actants with a name — that is, those worthy of the denomination «actant» — in the novel :

MALE	FEMALE
Basil Ransom	Verena Tarrant
Selah Tarrant	Olive Chancellor
Robert Burrage	Mrs Luna
Matthias Pardon	Mrs Tarrant
	Mrs Burrage
	Doctor Prance
	Miss Birdseye
	Mrs Farrinder

The predominance of female actants is at once apparent, even though in this case we leave out actants of the third category, those unindividualized, who make up the major part of crowds at feminist meetings.

The circumstances in which all these actants meet at once assign them their parts. Mrs Luna is the first woman to appear, playing hostess : she incarnates, at the outset of the novel, «society» in its worldly aspect ; she is noticeable for her insignificance, the only two striking aspects of her personality being wealth and loquacity ; she acts as introductress to Basil and Olive ; these two go together to a feminist meeting. This is to be a meeting in the literal sense, for here all the characters listed above are to meet, with the exception of the Burrages, who, being the incarnation of New York society, seen as a rung higher than Boston on the ladder of fame, will distinguish themselves by appearing later.

Not only is the meeting the occasion for the introduction of the characters : it will unexpectedly turn out to have Verena Tarrant for leading character in what is at this point conceived as a play : Verena steps on the stage ; in a «coup de théâtre» she assumes the part of the heroine, that is *the character everybody looks at* in the Jamesian tradition. All the other actants are onlookers ; yet two of them are active onlookers : Basil and Olive, who, by looking at Verena, are already forming the project of possessing her.

Not only are the actants' parts distributed at once, but the relative situation of male and female in the cosmogony of the novel is also established at once, in a conversation at the beginning of the meeting, before the action — that is, Verena's «coming out» — starts, between Basil Ransom and Doctor Prance :

> «Men and women are all the same to me» Doctor Prance remarked, «I don't see any difference. There is room for improvement in both sexes. Neither of them is up to the standard».
> And on Ransom's asking her what the standard appeared to her to be, she said : «Well, they ought to live better ; that's what they ought to do». And she went on to declare, further, that they all talked too much. This had so long been Ransom's conviction that his heart quite warmed to Doctor Prance» [15].

Now this is a very important segment of the novel. On the face of it, Basil Ransom and Doctor Prance seem to come to share identical opinions. This is striking when we know that Ransom represents the southern gentleman, and that in the novel the opinions he expresses regarding women are somewhat different :

> He held that they were delicate, agreeable creatures, whom Providence had placed under the protection of the bearded sex [16].

A further look at the way Ransom's agreement is expressed in the first quotation once more reveals the presence of ambiguity, this time through the use of the deictic *this*. The ambiguity here lies in the linguistic referent : does *this* refer to the preceding sentence only, or to Dr Prance's whole statement ? From a grammatical point of view, it seems impossible to decide : the problem of the field of reference of anaphoric operators is precisely a delicate factor in written language ; the stumbling-block being that the means at the disposal of written language for defining units, namely punctuation and italics, are extremely poor in comparison to the richness of intonation and sentence-stress in spoken language. Ambiguity is here seen to belong to the field of written language. In such a case the interpretation is left to the reader, who, one may believe, will establish his own boundaries.

This is of course an instance of the creative character of the reading process. However it is interesting to note how so conscious and — in some regards — dictatorial an author as James leaves the interpretation open at so crucial a point.

We believe that the creativity of reading is not a continuous process, that there are nodes at which the interpretation will take one direction or another, the direction chosen influencing later decisions. This is why a decision taken so early will be extremely important. The problem is not that of «reading errors» in the Freudian sense : since no objective criterion of choice can be retained here the problem is indeed that of the creativity of reading and not of reading errors. Depending on which choice is made, one's reading of the whole novel will be dominated by the following postulates : either :

1. Men and women are equal

or only

2. Men and women talk too much

At this stage one should remember that the conversation between Basil Ransom and Doctor Prance is introduced by Ransom's interior comments on her :

> She looked like a boy, and not even like a good boy (…).It was true that if she had been a boy she would have borne some relation to a girl, whereas Doctor Prance appeared to bear none whatever. Except her intelligent eye, she had no features to speak of. Ransom asked her if she were acquainted with the lioness, and on her staring at him, without response, explained that he meant the renowned Mrs Farrinder. [17]

In this passage Dr Prance's sexual neutrality is underlined, and we can also see that James knows how to use morphological marks of gender when he feels like it : Mrs Farrinder is «the lioness». We may infer from this that Ransom admits the equality of men and women in the absence of sexual tension. We might then say that the stressed feminity of Mrs Farrinder — who obviously feels that feminist convictions are no excuse for being unattractive — rouses in him a «male chauvinist» attitude : is Ransom, at once defeated as a Southerner, and having «an immense desire for success (…), a deep aversion for the ineffectual» [18], combining thus passivity and agressivity in his nature, afraid of women as women ? On p. 11, James writes of women — it is Ransom speaking :

> If they would only be private and passive, and have no feeling but for that, and leave publicity to the sex of rougher hide. [19]

So it appears that for Ransom two kinds of women are acceptable : those who, like Doctor Prance, have renounced feminity and are sexually neutral, and those whose feminity is atoned for by their remaining hidden in the gynecaeum.

But this only goes so far as to explain Basil's acceptance of Doctor Prance. That he agreed with her is already something , the problem of what he agreed with her about is still pendent. Solving the issue can be attempted through the analysis of unifying semantic features. The dominant feature in statement one being equality between A and B — men and women — we may wonder if the same feature will be found in statement two. The answer is yes : they *all* talk too much. *All* expressing the inclusion of two or several sets into one and the same larger set, statements one and two are seen to form an entity. We may thus believe that the reading : «Ransom agrees that men and women are equal and that, moreover, men and women talk too much», is to be favoured as the result of an investigation of language : still bearing in mind however that this admission was made to Doctor Prance, the particularities of whom have been stressed above.

To what point the unifying operators are perceived by the reader is uncertain ; but the very existence of the type of exegesis known as «explication de textes» would tend to prove that they are perceived imperfectly at normal reading pace.

The problem of the author's reasons for leaving the reader a choice at this point rests unsolved and will remain so since all investigations of an author's intentions are at best hazardous ; yet at least our underlying assumption that he did leave a choice — that the question is not due simply to carelessness on the author's part — seems verified by the way he effected later rewritings of his own novels. If we — from our point of view as reader and analyst — try to think of reasons why the option was left open, we may reason that Basil Ransom plays in this novel the part of an observer, but not of an impartial one however. He is thus sometimes made to expound what appear to be the author's views, and at other times solely his own ; the differenciation between the two is effected by the author's adding qualifications which may be impersonal, or expressed by authorial *I*. For instance the statement about the desirability of passivity in women on p.11 is followed by the sentence :

Ransom was pleased with the vision of that remedy ; it must be repeated that he was very provincial.

So we may choose a first interpretation, that Ransom — whose boorish side is regularly disapproved of by authorial comments — is purely and simply what feminists today would call a male chauvinist, and the novel will then take its regular course up to Verena's ill-boding elopement. If a male chauvinist himself, the reader may even go so far as to conclude that Verena is «served right», since she *did* talk too much, which is not at all a nice thing for a little girl to do, and Ransom saves her from the danger awaiting her at the hands of people like Mrs Farrinder :

> He stood appalled for a moment, as he said to himself that she would take her up and the girl would be ruined, would force her note and become a screamer. [20]

In that case James keeps in store for the imprudent reader the very last sentence of the novel :

> It is to be feared that with the union, so far from brilliant, into which she was about to enter, these (Verena's tears) were not the last she was destined to shed. [21]

Since Random himself has amply been described as a brilliant young man, it is indeed *the fact that Verena, herself a brilliant young woman, marries him* which is «far from brilliant». In order to see the outcome of the novel as the happy triumph of established order one would have to skip the last sentence which may properly be termed as an «unhappy ending». With the last sentence the unwary reader is caught in a trap in which James's love of suspense, ambiguity and irony are combined.

This interpretation having proved unsatisfactory, we shall decide upon the second possibility : Basil Ransom agrees with Doctor Prance because she is not sexually agressive. The real problem would then be, not that of war between the sexes, but that of war between agressive human beings. In order to develop this point we shall take a further look at the actants' constituent features.

*
* *

5. THE LAWS OF SURVIVAL OF THE SPECIES IN THE JAMESIAN FICTIONAL WORLD : AN INQUIRY INTO THE CONSTITUENT FEATURES OF MALE AND FEMALE ACTANTS, CONTINUED.

The structure of Jamesian actants consists basically in the presence of a certain number of key features. These are of course modulated in various ways, but in order to serve our purpose of clarifying the way in which the internal structure of actants influences the relations between actants we have schematized the basic internal structural features in the following table :

	positive			negative			
	beauty	charm	(1)	(2)	loquacity	wealth	violence
Verena	+	+	+	+	+	−	−
Olive	−	−	+	−	+	+	−
Mrs Luna	−	−	−	−	+	+	−
Mrs Tarrant	−	−	−	−	+	−	−
Mrs Burrage	−	+	+	−	+	+	−
Dr Prance	−	−	+	−	−	−	−
Miss Bridseye	−	−	−	+	+	−	−
Mrs Farrinder	+	+	+	−	+	−	−
B. Ransom	+	+	+	−	+	−	+
S. Tarrant	−	−	−	−	+	−	−
R. Burrage	+	+	+	−	+	+	−
M. Pardon	−	−	−	−	+	−	−
(1) intelligence (2) innocence							

This is of course schematic. By positive and negative features, we indicate whether the feature is favoured or not by the author or rather whether the impression conveyed to the reader, is that the author, acting as a god-like figure, arbiter of values inside the frame of his work, has a positive or a negative attitude towards this particular feature. For instance, since money is shown as a factor of corruption, it is a negative feature ; therefore the fact of not being endowed with that feature, that is, (—wealth) results in a positive aspect of the actant.

The presence or absence in a given actant of a feature which may in itself be positive or negative is not found in the same degree in all actants, and the presence or absence of the features are modulated according to the actants to which they belong, their importance, and the circumstances. Once again, we have deemed an actant worthy of the attribution of a feature if the overall impression is that *in the eyes of the reader*, the actant is endowed with the feature. Thus, Selah Tarrant, who has (—charm), is mentioned in the novel as having, as a mesmeric healer, some measure of success with certain ladies. However, as we shall see, the description made of him is in no way conducive to his having any measure of success with the reader, therefore he has not been endowed with the feature. Needless to say, by «the reader», we mean the author of the present study, a coherent subjectivity being what we aim at.

Among the positive features one, innocence, strikes by its rarity : it is shared only by Verena and Miss Birdseye. The most widely distributed is intelligence. The Jamesian world is indeed governed by intelligence, which is required to escape at least some of the traps and survive. If an actant has both innocence and intelligence — like Verena — he/she has a chance to get on, though likely to be caught in the end. If innocent and stupid like Miss Birdseye, the actant has no chance of success either in the world of the novel or in the reader's eyes ; in this James diverges from the laws of many Victorian writers.

The lack of positive features — still in terms of success, that is of actions of the actant — may be compensated by the presence of negative ones. The division into positive and negative features having been operated according the ethical criteria which appear to have been adopted by the author, the fact that a feature is negative — that is, ethically so — does not mean that it may not be an asset for survival in a world that is unethical — as we shall see further on. Negative features are, however, fewer than positive ones, something which is easily accounted for by the theory of the organic centre alluded to above. Since everything revolves round the heroine, and since it seems a law of the Jamesian world that a heroine must be good — good not like Thackeray's Amelia whose goodness lies in her acceptance of conventional Ruskin-type standards of feminine behaviour, but according to ethical laws applying to any human being — other actants will be determined mainly by the presence or absence of those features predominant in the heroine — the positive ones. To illustrate Verena's degree of perfection, here are some reflections by Olive :

She had come to consider the girl as a wonder of wonders, to hold that no human origin, however congruous it might superficially appear, would sufficiently account for her ; that her springing up between Selah and his wife was an exquisite whim of the creative force ; and that in such a case a few shades more or less of the inexplicable didn't matter. It was notorious that great beauties, great geniuses, great characters, take their own times and places for the coming into the world, leaving the gaping spectators to make them «fit in», and holding from far-off ancestors, or even, perhaps, straight from the divine generosity, much more than from their ugly or stupid progenitors. They were incalculable phenomena, anyway, as Selah would have said. Verena, for Olive, was the very type and model of the «gifted being» ; her qualities had not been bought and paid for ; they were like some brilliant birthday-present, left at the door by an unknown messenger, to be delightful for ever as an inexhaustible legacy, and amusing forever from the obscurity of its source. [22]

As we can see the heroine should be singled out by the greatest number of positive features. This is natural since she sets a standard to which all other actants will be referred. She is not altogether perfect — if she were it would hamper the development of the conflict necessary to the plot — and she possesses one negative feature, loquacity, which will prove her downfall since it is her «gift of gab» — to take up Dr Prance's words — that will expose her to being noticed by Olive and Ransom. All in all Verena is endowed with either too much, or too little ; this makes her vulnerable.

Let us now compare the structural patterns of the secondary actants, those who «ride in the coach» with the heroine.

The first of these is Selah Tarrant ; he belongs to this category for a very short time only, since he fades out as soon as Olive takes over. After that and for the greatest part of the novel he belongs to the third category. He is interesting insofar as he «starts Verena up», in the words of Matthias Pardon :

«She seems to have her father to start her up. It seems to pass into her». And Mr Pardon indulged in a gesture destined to signify the passage. [23]

At the beginning of the novel, Verena is under her father's influence ; the importance of this fact appears from the insistance with which the ritual which materializes it — the imposition of the hands — is described. However, Selah Tarrant — together with Mrs Tarrant and Matthias Pardon, who, we are given to understand, rode in the coach during the prehistory of the novel, before the events which find their chronological place inside the boundaries of the narrative, are noticeable for their insignificance : the only feature they are endowed with is the «gift of the gab» — a feature which would in the context be noticeable by its absence only. This again answers to functional logic since inside the limits of the novel these three actants are «has-beens».

To come back to Tarrant himself, the first actant to exert an influence upon Verena, let us examine the description the author makes of him :

> A slow, deliberate smile, which made his mouth enormous, developed into wrinkles, as long as the wings of a bat, on either sides of it, and showed a set of big, even, carnivorous teeth. [24]

James's contribution to fantastic literature is well-known, particularly in *The Turn of the Screw*, which develops the theme of the use of children by adults in order to reach their own perverted ends. Outside the fantastic genre, this theme is taken up in such novels as *What Maisie Knew* and *The Awkward Age*. It represents the extreme of the basic theme of Jamesian fiction — the destruction of the innocent by those whom experience has perverted. In *The Bostonians* the persecution of Verena the innocent by the experienced and corrupted shifts from her insignificant if vampiric father to Olive and later Ransom.

That Tarrant is so easily disposed with is justified by the fact that his interest in Verena is indirect. He does indeed at the beginning suck up her life in order to feed his own, but only because Verena is a means to procure money. As soon as Olive provides what he really wanted, he detaches himself from Verena. Verena's own easy detachment from her father finds the same explanation : he, too, was mainly an instrument to «draw her out» — for her to find an opportunity to grow up.

Verena has strongly oedipal characteristics. She does get rid of her father's influence, but only in order to be manipulated by another. She has no autonomy : «it isn't me, mother» she says p.48, denying that her accomplishments might indeed be her own. This neurotic side of her constitution is enhanced by her lack of wealth, which, if we take into account the conditions of the period, condemns her to be either obscure — which would be incompatible with her structure — or dishonest, which would be unsuitable since she is the heroine, or dependent. She therefore lets herself be drained out : Dr Prance remarks on p.40 that : «Yes, she was pretty-appearing, but there was a certain indication of anaemia».

Matthias Pardon is not even, like Selah Tarrant, a has-been, but a «might-have-been». At the beginning he stands waiting for

Verena, but is defeated at the portentous meeting ; his goal seems
to have been similar to Selah's :

> Young Mr Pardon remarked, in Ransom's hearing, that he knew parties
> who, if they had been present, would want to engage Miss Verena at a very
> high figure for the winter campaign. And Ransom heard him add in a lower
> tone : «There's money for some one in that girl : you see if she don't have quite
> a run». [25]

The description of Mr Pardon is slightly alarming ; he is :

> A young man with hair prematurely, or, as one felt that one should say,
> precociously white. [26]

> The young man with the side-whiskers and the white hair. [27]

Paleness is, curiously, a physical feature shared by almost all the
characters, even the least important ones ; Miss Birdseye for
instance :

> She had a sad, soft, pale face, which (and it was the effect of her whole head)
> looked as if it had been soaked, blurred, and made vague by exposure to some
> slow dissolvent. [28]

The white Mr Pardon being defenceless in the face of wealth,
Olive takes over. An examination of their respective features
makes Olive and Verena appear as opposite and complementary.
Olive is poor of nearly everything Verena is rich of ; her two assets
are intelligence, which constitutes the necessary basic link between
them, and wealth which Verena lacks. She has indeed a third
asset, that of being a woman ; it is easier for such an oedipal girl as
Verena, sexually immature, to attach herself to Olive rather than
to her rich suitor Robert Burrage when she rids herself of her
father.

The couple which Olive would have herself and Verena form
thus appears — leaving aside the homosexual aspect on which
James passes no judgment, such a thing as a positive sexual
relationship being unknown in his world anyway — clearly
neurotic. Verena's positive structure had been but slightly
perverted by the influence of her father, who, being himself
penniless, was in spite of his endeavours powerless to make her
enter a world of money — or rather enter it himself through her.

Olive has money and a negative structure. She wants Verena
both because she is strong — on account of her positive structure
— and fragile — on account of her lack of financial means, which
submits her to the influence of others, and her innocence, which
though morally positive is potentially dangerous. Therefore Olive

finds in Verena the positive features she herself lacks and to which she will cling as a parasite, feeding her own deficiencies with them, but in order to do so she must put Verena in a situation of inferiority by creating in her a deficiency — the need for money which had been less perceptible in her previous world of shabbiness. Verena will comply all the more easily as, to her, Olive's tutelage — or should we say vampirism — is but a prolongation of her father's, plus a promise of coming out into the world. The need for money is introduced by Olive into Verena's positive structure, so that each partner of the couple will have to lean on the other, the couple being held together by their complementary deficiencies.

At this point two aspects should be stressed. The first, which is characteristic of the archetypal Jamesian structure, is the antinomy, complementarity and ambivalence of the features innocence and wealth. To be caught between innocence and wealth is the common plight of the Jamesian heroine. As we have already hinted, innocence appears as both an asset and a handicap. An asset in that its possession implies moral qualities, it is a handicap in that it implies a lack of experience — of knowledge. On the other hand, money gives power, and with the power comes knowledge : therefore, the possession of money, which comes to be coveted by the heroine as a means of acquiring power — and therefore of fulfilling the ambition which results of her endowment of both moral and intellectual qualities, had a negative effect. Once in a position of power, but denied the ruthlessness which permits an efficient use of power by her innocence, money does not corrupt her — she is morally too positive — but, corruption being the only way in which she could survive this situation, she is destroyed ; at the end of the novel the only future the author allows her is that of the traditionally oppressed woman :

«Ah !Now I am glad !» said Verena, when they reached the street. But though she was glad, he presently discovered that, beneath her hood, she was in tears. [29]

Instead of appearing on a platform clothed in light, the focus-point of the crowd's eyes and ears, she is reduced to pretence, shadow, acquiescence.

A smile of exceeding faintness played across her lips — it was just perceptible enough to light up the native gravity of her face. It might have been likened to a thin ray of moonlight resting upon the wall of a prison. (...). He observed

that Miss Chancellor's hand was at once cold and limp ; she merely placed it in his, without exerting the smallest pressure . [30]
She was so essentially a celibate that Ransom found himself thinking of her as old, though when he came to look at her (as he said to himself) it was apparent that her years were fewer than his own. He did not dislike her, she had been so friendly ; but, little by little, she gave him an uneasy feeling — the sense that you could not be safe with a person who took things so hard. (...) Her white skin had a singular look of being drawn tightly across her face (...) The curious tint of her skin was a living colour ; when she turned it upon you, you thought vaguely of the glitter of green ice. She had absolutely no figure, and presented a certain appearance of feeling cold. [31]

It is therefore not to be wondered if Ransom at first appears as a positive influence upon Verena : it is positive in so far as it enables her to detach herself from Olive, just as Olive had helped Verena's detachment from her father. Basil Ransom has a great number of positive features : in fact he has the same structure here as Verena's other suitor, Robert Burrage ; we may note that both these actants have the same initials, reversed. Ransom's advantage over Burrage resided, first, in laying a claim upon Verena after Olive, and thus when she was already more emancipated and growing restless with Olive's domination ; second in his resorting to the use of force, something Burrage would be too civilized to do, and which is suggested by the name Ransom.

Ransom and Burrage also share a predominance of negative features, two out of three ; but Burrage's are loquacity and wealth, and the last has already done its work for Verena : Ransom's strength lies therefore precisely in his being the only actant endowed with the feature force.

Verena and Ransom have a lot in common ; however, the loss of innocence as we know is for Jamesian actants the original sin, the indelible taint which makes it impossible for them to develop harmoniously hereafter. In Ransom's structure also innocence and money — his two deficiencies — are correlative though in a different way from Verena's : for Ransom the loss of innocence was provoked by the loss of, not the access to, money.

Basil Ransom had lived, but she knew he had lived to see bitter hours. His family was ruined ; they had lost their slaves, their property, their friends and relations, their homes ; had tasted of all the cruelty of defeat. He had tried for a while to carry on the plantation himself, but he had a millstone of debt round his neck, and he longed for some work which would transport him to the haunts of men. The state of Mississipi seemed to him the state of despair ; so he surrendered the remnants of his patrimony to his mother and sisters, and, at nearly thirty years of age, alighted for the first time in New-York, in the costume of his province, with fifty dollars in his pocket, and a gnawing hunger in his heart. [32]

Like Madame Merle and Osmond in *The Portrait*, Kate Croy in *The Wings of the Dove* ; Charlotte Stant in *The Golden Bowl,* Fleda Vetch in *The Spoils of Poynton,* he is corrupted and presents only the appearance of life.

In Jamesian actants, loss of innocence, instead of being compensated by a beneficial acquisition of experience, is totally perverting ; the actants never grow up ; if they grow, they grow sideways, warped. In a Jamesian novel, an innocent heroine loses her illusions ; there the novel stops. Beside her there are other actants who have lost their innocence *before* the beginning of the novel. The heroine and these other actants (secondary actants) interact, for the final defeat of the first ; the fight between the young and good, and the bad and old goes on, but we are not shown the total course of a life — from young and good to old and bad, from Isabel Archer to Madame Merle : instead of :

crisis of experience

Life	developing	Death

We have :

Life	Crisis

Versus

Post-crisis	Death

The nefarious effect of access to wealth, which results either in perversion or in the destruction of the personality, is not however characteristic of all actants : for instance, Mr Touchett or Gaspar Goodwood in *The Portrait* come out unscathed. For them money is indeed a source of strength and fulfilment. The reason seems due to simple ethics : those actants are self-made men. Money has made them tough, not bad. Money destroys or corrupts those who acquire it in a debasing way : and precisely, in the 19th century there was no way for a woman to acquire money except by receiving it in a totally passive way, by heritage, in which case the lack of action on her part could not be expected to yield any strengthening results, or by debasing herself in some way, which could only, in a highly ethical if pessimistic world, have negative results.

That Basil's influence over Verena will in fact eventually prove as destructive as Selah's and Olive's is signalled by the use, for Ransom also, of the imagery of vampirism :

> He ever looked a little hard and discouraging, like a column of figures, in spite of the friendly face which he bent upon his hostess's deputy, and which, in its thinness, had a deep dry line, a sort of premature wrinkle, on either side of the mouth. [33]

Ransom's wrinkle is premature because he has not yet taken possession of Verena : remember Selah's «two wrinkles, as long as the wings of a bat, on either side of it» already quoted.

The passing of Verena from Olive's hands into Basil's is not, however, as easy as that from her father's to Olive's. Going with Ransom means becoming a woman with the implications of this status at the time, that is, not fulfilling herself but denying herself, whereas, up till now Verena's «protectors» had been a way of accession to greater fulfilment, however heavy the price.

We may now see why woman was such a privileged subject for the author. We shall not here try to probe into the reasons why the growth of the Jamesian heroine must be a stunted one ; this would be speculation. But woman did indeed fill perfectly the structural pattern of the Jamesian novel, which is that of tragedy, even though a strain of comedy is intertwined. The author writes of Olive (Ransom is speaking) :

> He was sorry for her, but he saw in a flash that no one could help her, that was what made her tragic. [34]

Indeed, the final treatment of Olive is highly interesting. She at least is not in a situation of financial dependence, though her wealth seems to her a burden as well as an asset ; but her neurotic leanings make her wish for self-destruction :

> The most secret, the most sacred hope of her nature was that she might one day have such a chance, that she might be a martyr and die for something. [35]

One must emphasize the expression : «the most sacred hope of her nature», and not : «her most sacred hope». Thus in Olive the conflict is between her death-wish and the will to live, which can only be satisfied by living at someone else's expense, since she seems to have too few resources in herself. What happens, however, is that Verena, the stronger of the two, somehow gets the better of Olive, and finally Olive comes to depend on her rather than the reverse, as Verena's success is about to give her the possibility of earning her own living. At this point both Olive and Ransom are about to lose her, when Ransom's recourse to force brings her back to dependence. One might have expected Olive to go to pieces after Verena left her : but on the contrary, since she had come to be dependent upon Verena, severance from the latter rather seems to bring about Olive's liberation. This denouement is full of suspense :

> As soon as Ransom looked at her he became aware that the weakness she had just shown had passed away. She had straightened herself again, and she was upright in her desolation. The expression of her face was a thing to remain with him for ever ; it was impossible to imagine a more vivid presentment of blighted hope and wounded pride. Dry, desperate, rigid, she yet wavered and seemed uncertain ; her pale, glittering eyes straining forward, as if they were looking for death. Ransom had a vision, even at that crowded moment, that if she could have met it there and then, bristling with steel or lurid with fire, she would have rushed on it without a tremor, like a heroine that she was. (...) She might have suggested to him some feminine firebrand of Paris revolutions, erect on a barricade, or even the sacrificial figure of Hypatia, whirled through the furious mob of Alexandria.(...) As they mingled in the issuing crowd he perceived the quick, complete, tremendous silence which, in the hall, had greeted Olive Chancellor's rush to the front. Every sound instantly dropped, the hush was respectful, the great public waited, and whatever she should say to them (and he thought she might indeed be embarrassed) it was not apparent that they were likely to hurl the benches at her. [36]

So Olive and Verena's destinies are sealed. The financial transaction through which Olive had acquired Verena having failed, she is in a sense washed of the sin of possessing money ; she has paid for her wealth. In fact, through Verena, she has acquired independence and the possibility of action ; while through Ransom Verena has been brought to dependence.

Their end is expressed through the same device of litotes : Verena's union is «far from brilliant», her tears are «not the last», whereas Olive's spectators are not «likely to hurl the benches at her». Verena's end is the negation of positivity ; while Olive's is the negation of negativity. On this the novel ends ; but we must not forget that Ransom's use of force has not only provoked Verena's defeat ; it has also insured Olive's success.

The real winner, however, appears to be Ransom, since the crisis is solved through his intervention — the recourse to force. This intervention solves the unending dilemma of Verena's hesitation between Ransom and Olive, which is in fact that of a hypercivilized society no longer capable of making its own choices, a society which can no longer act but only talk. In this situation it is not surprising that Ransom's action should be a catalyser — but only at the cost of the only worthy member, Verena, being sacrificed. Verena is the incarnation of goodness, and also of woman ; as we already mentioned, positive values and feminity are equated, one may think because the situation of women at the time fitted so well the pattern of the defeat of innocence. One of James's short stories has for a title *The Beast in the Jungle* : and the outwardly polished society he described is indeed a ferocious place in which human beings try to regain the life they have lost by devouring others. The analysis of the mesh of relationships showed that the impulse of attraction — of love — is in fact an attempt at acquiring the beloved object, at reducing it to slavery not in order to enjoy its qualities but to procure them for oneself in a cannibalistic process expressed through images of vampirism. In this world one acquires the defeated warrior's courage by eating his heart. Woman fits the overall pattern best : but the problem is, over and above that of feminism as an attempt at breaking the pattern, that of human relationships at large. In that light, the ambiguity of the title can be solved.

NOTES

1. The term «actant» designates, in our vocabulary, those substantives endowed with the semantic feature (+ human) ; the multiple subject-predicate relations into which they enter constitute the «plot» of the novel — or «action». The term «character» has been avoided because, together with a certain number of words in the vocabulary of criticism, such as «stylistics» for instance, it has been grossly misused. Characters have been made into persons in the way that a child playing with her doll «pretends». Characters only «live» in the phantasmatic elaboration that goes on in the reader's mind. When one is not only reading, but analyzing, the reading process, one should be able to effect a reasonable amount of distanciation.

2. Since this study will come to bear on problems of the structure of the novel, we shall here concentrate on this genre, leaving the short stories aside.

3. R. Barthes, **Le Degré Zéro de l'Ecriture**, coll. Points, p. 29.

4. We should make it clear that we do not disregard the importance of successful illusions in fiction, but we must stress that this illusion is the consequence for the reader of a successful manipulation of language on the writer's part.

5. Cf : C. Rihoit, «Waiting for Isabel», in Joly ed., **Studies in English Grammar.**

6. **The Great Tradition**, Penguin, p. 142.

7. H. James, **Preface to the Golden Bowl**, Penguin, p. 8.

8. H. James, **The Portrait of a Lady**, Penguin, p. 1.

9. Preface to **The Portrait of a Lady**, p. XV.

10. **The Bostonians**, Penguin, p. 6.

11. H. James, Preface to **The Golden Bowl**, p. 8.

12. «She thought him very handsome as he said this, but reflected that unfortunately men didn't care for the truth, especially the new kinds in proportion as they were good-looking. She had, however, a moral resource that she could always fall back upon ; it had already been a comfort to her, on occasions of acute feeling, that she hated men, as a class, anyway». **The Bostonians**, p. 21.

13. «'Olive, Olive ,'» Verena suddenly shrieked ; and her piercing cry might have reached the front. But Ransom had already, by muscular force, wrenched her away, and was hurrying her out». **The Bostonians**, p. 21.

14. Preface to **The Portrait of a Lady**, p. VI.

15. **The Bostonians**, p. 37.

16. **The Bostonians**, p. 12.

17. **The Bostonians**, pp. 36-37.

18. **The Bostonians**, p. 16.

19. **The Bostonians**, p. 11.

20. **The Bostonians**, p. 57.

21. **The Bostonians**, p. 390.

22. **The Bostonians**, pp. 110-111.

23. **The Bostonians**, p. 47.

24. **The Bostonians,** p. 41.

25. **The Bostonians**, p. 56.

26. **The Bostonians**, p. 97.

27. **The Bostonians**, p. 38.

28. **The Bostonians**, p. 24.

29. **The Bostonians**, p. 389.

30. **The Bostonians**, p. 9.

31. **The Bostonians**, pp. 17-18.

32. **The Bostonians**, p. 13.

33. **The Bostonians**, p. 56.

34. **The Bostonians**, p. 12.

35. **The Bostonians**, p. 13.

36. **The Bostonians**, p. 388.

Kathleen HULLEY

From the Crystal Sphere to Edge City :

ideology in the novels of Dashiell Hammett

A large octavo volume revealed to him
the teachings of Israel Baal Shem-Tob,
founder of the sect of the pious ; another
volume, the virtues and terrors of the
Tetragrammaton, which is the ineffable
name of God ; another the thesis that
God has a secret name, in which is
epitomized (as in the crystal sphere
which the Persians attribute to
Alexander of Macedon) his ninth attribute, eternity — that is to say the
immediate knowledge of everything that
will exist, exists, and has existed in the
universe.

Death and the Compass
JORGE LUIS BORGES

Detective fiction had been, until Dashiell Hammett and «The
Black Mask» magazine introduced the *hard-boiled* school,
structured on the principle of the crystal sphere. Its logic, its
temporal and narrative structure, its theme assured a clear,
unified, knowable universe. Its metaphysic rested on the
assumption that time and space have continuity and coherence,
that events are not merely contiguous but filled with cause and
direction. Any fiction which moves towards climax, no matter what
its subject or tone, is both a displaced mimesis of apocalypse,
affirming the notion of space filled with God and time which
moves toward Him and also a mimesis of the myth of rationality [1].
In the classic murder mystery events and objects achieve metaphysical and ideological significance by containing within
themselves, from the beginning, the solution to the crime, so that
the dénouement of discovery vests every object, event, and person
with a logical significance — a significance established the
moment the crime has been committed. Although such a story
seems to move forward, it is static, its end contained in its
beginnings — a perfect cristal sphere.
   Thus the traditional conjunction of ratiocination and criminal
apprehension in the classic «whodunit» which arose in the 19th
century affirms and constructs a notion of social reality upon
which democratic social order rests. It is a child of the
Enlightenment, mirroring empiricism, logic, and the necessity for
«social» order. In the traditional whodunit, as soon as a crime is

committed, the dectective-hero brings together these myths in order to restore justice. His story of crime, search, and capture merely reinforces the Enlightenment myths of order on which the whole political and economic structure of modern democracy was erected. He collaborates with society to define social aberrency as evil ; crime and its solution are both socially defined and socially protected fictions.

Earliest fictional detectives were fully aware they paid a high price to maintain a particular myth of social order. Edgar Allan Poe's Augsute Dupin lived a solitary life, in the dark, never venturing into the light ; Arthur Conan Doyle's Sherlock Holmes was an opium smoker. Dupin was so aware of the particular view of man he was upholding that he once said, «deprived of ordinary resources, the analyst throws himself into the spirit of his opponent, identifies himself therewith, and not unfrequently sees thus, at a glance the sole methods... by which he was to seduce into error or hurry into miscalculation» [2]. He saw that the killer is merely the hero's «doppleganger», a repressed mirror image of socially forbidden desires. Dupin's theory of ratiocination admits that crime solution has only superficially to do with the observation of empirical data and profoundly to do with the hero's own ability to contact his own aberrent desires. Both classic|heroes had, in fact, moved to Edge City — the edges of the civilized world, the edges of evil, the edges of their own suppressed capacity for chaos and disruption. Each dwells in the dark precisely to uphold the social fiction that the irrational *is* merely aberrent.

But before Dashiell Hammett, this risky edge of detective fiction, so fundamental to Poe and Doyle, had nearly disappeared from the pages of the traditional whodunit. Hammett's fiction, however, plunges to the center of those frightening desires. His heroes move from the arm-chair and dark house into the «mean streets» of Edge City, where the fantasy of violence and chaos belongs to everyone, and to the hero in the name of the law. In Edge City the hero need no longer *imagine* himself the criminal ; he may enact his own dark and murderous fantasies. Clearly this narrative shift has its own ideological implications about the social construction of reality.

But Hammett expresses these implications only by duplicity : his novels pretend to preserve a mythical social contract but instead challenge all its assumptions [3]. His works strike us immediately by their ambivalence — a lack, a shocking reversal of our expectations. As soon as his Continental Op goes to solve a crime, the client is usually murdered. Further violence mushrooms from this singular and repeated failure. Moreover, we are faced with a tangle of lies and stories ; truth is measured only in terms of capture and death. The interior life of all the characters, which seems wholly absent, is entirely exteriorized in violent action : There seems to be neither a recognizable social nor sexual order ; crimes are solved, but nothing returns to its normal place. The only moral center is a personal code the hero adheres to, but within this code ends become confused with means or even destroyed by them. In these stories the myth of social order cannot restrain the rampant and undirected desire on which it depends. Instead, another world emerges, underneath, behind, its obverse underwolrd image — Edge-City.

Hammett, therefore, chooses a hidden negative pole as the setting for his fiction. His heroes dwell literally and psychologically in the socially negative world which is in fact the foundation on which «order» is structured. This suggests that what the order denies is an a priori «Primal delirium», amoral, irrational, chaotic —a pure negation which is «beyond all foundation»[4] ; yet it is the source not only of power and disruption but of creative energy as well. Such unrestricted desire is the opposite pole of our fictive world ; it is The Other which makes itself known only indirectly in dream, in fantasy, in fictions. When in «The Tenth Clew» the Op nearly submits to his impulse to drown, we are aware that this impulse is only a metaphor for the overwhelming power of this repressed Other.

By breaking with the conventions of crime fiction, Hammett is able to explore this opposite pole of social order while seeming to uphold its traditions. In fact, that pretense becomes a strand in his hero's own fantasies, so that the socially defined «crime» is merely the catalytic event which gives rise to new fictions that toy with and expose the «order» which denies their potency.

Red Harvest (1929) and *The Glass Key* (1931) best exemplify both his methods and his ideological implications [5]. Both these novels repeat patterns which turn the myths of western civilization inside out in a devasting criticism of its moral and social duplicity. They challenge social myth by insisting on the personal and unique assertion of the individual over law and institution. This challenge, which is repeated in differing and complex forms in all his novels and stories, aims not at the conventional reaffirmation of social myth, but at disruption ; and this disruption continues on all levels of the narrative.

The pattern is clearest in *Red Harvest* and *The Glass Key* because in both these novels there are four explicit levels of narrative, each of which disrupts the other even while giving rise to the next. There are stories within stories, a Chinese puzzle box whose solution is to self-destruct. These four stories are the story of a murder, the story of the restoration of power, the story of the hero's solution to both these problems, and the story of the hero's story. Each of these narratives provides its own criterion of social order. For example, the story of murder depends on an external social order which defines certain acts as socially disruptive and other acts as socially constructive. But in the story of the restoration of power, the hero himself defines that power in his own terms. The third story — the solution — is especially deceptive for while it appears to be a story which restores order, we shall see from analysis of the psychological structures of relationships that it is a story which preserves disruption. This third story is created by the fourth story — the story of the hero's stories, stories which only pretend to mirror rational fictions, but which instead undercut the fiction of crime and solution, parodying all its assumptions.

In his «Introduction» to the recent issue of *Continental Op Stories* Steven Marcus is the first to point out that the Op's real task is not to solve crimes but to «deconstruct» fiction :

> ... He soon discovers that the «reality» that anyone involved in will swear to is in fact itself a construction, a fabrication, a fiction, a faked,and alternate reality and that it has been gotten together before he ever arrived on the scene. And the Op's work, therefore, is to deconstruct, decompose, deplot, and defictionalize that «reality» and to construct or reconstruct out of it a true fiction. i.e., an account of what «really» happened [6].

But clearly Hammett goes one further step. The Op's story of what «really» happened is simply another fiction — a lie, a «hunch», a fantasy which happens to fit the social requirement that the crime be solved. The hero creates the illusion of order by bowing to this requirement but, in fact, his obsessive story-telling disrupts the myth of «reality». As one fiction explodes the myth of another, the story-making process itself is revealed as the foundation of reality.

This narrative compulsion creates the suspicion that there is subversive moment in every story about a crime, an instant when we suspect everyone, when every detail seems relevant. In the mushrooming, bloody chaos of *Red Harvest* it is especially evident that an ideology that requires the fiction of significance and connection casts guilt on everyone and everything. Thus, in a sense, any story his hero tells will do, so long as it fits the most elements into the most coherent pattern. The story is a game, not a solution.

Furthermore, that subversive moment when everything becomes possible possesses its own erotic disruptive resistance to the forward motion of the narrative and tempts the narrative to destroy itself. While the detective gropes to tell the «right» story, he must continuously resist the auto-erotic pull of this narrative ; he must select only those elements which will fit a socially required pattern of solution. But the myth of significance resists the very desire for form which gave impetus to the original search. Only an outside presure to affirm its own rationality pushes the story forward, towards conclusion and away from the compulsion to remain locked in its own action.

Thus while the conscious desire of the detective-hero's text is to move towards solution, towards dénouement, towards coherence, its unconscious compulsion is toward regressive repetitiveness which pushes the text toward entropy[7]. The «detective» stories of Thomas Pynchon, for example — V and The Crying of Lot 49 — are stories of a search in which everything and anything may be a clue. As the search becomes more and more its own motive, the text reveals an uncontrollable desire to include all of reality, all of history, all of the imagination as it drives towards significance. Psychon's novels rest in that subversive moment when everything is implicated ; they turn that moment inside out so that we may see that at bottom the search for significance is a drive so urgent that it obliterates itself. Detective fiction has traditionally resisted the urge to become trapped in its own search, but the narrative moves forward only by evading its own motives and submitting to the demands of the communal myths it simultaneously upholds and relies upon.

Hammett's novels amplify the tensions between the social myth and the obsessive fantasies of his heroes. His second story, the restoration of power, resolves that tension by taking up the narrative residue of coherence demanded by the story of solution. Instead of becoming caught by his desire to turn everything into a «clue», the hero lays bare the dialectics of power within the community. This second story does not trap events in a linear labyrinth of solution ; instead it allows the hero to kill whatever does not fit his story of communal power. This latter story uncovers the hero's ideological stance because it diverts the language from conventional narrative forms and because it reconstructs the pattern of relationships so that the hero supports an essentially disruptive power structure.

Language, first of all, is deflected from its functions of rational discourse towards a fantasy which unleashes violence outward but which turns eroticism linguistically inward. Words, accusation, fable,lies,create events, suspects,victims, and killers. But while the hero's fantasies of violence take form in action — gunfights or murder — his erotic fantasies remain locked in the descriptions of violence. Thus violence and especially death is the only permissible orgasmic expression. From the point of view of story-telling eroticism must be repressed because, with the exception of Nora Charles of *The Thin Man*, all women are dangerous competitors. They lie, cheat, and fantasize as well as the hero, but in addition they possess a seductive power which can divert the story into new channels. «Good» women are reticent, and they die quickly.

In such confusion, the language of violence absorbs the dangers of erotic desire and gives it release. There is a scene in a short story called «The Tenth Clew» in which the Op questions the seductive Creda Dexter. He says, «I went up against Creda Dester again spending an entire afternoon in her apartment, banging away with question after question, all directed toward her former love affairs». Poking, prying, «banging» her sexual life, the Op is oblivious to the eroticism beneath his persistent pursuit of verbal response. This substitution of mental attack for sexual attack is, in part, conventional — in American literature violence has always been a suitable defense against the threat of sexuality — but Hammett's heros fantasize a verbal penetration which is so unconsciously sexual that it parodies that convention and exposes the socially suppressed ideology which separates sexuality from virtue and associates it with crime.

Red Harvest, the most erotically violent fantasy of the omnipotency of words, opens with a metaphysical pun arising from the confusion of pronunciation between Personville and poison-ville. It continues with the sexually disinterested, but verbally procreative Op whose psychically confused language turns a whole town to seething violence. For him words and guns achieve equal power, subordinating the distinction between eroticism and violence. He «burns» cigarettes, «loads» his stomach, gets «twelve solid hours of end to end sleep», while bullets «kiss holes in the door» above his head. His body becomes simply another element in his fictions, and objects themselves threaten to take on a deadly life of their own. It is no wonder that Dinah Brand, Poisonville's «deluxe hustler», dies, the Op's hand on the ice-pick thrust in her ample breat, just after the Op has verbally ejaculated his own self-doubt before her. What is ideologically important in this use of language is its deceptive creation of a myth that the social tradition of sexual supression and the substitution of violence are necessary to the order the Op defends, while, in fact, this confused naming subverts that order.

In *The Glass Key* Ned Beaumont's language is the obverse reflection of the Op's. Instead of using language to exteriorize subversion, he turns it inward against himself. Nevertheless, their ideological goals are precisely the same — the disruption of the social mythology and its submission to the hero's personal code. It is merely as if «lean» Ned is what remains after the «fat» Op's psychic reduction in violence. The nightmare repetition of murder in which the Op indulges achieves reconciliation only by abstention and withdrawal. As catalyst, the Op is absorbed in events ; Ned, on the other hand, prevents these fantasies from becoming event by maintaining a self-conscious barrier between objects and himself. For example, while the Op remains perpetually anonymous, Ned Beaumont's name is reiterated obsessively as if to assure his own solidity. This shift in perspective on naming is significant, for by mastering and exteriorizing language, the Op has hidden the disruptive aims of his story. Ned, on the other hand, turns our attention to its literal psychic dangers.

Secondly, by turning words inward, Ned's fiction makes more explicit the role of the reader in filling out and completing his own fiction. In *The Glass Key* many simple declarative sentences end either with concrete nouns or with intransitive verbs, isolating the thing perceived and giving sentences a static quality. Each sentence, managed through Ned's point of view, becomes a separate universe, our attention focussed on its object, or on the active verb which has become stilled, part of a frozen gesture :

The dice rolled (p. 1).
He took his hand from the door-knob (p. 6).

The rolling dice become a static image of rolled dice ; the knob, the hand, the turn each become a single fragmented image. as if a photo flash had gone off, revealing the gesture in an otherwise darkened room. Within such sentences, words become isolated ; they seem to have only a one to one relation between «signifier» and «signified», unable to motivate meaning. This absence of signification involves us in trying to discover the meaning we want —it involves us in telling the tale. But by becoming implicated in the socially approved drive toward resolution, we become victims of irony. For when we fill in the gaps, we write still another story, and assert our *own* omnipotent control ever events.

Hammett, thus, makes us believe that we participate in the story of the archetypal quest, while he really tells a story of his capacity to involve us in a fabulation of the negative. He destroys his own fictions to expose their false foundations. If we shut a Hammett story satisfied that order has been restored, we have written our own story. For in truth his stories allow suffering and fragmentation to continue on every level of narrative : murder is solved by more murder, the power he restores is corrupt, sexual and social relations have been perverted and remain perverted. We write a deceptive solution so that Hammett's language may submit to its own erotic desire to subvert itself, to plunge, in short, into the negative.

It is for this reason that *Red Harvest* and *The Glass Key* are so at ease with the rise of gangsterism during Prohibition (the negative made law). In *The Glass Key* Ned's best friend, the man who runs the town, is a racketeer himself. In *Red Harvest* a «robber baron» has built the town. In both novels this patriarch runs or has run every political office in the territory ; gangsters run the speakeasies where all the town-folk buy their booze ; prostitution and gambling have the tacit sanction of the community. Even the police are gangsters in *Red Harvest*, and in *The Glass Key* Paul owns the whole apparatus of law. There is no such thing as «law and order» for law is subservient to power.

Because law serves power, the hero is able to define justice in his own terms, even as he complies with the communal fiction that justice is impartial : The Op decides he'd rather unleash a blood-bath to purge Personville because «the courts are too slow for us». or Ned holds a gun on Shad O'Rory while Shad is strangled by one of his own henchmen, but later Ned prevents the Senator from committing suicide because he must «take what's coming» to him. The hero remains the real power behind all communal myths while exposing their fictive foundation.

This picture suggests the standard Wasteland theme of American literature and it has suggested to some critics that Hammett's treatment is again a nostalgic longing to restore the purity and innocence of the American Dream. But this is not at all the case. Hammett's heroes are not modern Leatherstockings bringing civilization to the jungle of the cities, nor are his novels realistic portrayals of the American nightmare. They are pure fantasy and pure assertions of fantasy — an ironic attack on the dream and on the traditions it has fostered, an attack on order itself. Hammett's nightmare is not caused by the failure of the American Dream, it is its wish fulfillment. His hero is not the sad and violent knight protecting the social contract at the cost of his own interior life, he is the vital embodiment of the community's hidden desires. The story *is* his interior life.

This inner life reveals itself in the story which takes up the residue left over from the story of murder — the story of the restoration of power in which the hero projects a fantasy which uncovers the ideology of his hidden desires. In both *Red Harvest* and *The Glass Key* the hero decides to restore a patriarch to power. Such a task is clearly «undemocratic», but if we examine the complex relationships this restoration of power allows the hero to maintain, we shall see both the causes for his obsessive substitution of violence for eroticism and the ideological stance which lies behind his disruption of traditional fictive forms. This story is *his* story, not the community's. It is a story he structures by and for himself in such a way that his own disruptive fantasy evades all opposition.

In this story the hero finds himself confronted with a problem of restoring order to a town on the verge of collapsing into «criminal» chaos. One of the elements of this problem is the patriarch who has built the town : he is middle aged, widowed, with grown children. He has always been corrupt in terms of the law, but he has maintained enough institutional order that only more disruptive tactics have disloged him. But in both stories the patriarchs are without a proper mate, while the sexual desires of their sons are directed, properly, towards the daughters of the community. Sexual power is, therefore, divided from social power. Taylor Henry of *The Glass Key* courts Opal Madvig, the dauther of the patriarch, while Donald Willsson, the patriarch's son in *Red Harvest* is married. Nevertheless, both of these young men die as soon as the patriarch reasserts his sexual power by himself courting one of the daughters of the community. In *The Glass Key* a son is murdered by his real father, though that father is not the patriarch. *Red Harvest* parallels this theme, for Elihu Willsson, the patriarch, is in love with Dinah Brand while his son only appears to have a liaison with her. Nevertheless, when that son is murdered by another of Dinah's suitors, it is clear that rivalry over Dinah is cause of murder. Each novel reiterates the pattern of the murder of a son in a father/son rivalry for the love of a «daughter» [8].

When this perversion of the normal order of succession becomes evident by the murder, the hero enters the story. He must solve the crime and restore communal order. And to do this he has three possible choices : he may submit to the criminals, eliminating the conflict between them and the patriarch ; he may oust both the criminals and patriarch to restore a «democratic» contract ; or he may oust the criminals and restore the patriarch. In both stories he chooses the last strategy. But as soon as he chooses, the «daughters» whom the respective patriarchs love become attracted to the hero, so that the hero replaces the dead son in the structure of emotional relationships.

By both repeating the pattern of father/son rivalry and preserving that rival/father's power, the hero's strategy is pure disruption. First of all, he reveals that what lies behind all socially constructed fictions of communal stability is the oedipal rivalry. But he brings this desire out into the open. Secondly, by telling a story in which he neither defeats nor replaces the father/rival, he seems to guarantee his own neurotic alienation : whether or not he wins the daughter, he cannot take his place in the community, but must remain outcast. Finally, both these strategies hide the hero's deeper desire which is to assert his superiority over any socially constructed myth of order. His role as outcast is more important to this pattern than would be any attempt as assimilation.

He begins by entering a story where the daughter is already fixed in an anti-social, erotic role by the father's desire and the rival/son's murder. She arouses only the anti-social emotions of lust and murder, and cannot sustain community because she can never assume her socially preservative, «maternal» role save by marrying the father [9]. By perverting incestuous desire away from the mother, both the father and the son assume the anarchic right to divert incestuous desire from its traditional and, in a sense, stable forms, towards purely disruptive forms [10]. Even when the daughter chooses her proper mate — the hero — the father's desire for her forces her to remain outside the community, a perpetual object of erotic disire and the hero's unwitting accomplice in ideological irony.

The second element in the hero's strategy depends on the weakness of the father. Unsure that he even wants to maintain the difficult tasks of power, the father seems drawn to his own failure. Thus there are two apparently contradictory directions to the hero's story : one is to support the father and return him to power, the other is to humiliate him by becoming his sucessful rival. The father's own reluctance or inability to reassert political power merely makes him more dependent on the son who restores his power. By choosing this pattern the hero assures the perfect «set up» not only to expose the father's weakness, but also to assert his own effaced dominance.

The ideological implications of this abnormal reversal of power can be clarified by looking at Gilles Deleuze's discussion of the ideology of sadism and masochism. He offers a description of the psychology of law, institution, and contract which illuminates the ambiguities of our hero's manipulation of story. Deleuze writes :

> The contract presupposes, in principle, the free consent of the contracting parties and determines between them a system of reciprocal rights and duties ; it cannot affect a third party and is valid for a limited period. Institutions, by contrast, determine a long-term state of affairs, which is both involuntary and inalienable ; it establishes a power or an authority which takes effect against a third party. But even more significant is the difference between the contract and the institution with respect to what is known as the law : the contract actually generates a law even if this law oversteps and contravenes the conditions which made it possible ; the institution is of a very different order in that it tends to render laws unnecessary, to replace the system of rights and duties by a dynamic model of action, authority and power....the specific impulse underlying the contract is towards the creation of a law, even if in the end the law should take over and impose its authority upon the contract. Whereas, the corresponding impulse at work in the case of the institution is towards the degradation of all laws and the establishment of a superior power that sets itself above them [11].

Deleuze associates institutions with the arbitrary and anarchic whim of the father ; law with the conservative and democratic impulse of the mother. According to his definition, law and contract are the impulse of democratic constitution ; institution the impulse of the monarchy which democracy opposed.

Hammett's stories reverse and parody both these situations. In *The Glass Key* Ned exalts the father to his transcendent position while the father perversely aligns himself with the forces of his own expulsion. It is this very weakness of the father which attracts the hero, for it is this weakness which inherently parodies the social order. That is to say , the patriarchy itself is a form of institution. But ironically, the hero must force the patriarch to struggle for his own institution by binding him to a contract. This is one function of the hero's code of absolute loyalty ; it is the contract by which the hero binds the patriarch to preserve his own institution.

Because they must be bound by a contract to save their own institution, both Paul of *The Glass Key* and Elihu of *Red Harvest* suffer from a kind of masochism. Paul's is especially clear : because he desires Janet Henry — a woman who does not desire him — he hides the facts of Taylor Henry's death in such a way that not only is he promoting the murderer for Senate, but that he himself is the prime suspect. It is thus inevitable that he will lose both the girl and control of his community. Elihu also masochistically seeks the instruments of his defeat, first bringing the gangsters to «Poisonville» and then refusing to dislodge them. Each father binds himself to a contract for his own humiliation and impotence. The hero instinctively recognizes this self-destructive drive and offers an opposing contract that will free the patriarch from his own obligations to anything but the desires of the hero.

In *The Glass Key* there are clear indications that Ned has shaped relations to Paul precisely in order to be in on the kill. There is an obvious element of glee as Ned watches Paul's downfall. For example, when he discovers that Janet, instead of loving Paul, suspects him of murdering her brother, «a glad light came into his eyes, gladness spread over his face. He laughed, not loud, but in complete delight». And even though Ned has never expressed the least desire for this woman whom Paul has loved, he takes her away with him at the end of the story.

The Op is even more possessed by his desire to parody the father's power. The Op literally binds Elihu to a contract whose very terms make Elihu totally dependent on the Op while freeing the Op to find any solution he likes. When that solution turns out to be a violence that spreads like a bruise beneath the skin, death upon death upon bloody death, we realize we are locked within a fantasy of omnipotence, directed not against order, but against the fictions on which order is constructed. His contract with the father frees the Op to unleash the negative eroticism underlying repressive fictions of coherence.

Clearly, by making themselves the heroes of a story of the restoration of the Patriarch's power, the heroes create a situation whereby they may exploit disruptive drives to the full, under the guise of social virtue. The hero keeps the father, so to speak, in his place precisely so that the hero himself may remain a free principle of negation. He is thus able to turn the myth of democratic contract inside out, uncovering the inherent sterility of its form. By telling the story in this way, the hero preserves a totally ironic situation which allows him to remain outside and above the fictions of both law and institution.

Hammett's heroes manipulate the structure of power so that the circle of parody is complete. The patriarchy which is the real power beneath the appearance of democracy undercuts both contract and law while the Patriarch's dependence on the son undercuts the fictions which support institutions.

In conclusion, the traditional hero of the «hard-boiled» school of detective fiction has been described as a modern pioneer, or even a modern Christ figure — lonely, suffering, quixotically fighting to rescue Innocence from the perversions of the law and the failures of institutions. His fundamental task is to restore one or the other. These heroes often work for nothing, they are always outcast, taking amazing amounts of physical punishment from both cops and robbers. Still, their job is essentially restorative ; they uphold the fundamental idealism of both law and democracy, sacrificing themselves to affirm the purity of the social contract, and thus their own innocence. None of this is true of Hammett's heroes.

Nevertheless, because they confuse a similarity of setting with a similarity of ideological structure, many critics have misunderstood Hammett's heroes, identifying them with the heroes of his followers in order to reconstruct the myth of the crystal sphere. But Hammett was far more «modern» than his successors. His heroes are neither masochistic versions of a new Christ, nor knights fighting to restore the social contract. His heroes are beyond such innocence. They have become story-tellers, myth-makers and myth-breakers, disrupting their own fictions and the fictions by which social order is constructed. These heroes are revolutionaries whose desire is to preserve a mythical state of revolution — that obverse image of the promise of democracy.

Thus, if as we reconstruct our own myths of social order in reading Hammett, we feel a certain horror at the 17 deaths in Red Harvest or a disquiet before Ned's ambiguous commitment to Paul in *The*

Glass Key, that horror is a recognition of the revolutionary residue left behind the order we have imposed on his hero's stories. For beneath that order Hammett creates a world of unrepressed desire, a fantasy of the dream of disruption, omnipotence, and conquest which is at the root of the American Dream. Hammett's hero does *not*, however, kill the father in another recapitulation of the flight from Europe, he castrates him by keeping him in a false position of power in a false social order.

Detective fiction provides an excellent myth on which to base a story of a culture hero who parodies that culture, since in the detective story the hero stands between what the community defines as good, or socially preserving, and what it defines as evil, or socially disruptive. By refusing both definitions, Hammett's hero turns «good» and «evil» into elements of a private fantasy created to reveal that both are relative and socially created fictions. He, instead, maintains a revolutionary, disruptive position between the false polarities of good and evil, refusing to close the gap.

FOOTNOTES

1. Both Frank Kermode, in **The Sense of an Ending**, and Ian Watt in **The Rise of the Novel** show that traditional forms of fiction have metaphysical and ideological implications that reinforce the rise of the middle class in the 18th and 19th centuries.

2. Edgar Allan Poe, «Murders in the Rue Morgue», in **Dective Fiction : Crime and Compromise**, eds. Dick Allen and David Chacko (New York : Harcourt Brace Jovanovich, Inc., 1974), p. 80.

3. D.H. Lawrence in **Studies in Classic American Literature** was first to point out that American literature is duplicitous — it pretends to an innocence it does not possess.

4. Gilles Deleuze, **Masochism : An Interpretation of Coldness and Cruelty** (New Yord : George Braziller, 1971), p. 25.

5. All the references to Dashiell Hammett's works appear in the text : **The Glass Key** (New York : Vintage, 1972) ; **Red Harvest** (New York : Vintage, 1972) ; **The Thin Man** (Harmondsworth : Penguin Books, 1961) ; **The Maltese Falcon** (Harmondsworth : Penguin Books, 1963) ; **The Big Knockover** (New York : Random House, 1966) ; **The Continental Op** (New York : Random House, 1974).

6. Steven Marcus, «Introduction», **The Continental Op** , Op. cit. p. XX.

7. **Entropy** is defined in **Webster's Third International Dictionary** :
(a) a quantity that is the measure of the amount of energy in a system not available for doing work.
(b) the ultimate state reached in the degradation of the matter and energy of the universe.
(c) state of inert uniformity of component elements.
(d) absence of form, pattern, hierarchy, or differentiation.
(e) the general trend of the universe toward death and disorder.

8. The theme of impotent fathers and sexually destructive daughters runs throughout Hammett's fiction. In **The Thin Man** Nick and Nora must vindicate a father who has disappeared but whom the daughter believes guilty of murder. They must uncover a false father and discover the true one, who turns out to have been dead all along — the ultimate impotence. In **The Dain Curse** a father dies to shield a daughter who hates him. Only **The Maltese Falcon** hides this theme ; but Brigid O'Shaughnessy is, indeed, a sexually powervul and murderous daughter whom the hero must finally renounce, while his paternal rivals are the corrupt «fat man» and the effete Joe Cairo — an impotent duo of evil.

9. Simone de Beauvoir, **The Second Sex** (New York : Bantam, 1970). Simone de Beauvoir has a long discussion about the revolutionary, disruptive power of eroticism. She argues that in patriarchy, eroticism is associated with the woman in order that the father may repress what is hostile to the social order.

10. Deleuze points that «what makes Sade's heroines sadistic is their sodomic union with the father in a fundamental alliance against the mother. Sadism is in every sense an active negation of the mother and an exaltation of the father who is beyond all laws». **Op. cit.,** p. 52.

11. Deleuze, **Op. cit.,** pp. 67-68.

Roland TISSOT

The ideology of Super-Realism

Thus, willy-nilly, paintings have more meaning
in them than appears at first sight. In them,
there always abides some kind of truth.
    G. Aillaud, *French super-realist.*

The cruel agressiveness, the unbearable tension that seem to
characterize all super-realist endeavors are disquieting qualities
compared to which even Hopper's bleak patient insights into the
«new nature» of American landscape appear endowed with human
kindness. Among other trappings, emotion is precisely what they
first discard. They deliberately take the stance of antiseptic
cleanliness, of the architectural puritanism of the Bauhaus
formalists, and also greatly favor the efficiency of industrial
design. Colors, once the syntax of feelings, now fall into discredit.
Flat tracts of dull tints can be laboriously glazed over, but mostly
they stand neglected, and bear witness to the painter's total
unconcern. On the other hand, «they can be used as eyesores in the
jive, strident rhetoric of their brutal chemistry : thalo blues,
dioxazine purples, acrareds» [1]. In both cases, however, these
artists tend to avoid the slipshod hedonism of lyrical abstraction.
They shun the expressive accumulation of brushstrokes. They
would rather play with the gloss of surfaces — mechanized scraps
in junkyards, smashed chassis, gleaming chrome-plated exhaust-
pipes on Japanese motorbikes, austere façades of government
buildings — coolly devoted as they all are to the banal and the
anonymous. Such paintings intentionally reject the contingency
and originality of personal style. They merely aim at being
processed like any other industrial product. The super-realists'
vision is dry, cosmetic. It distrusts interpretation. Ideologically, it
seems to hark back to the past, as though since Tom Eakins's days
these painters had been mothballed into a smooth time-sphere
altogether untroubled by history. We contend, however, that a
particular art-style is a subconsciously projected image of a
political order, and that reality is less visualized than it is
fabricated. Willy-nilly, ideologies will creep through any kind of
practice as surely as weeds through crannied walls. Therefore, to
investigate into the various techniques of the super-realists is to
realize that these artists keep on producing — but unawares — the
ideology they are so heavily dependent on.

The first thing that may strike us when we look at such paintings is their strong pull towards the center of the canvas. Obviously, the ideology of the super-realists' vision is grounded on the western metaphysical tradition, whose main assumption is that the human eye stands at the very center of the system and accepts the intrusion of a third dimension within a bidimensional surface.

It is interesting to note that the invention of photography, if it did liberate the progressive painters from the shackles of realism, came also as a kind of godsend to the traditionalists. As a matter of fact, the camera lens was the foolproof mechanical device reduplicating the human eye, thereby allowing the Renaissance codes of the specular and perspective visions to perpetuate themselves and increase the belief in the criteria of normality and scientifically proven truth. Thus helped by the camera lens, people forgot the fact that human vision, like photography, is based on an optical illusion. We thus owe some of the enduring famed of Uccello's cube to the camera, a brand-new technological device which, paradoxically enough, helped perpetuate a certain code of vision that no longer fits the picture of the world imposed by twentieth-century science. Instead, it conveys the nostalgia of an art and times gone by, that had built up a certain kind of order and nursed the fond hope of acquiring the capacity to pierce the secrets of the objective world. So that the kind of formal revolution that Cézanne forced upon us with the tense equilibrium of his painted objects, with his slightly off-balance pitchers, with his barely biased perspectives, in brief all the dis-illusions that he originated, were more than compensated in the public mind by the inscription of the normality and (apparently) neutral objective centrality of the camera-eye.

Now the great majority of painters among the super-realists accept the hegemony and centrality of a lenticular, monocular vision focussing on a mythic point on the horizon (that perfect nexus of power) upon which all spatial forces must converge. They likewise accept the overall adequation of reality to a mental construct in which «I see» also means «I understand». This implies in turn a sort of transfixation of reality, a state of arrested flux, an ordering of the visible around a central eye. It also implicitly proclaims the total acceptance of the principle of leadership that pervades the classical perspective. In order to reach the kind of cosy optical comfort that perspective can afford, our eyes have been patiently tamed since da Vinci to comply with a rational, wholly intelligible universe, by candidly eliminating all solutions of continuity, all imaginary ramblings, all blind spots, assuming in fact that Reason forever is a gifted painter who can comprehend all the visible order within the slick mastery of his touch.

We now understand how culturally dependent the old masters were upon a normative code of vision, remote yet wonderfully resistant to change, whereby reality was perceived as an *analogon*, less to be deciphered than to be merely read. On the one hand, the super-realists have unquestioningly borrowed from them. This may well account for their swift success and for the general feeling of reassurance in the public. With them, the onlooker stands in a position of secure knowledge, that of the privileged perceptive subject in a strongly hierarchic, power-oriented picture organization, wholly relieved from the eccentricities of, say, Jackson Pollock's *all-over* patterns and dizzy arabesques.

Yet, on the other hand, the super-realists differ widely from their masters on one particular point : they do not trouble themselves with the atmospheric in-depth perspective. A shallow, glaring uniformity has taken the place of the exquisite color variations and misty backgrounds of the past. Try as you may, such a painting as Richard Estes' *Urban Landscape* will thwart your desire for penetration. Despite its orderly symmetry, its neat converging lines that draw all visual energies towards the center, you will always be foiled by all this interplay of mirrors, this revolving door opening on an architecture of silence (or is it the void ? or the glittering reflections of the street upon the window-panes ?). A spectral disquiet haunts the loveless, insignificant surface. Our eyes are caught in the vain quest of desire by this trap-door gaping over a vacuum. The super-realists have indeed forsaken the age-old principle of anchoring the subject into some exterior reality, whether it be a Platonic Idea or God's decree. They merely assume the superficiality of the canvas, thereby stealing away from the romantic notion of the loving, suffering, tragic creature of yore helplessly floating between two worlds. Here, on the contrary, the perceptive subject (fallible, sensitive) seems noticeably absent. We are always hoodwinked by the *trompe-l'oeil*, by the cold-blooded, spine-chilling assertion of bidimensional illusion. This is further enhanced by the particular mode of reproduction from color-slides : the painted object asserts itself in its *thereness*, devoid of all semantic content, a flat colored film for ever blocking interpretation, because its centrality is not so much ordered around a human eye as it is around a mechanical, «instamatic» blank. Here the French term *nature morte*, for once, makes sense. Avoiding as they do the second aspect of the artificial perspective, the super-realists show that they are steeped in their century and that they share in the general feeling of suspicion towards what they believe are but imaginary fallacies.

Another aspect of the super-realists' ideology of vision is their deliberate choice of the rectangular, traditional «open-window» canvas. To emphasize this, some artists, like Audrey Flack for example, will even paint a frame around their canvases. In the recent past, we may recall (presumably because they had grown impatient over the spatial imitations of that classic form) the open-window theory had been overtly transgressed by such painters as Hinman, Frank Stella, Ellsworth Kelly. Such a theory, however, was itself a cultural, historic, institutionally coded norm, answerable in the last instance for the chosen center, the Eye of the sovereign subject who brings order to chaos, for there is an obvious complicity between that technical contrivance and an enduring anthropocentric creed. Besides, the open-window frame also performs a specific function (significantly enough, it is seldom put around the canvas by the artist himself, but by the art-gallery or the buyer). It helps focus our attention on a privileged portion of space. It cuts off the essential from the frivolous, the orderly from the irrelevant. It blots out what we might call, using the language of film-critics, the disorderliness of the «off-space». «O blessed rage for order !» cried Wallace Stevens even if Mallarmé, with nostalgia, could speak of the «oblivion outside the frame», the rich forgotten possibilities that it closes out forever.

Yet, there is ample reason to believe that the super-realists' choice is as much ironical as it is nostalgic. Their attitude might be theatrical, almost a stance on «the vanity of all art», as Marcel Duchamp would have said. George Deem, for instance, in *An American Vermeer*, makes a triptych out of three well-known Vermeers put side by side. We all feel the ironic put-down of the pastiche, which equivocally consolidates the pre-existing order while trying to debunk it. But the same feeling of inadequacy and malaise towards the transcription of space that had badgered the lyrical abstractionists is still at work here ; but it is resolved through the use of irony rather than bathos. Despite these cautious remarks, we may say that the rectangular canvas ingenuously discloses a universe in need of stability, symmetry, selection, law and order. Such pictorial behavior might hold up the mirror to the growing political centralism, the steady re-inforcement of leadership in the United States in the last decade. It might also run counter to the biased, jolting perspectives, the off-center turmoil of abstract lyricism, that evinced the perturbed confidence and disorientation of the artists who had come of age in the era of the Great Depression and had reached fame after World War II.

The frontal pose is the fourth interesting aspect of the super-realists' ideology of representation. To determine the present unconscious motivations of that practice is no easy task. Gigantic and threatening, Chuck Close's portraits seem almost irrelevant in a democracy, despite the painter's professions of faith to the contrary. The influence of the motion-pictures must be paramount in their utter concern with the spiritual election of the hero (objectified on the screen by the close-up). Those blown-up portraits, like vast emergences of Being, monopolize our attention, focussing it on the head as a part for the whole person. All motor and bodily impulses are thus repressed and sublimated into the conscience that lurks behind the eyes, flashing forth meaning in fleeting epiphanies. Besides, concentrating the universal into the ego, such narcissistic ostentation, when it does not betoken the transcendence of mind over matter, points to the ideology of rugged individualism, conspicuous consumption or any other kind of elitist motivations. It also stems back to times gone by, to the long gallery of portraits in a theocentric universe that sought to link the image of Man to his Creator. The tradition remains, but God is now absent. In the patrology of the Republic, if Mr Everyman looms large at last in Chuck Close's portraits, he must feel like a lay, bemused Pantocrator of sorts.

Despite the unsettling quality of his production, Chuck Close is no anomaly. His portraits are part and parcel of a constant American effort to gather the scattered energies of the *demos* without subverting democracy in the process ; part also of a plan to constitute a heroic iconography that would give epic grandeur to the ordinary citizen. If we are to believe Mr Kavolis, «democratic systems tend to favor art-styles characterized by informal spontaneity and lack of glorification in their subject-matter. In their search for equality *vs* need for hierarchy, they shun sharp-focus attention in favor of all-over patterns. Conversely, loss of democracy favors a tendency towards oversized canvases, a reflection of a trend toward increasing centralization of political and economic power». But power, he adds, «in the democratic type of bureaucratic authority is largely impersonal, hence the rigidity, standardization and monumentality of the non-objective subject-matter» [2]. Chuck Close's portraits are perhaps a vain attempt at reconciling the self of Walt Whitman's *Song of Myself* with Man *en masse*. But gone now is the 19th century poet's optimism. As a matter of fact, these giant portraits could well be the answer of the painter to the progressive deterioration of representative democracy, the illusions of «democratic vistas», the malaise of the prevailing ideology through the turbulent decades of the sixties and seventies. Moreover, what we can also visualize here is the frustrated concept of equal fraternity. No ideal and imaginary City of Brotherly Love could stand the diversification and stratification of a society disunited by the mind-boggling itemization of work. Lastly, in their massive frontality, Close's portraits do not really bear witness to the irrepressible intrusion of the sacred upon existence, but rather, in their monumental aloofness, pay their icy tribute to Death, the only true democratic Leveller. No, not even to death, for like the famous snowman

> Who, nothing in himself, beholds
> Nothing that is not there and the nothing that is.

these are but mummies, ritualistically embalmed by a thrifty mortician. Such disquieting strangeness grates upon the smooth language of bourgeois idealism that Close technically tries to emulate. But as we shall soon see, he only operates on the illusion of such representation, on the fantasy of Man as a self-sufficient monad bursting into view against a repressed historical background. With Close, all is eventually deprived of its sacral quality. The transcendental Ego, no longer guaranteed by any mirror-identification, breaks up into smithereens.

Another technique worthy of notice is the super-realists' constant device of painting from color-slides. Both Plato and Pascal may well feel posthumously vindicated, for such painting is indeed the acme of make-believe. Often enough, however, the inscription of the painter's work is easily traceable in the visible photograms and gridiron patterns. But in conformity with the dominating ideology, which aims at the sleekness of the «finished product», the photorealism of the camera oscura creates wished-for links with the machine-age. This affinity with the machine (a state of mind that Andy Warhol was the first to boast about) the super-realist painters do not romantically reject, but take for granted. In doing this, J.F. Lyotard contends, the painter directs us «towards problems of production and reproduction that are simply those of modern capitalism, in turn denounced by marxism, romantic humanism and the workers'movement» [3]. That wonderful machinery produces baits and decoys to ensnare our phantasms in order to eventually form an art-market. A painting, in that case, is first and foremost a product, neither more nor less than a package of detergent, a reach-me-down suit, let alone a big advertising poster. For the super-realists comply with this sole rule : that of the utter equivalence of all things under the sun, whether they be natural or man-made. Eventually, all become magically transformed into wads of greenbacks. Consequently the artist does not care about the subject-matter any more. There is nothing sublime. There is nothing vulgar either. In the long run, everything becomes a semblance of something else. Fake like fiction. What remains desirable is merely the «making» of all that is ultimately sham and mockery. All those masks and parodies of reality can be swapped at random, a family portrait by Bechtle trucked for a Volkswagen by Don Eddy, for instance. For all items are standardized in the most hallucinatory way, processed like corn-beef in Chicago.

And so, like latter-day Bouvards and Pécuchets awesomely copying final catalogues, the super-realists' only desire is to become the reproducing machine itself. The machine is precisely what traps the libidinal impulse and changes all that energy into wealth. Forsaking all humanity, the artist longs to dwell in the very core of desire, inside the wonderful technical contrivance that can endlessly reproduce. He then becomes not so much the capital as the means of capitalist reproduction, the locus of desire where value is added and money accrues. The painters are still alive. They even hold a brush at times. But standing stiff in iron stays, they seem to paint with artificial limbs, in complete subservience to the machine. For none of them could match a Kodakprint or a Xerox for sheer efficiency. Such is the price that they have to pay in order to vie with the system.

On the other hand, if we observe the finished product, we soon realize that a slight difference does exist between it and the projected color-slide it was painted from. The former seems to have undergone some sort of chromatic intensification. Colors are harsher, as if to avoid the loss which is bound to happen in the process of reduplication (according to the law of thermodynamics). Henry Adams, we may recall, had built up a whole vision of history around the principle of entropy. Capitalism and profit, though, ignore such romantic pessimism and run counter to that principle. The avid maw of capitalism reconciles the Virgin with the Dynamo, as efficiently as do R. Lindner's cruel prostitutes lusting for blood. The super-realists' thought-processes, therefore, unconsciously obey the law of profit. And so, solely by interposing their libidinal selves between camera and canvas, by «mixing memory and desire», they put the complex but indifferent machine slightly out of order, making it give a bit more than it ought to, thus providing the incremental color surplus that businessmen would call an excess yield or an increase in value.

The super-realists' fantasy of formal perfection, linked to the fetishism of technology, may yet come as a further and last proof of the alleged complicity of their language with the language of industrial power. Their slick, sophisticated surfaces, their endless celebrations of minutiae smack of an open desire to emulate the finality of industrial design. Ideally, then, fiction must be repressed, screening off in its smooth texture the discontinued, heterogeneous *Anderer Schauplatz* of sheer work, for the *other scene* of history must be blotted out by the wholly imaginary scene in front of us, with the spectator's eye looping the imaginary loop. The ideal viewer of such paintings is not supposed to know anything about the way they have been produced. His fixed, uncritical point of view, in and out of time, non-dialectical, conceives of itself as anhistoric (as by the way does the bourgeoisie), and imagines the work of art as something «achieved», never «in progress», and above all unsullied by the scars of its own production. He loathes whatever is amateurish and always prefers the cool efficiency of professionalism. All the gear, clang and clatter of the machinery necessary for the making of that resplendent display is repressed into the canvas, glossed over, and wholly replaced by the watcher's willing suspension of disbelief.

We now understand why the super-realists are so given over to the camera. Is it not simpler, neater, more efficient ? Is is not the easiest means to acquire mastery without the long frustrating years of apprenticeship ? No wonder that so many of our painters are but recent converts from Madison Avenue : the miraculous robots of technology helped them process those neat eye-catching appliances ready to form an art-market, relying on a good PR campaign and on our neurotic impulse to buy. The «super» in super-realism may mean just that : realism is of a ghostly, fantasmatic nature. As one critic put it, those paintings are but «lures for sale» [4]. This is the last inventory at Mme Tussaud's, and the devil take the hindmost.

There is perhaps, one must admit, a certain abnegation in giving up (for the sake of impersonality) all the conquests of the past century, and also the notion of artist as creator for the lowlier ones of maker, craftsman, worker, let alone adman. But even the debunking of originality has its ideological connotations.

Acrylic colors, we gather, and the technique of glazing are such castmarks of impersonality. Layers of varnish shine over arrested clichés, without evanescence, each tiny particle of liquid caught in its ordered place, assuring continuity, intelligibility, homogeneity, casting off the personal brush stroke and hiding the «working through» of history. Like the liquid syntax of bourgeois narration, which aims at resolution, exhaustiveness, glazing spreads across the surface an elegiac layer of wholeness, a saturated, even field of linked molecules, a thin homogeneous film of polymerization. With polymerization all is effaced under a veil of neutrality ; antagonisms are resolved, differences annulled. We may then apprehend time and space as a continuum, forgetting meanwhile that realism is unable to render the random plenitude of experience and its opacity. As a matter of fact, what is sought after under the layer of varnish is the efficacy of ideological captation, the obliteration of exalted violence, all the raw energies ready to be released in Wall Street, the Pentagon or even Times Square. Lacquer aims at a cover-up of any sort of violence, whether it be economic, political or sexual. In the same vein, it would not be wrong to say that an escalator by Estes, a Starfighter by Paul Staiger, or an automobile by Don Eddy are both metonymies of American space and metaphors of the huge Western technocratic empire. At this point we could draw a parallel between super-realism and Italian Futurism whose exaltation of the ideology of violence, of the speed and progress of industrial society once led its zealots to support a perverted regime. But we must not push the comparison too far. Not only are historical contexts poles apart but, besides, its seems highly unlikely that the super-realists could for one minute envisage their insertion into society in the light of that foreign school of painting. It never dawned upon them that they could use their art as an active political firebrand. They would brush aside the idea of being considered the unwitting propagandists of the reigning ideology. Such thinking is alien to them.

On the whole, the bad quality of their artistic production leads one to conclude, halfheartedly, that they were only intent on using a system that so lavishly drowned them in quick, easy money. We must bear in mind that super-realism has taken hold of America and of the rest of the world with an efficiency that could be dubbed a miracle of marketing and advertizing. In the last analysis, why they chose to ape the ways and means of advanced technocracies was less a matter of innocent — or rather guileless — subservience to the prevailing art fashion, than a matter of cunning business wisdom.

To conclude, what the super-realist ideology endeavored to conceal again after so many years is that the Western consciousness feeds upon illusions, and furthermore that it doggedly aspires to be unconscious of the system of values that shapes its vision of reality. So doing, like a solemn valedictory, it forcefully denies all the efforts and formal revolts of all the lucid painters from Cézanne onwards. Recoiling upon a cluster of core values, the ideology of super-realism is plainly and unabashedly reactionary. A cowardly sigh of relief seems to breathe through (or is it across ?) those doomed archives of the American silent majority. Frustrated after so many abhorred radical threats or even revolutionary outbursts, after so many unrequited services, at once guilty of, yet lusting after, the exultation of power, those were the very same men who spurned abstract art as «foreign and decadent» when it came out, and triumphantly reelected Richard Nixon in 1968 when he campaigned under the catchword of «Law and Order» [5]. It is a school of painting fit for the mythic heirs of that other frustrated pair in *American Gothic*, painted by Grant Wood at the time of the Great Depression. The American middle-class, it appears, narcissistically looks at itself in those ice-cold mirrors that so bleakly double the machine-age they live in. Cold comfort, uneasy security but cool political certitudes hold sway upon their supermarketed lives as they do on the spooky lives of Duane

Hanson's plastic puppets, obese ladies and malevolent rockers.

We suspect that whenever those people look deep enough into those paintings, beyond realism into super-realism, they cannot fail to see the raw, naked violence of power, the destructive force behind it all. To quote Stevens once more,

> The lion sleeps in the sun.
> Its nose is on its paws.
> It can kill a man.

NOTES

1. H.D. RAYMOND : «Beyond freedom, dignity and ridicule», **Arts Magazine**, Feb. 1974, p.25 et **passim.**

2. V. KAVOLIS : **Artistic Expression, A Sociological Analysis,** Cornell U.P., 1968. (voir aussi Fairfield PORTER : «Class Content in American Abstract Painting», **Art News**, 61, Apr. 62, p.49.

3. J.F. LYOTARD : **Figurations, 1960-1973,** Paris, Seuil, 1973. «Esquisse d'une économique de l'hyperréalisme», **Art Vivant**, 36, p.9.

4. C. BACKES-CLEMENT : «Leurre en vente», **Art Vivant,** 37, p. 7.

5. J. CLAIR : **«Situation des réalismes»,** Art Vivant, 48, p.21.

BIBLIOGRAPHY

P. LEIDER : «Artists and Politics : a symposium», **Artforum**, 9, Sept. 1970, pp. 35-49.

T. SCHWARTZ : «Politicalization of the Avant-garde» **Art in America**, 59, Nov. 1971, pp. 97-105.

E. FISCHER ;«Art Against Ideology reviewed» **Journal of Aesthetics**, 29, n° 4, Sept. 1971, pp. 537-38.

H. KRAMER : **The Age of the Avant-garde**, Secker & Warburg, 1974.

PART II

Michel FABRE

Introduction

Blacks and whites implicitly agree that Afro-American literature has always been committed, if not militant. The proof itself is that establishement critics have often reproached this literature for being inferior because it was propagandistic, and black nationalist critics have charged a number of Afro-american writers like Jean Toomer, Robert Hayden, and even Ralph Ellison, with being pro-white because they did not address blacks first and refrained from militancy, even though they dealt with authentically black themes.

This is not the place to debate the art versus propaganda issue but simply to emphasize the complexity and peculiarities of the relationship between literature and ideology which are, so to speak, compounded in the case of black writing. To the class consciousness which may inform white American literature, the dimension of ethnic consciousness must be added ; then, an open racial perspective inevitably duplicates, corrects or confuses, the social outlook.

Very roughly, Afro-American ideological currents can be measured by the double yard-stick of race and class in the fields of political, social, and cultural expression ; the combinations thus obtained fall into a number of potential attitudes on the part of the individual writer. According to the vicissitudes of Afro-

American history within the context of American and internation history, the black writer thus often had to create with several aims in mind expressing his «individual black self», as Langston Hughes claimed in 1926, but also, of necessity, his American personality ; addressing a potential black readership but also, of necessity, a Western audience ; and often deliberately aiming at the development of (black) group solidarity but also, of necessity, at winning allies within the white (liberal) community.

Considered in chronological order, the writings and issues explored in the following articles all exhibit the multiple preoccupations and problems of the Afro-American writer. They all emphasize the close, and often direct relationship between socio-political context and individual artistic output.

The first article deals with Booker T. Washington, who, during the nadir of Afro-American history, confronted the dire segregation which succeded an abortive Reconstruction ; he often had to resort to the strategy of the oppressed, as well as to the techniques of black church oratory, in order to convince the power structure that blacks should be allowed to walk their «separate but equal» way towards the golden aims of capitalism.

A few decades later, Jean Toomer seemed to personify the inner conflict which Booker T. Washington's political opponent, Willian E.B. Dubois had described as that of «two souls warring within the same breast». Toomer struggled to unite, in artistic terms, his dual racial and cultural heritage into a meaningful whole ; passing from the aesthetics of a Waldo Frank to the «unitist» philosophy of a Gurdjeff, he sought to transcend any provincialism, in order to reach a universally human definition. His book, Cane, *in many ways far ahead of its times, may be an ideological failure, yet it remains a splendid evocation of rural black life during the Harlem Renaissance.*

Toomer's contemporary, Claude McKay, had a more realistic approach. He was well aware of the major nationalistic currents of his period and tried to use their potentialities, not only in the literary field, but in order to promote the acceptance of blacks into a pluralistic American society. Like Toomer, he refused to be defined only in relationship to the black community, be it the broader international scene depicted in Banjo *; he insisted upon the artist's right to his vision and upon the universality of a personal outlook.*

As Ishmael Reed put it wittily in Mumbo Jumbo *(1972), «Jes Grew, the Something or other that led Charlie Parker to scale the Everest of the Chord» —let us call it «soul» or the dynamic principle opposed to cold intellectualism — is, in itself, an aspect of cultural resistance which informed the Black Power period, as well as the Harlem Renaissance. This aspect is particularly noticeable in the socio-political interpretations of jazz and the blues, propounded by Le Roi Jones. Moreover, free jazz has minimized European borrowings and promoted «African» aesthetics capable of asserting the authenticity of blackness, while adding to the political commitment of black music.*

In recent years, this dimension of black ideology has become more apparent politically, as, for instance, in the case of the «reverse quotas» advocated to remedy some of the inequalities in employment that beset black Americans. If we remember Booker T. Washington's attempts at securing jobs for Negroes a century ago and the reactions of the white majority then, it is revealing and somewhat ironical to watch the contemporary response of trade union leaders, the Jewish community, or the average white to the «quota system». In the name of individualism, gradualism, or the preservation of order, each of these groups tries to prevent the underprivileged from achieving equal opportunity.

We are far, here, from the field of literature, yet adverse white reactions —political in essence, though often couched in cultural terms— are precisely those which negatively affect much of black writing today. This may explain why Afro-American writers feel compelled, more than ever, to affirm group solidarity and the growing importance of the colored world in their attempts to mold American society into a truly pluralistic one. One illusion is gone, that of the so-called melting pot, and «integration» has become a dirty word ; rather, tokenism and the need to shed one's cultural specificity in order to become accepted have been denounced. Indeed, one of the major tasks of Afro-American literature and criticism today still consists in clearing cultural and ideological issues and in destroying stereotypes in a world where change does not necessarily mean progress.

Pierre DENAIN

An educator's education :

notes on the makings of Booker T. Washington's ideology [1]

In September 1895, shortly after his Atlanta Exposition Address, Booker T. Washington was catapulted to the foreground of the national scene by a substantial proportion of the American press which hailed him at the new spokesman for the Negro race. [2] From then on till his death, although he was no undisputed leader among his own people, the Principal of Tuskegee Normal and Industrial Institute played a major role in the development of race relations in the United States. He thus became, and remained for the next twenty years, the foremost representative of an accomodationist school of Negro thought and the forceful proponent of a conservative, gradualist ideology which aroused bitter opposition among the Negro «radicals» of his age and, later, drew contemptuous criticism from the Black militants in the 1960's.

Washington's gradualism was grounded on the premise that the newly-freed slaves had been lured into the traps of Reconstruction. His youthful experience of the period had showed him

> that the Reconstruction policy, as far as it related to my race, was in a large measure on a false foundation, was artificial and forced. In many cases it seemed to me that the ignorance of my race was being used as a tool with which to help white men into office, and that there was an element in the North which wanted to punish the Southern white men by forcing the Negro into positions over the heads of Southern whites. I felt that the Negro would be the one to suffer from this in the end. Besides, the general political agitation drew the attention of our people away from the more fundamental matters of perfecting themselves in the industries at their doors and in securing property. [3]

As a result of the mistakes of Reconstruction, the Negroes had been frustrated in their hopes of enjoying their rights of American citizens. Now, in the Tuskegeean's perspective, these rights were to be actually secured and enjoyed at some future date and by indirection, i.e. through a slow growth resulting from the steady application of moral and economic virtues : thrift, industry and character. Deprecating political agitation, Washington emphasized the primacy of economic progress. As the mass of American Negroes were likely to live by the production of their hands, they should learn trades, and thus gain a foothold in the lowest rungs of the economic ladder : «It is at the bottom we must begin and not at the top.» [4] By seizing the opportunities at hand («Cast down your bucket where you are»), they would manage to make themselves indispensable to the Southern whites, who would trust them the more readily as they appreciated the qualities of docility and self-help of the race. [5] Under these conditions, the question of political rights would settle by itself :

154

My own belief is, although I have never before said so in so many words, that the time will come when the Negro in the South will be accorded all the political rights which his ability, character and material possessions entitle him to. I think, though, that the opportunity to freely exercise such political rights will not not come in any large degree through outside or artificial forcing, but will be accorded to the Negro by the Southern white people themselves, and that they will protect him in the exercise of those rights... 6

In 1895, however, Booker T. Washington, his statement to the contrary, was not «merely a Negro School teacher in a rather obscure industrial school.» 7 He had served for several years as President of the Alabama State Teachers' Association, and, as such, had started building up a nation-wide reputation for accomodationism as early as 1884. That year, he advertized his theory of industrial education at the annual conference of the National Education Association in Madison, Wisconsin, and presented it to an audience of four thousand as part of a coherent conciliatory philosophy. His rationale was that, as the Negro's home would be «permanently in the South», it was necessary to help him «prepare himself to live there as an independent, educated citizen», one who would «live friendly and peaceably with his white neighbours socially and politically.» 8 The best means to reach this goal was to develop industrial education for the Negro.

In view of the fact that «it 'kills two birds with one stone', viz. secures the cooperation of the whites and does the best possible thing for the black man» 8, industrial education was the cornerstone of Washington's social philosophy. The industrial school, indeed, was the only institution that could admit a majority of poor students : nothing was bought at Tuskegee that the students could produce, which allowed them to pay for board mostly in kind. They were taught those trades of which the race had a monopoly in the South, so that they could begin to support themselves even before they left school and make a living as soon as they graduated. The students' manual work was not only a useful, marketable commodity inside and outside of the school ; it also served to inculcate in them the dignity of labor, a notion to which more than two centuries of slavery seemed to have made the Negro forever impervious. 9 This combined training of «hand, head and heart» aimed at integrating American Negroes into the mainstream in a manner both suitable to their pressing needs and agreeable to the White Man. In white circles, Washington's statement «In all things that are purely social, we can be separate as the fingers, yet one as the hand in all things essential to mutual progress», was construed as an acceptance of Jim Crow, in the wake of his commendation of the railroad commissioners of Alabama for ordering in 1884 «equal but separate accomodations for both races» on all intrastate trains. [10] Selected by the Board of Directors of the Atlanta Exposition on the basis of his accomodationist stance, Booker T. Washington became the leader of his people because of his adaptability to white America.

Twice in the year 1901, William E.B. Dubois said of the Tuskegeean : «He represents in Negro thought the old attitude of adjustment to environment.» [11] The truth of this judgment is corroborated by the development of Booker's career up to his Atlanta Address. As a slave on a small Virginia plantation, he had no choice but to adapt himself to his environment and to do odd jobs as a houseboy for about nine years. His early experience of «freedom» was even more bitter than the years he had spent in slavery. His stepfather compelled him to work in the mines at Malden, so that the boy was practically unable to fulfill his dream of attending school until he served once more as a houseboy, at the home of Mrs. Ruffner. While befriending the young mulatto, this fastidious Yankee woman indoctrinated him. She taught him the rules of neatness and system along with the virtues of cleanliness, industry and honesty, encouraged him to read and permitted him to go to school in the afternoons. For all of this teaching Washington was immensely grateful to her : «The lessons I learned in the home of Mrs. Ruffner were as valuable to me as any education I have gotten eversince», he acknowledges. [12] He received a decisive reward, indeed, when he passed the peculiar Hampton entrance examination assigned to him by Miss Mackie. He had to sweep a recitation room. He then implemented Mrs. Ruffner's lessons so well that the examiner, another «Yankee woman who knew where to look for dirt, was unable to find one bit of dirt on the floor or a particle of dust on any of the furniture.» [13] The boy was overjoyed and determined to make the most of this long-sought opportunity to get an education. Two days later he met Samuel Armstrong, founder and Principal of Hampton. The black boy and the white man clicked from the the first. Armstrong made upon him the impression «of being the most perfect specimen of man, physically, mentally and spiritually, that I have ever seen», and, Washington adds, «I have never had occasion to change my mind eversince.» [14]

Upon entering Hampton, Booker T. Washington had struck up

with Armstrong a relationship that was to last for more than twenty years. An outstanding student, he was the more flexible as he was given special attention by Samuel Armstrong, who channeled his ambition into a missionary vocation for the service of a sacred cause and stood behind him to the last. In the eyes of the student, the Principal assumed the proportions of an ideal father figure, which led him to interiorize the philosophy of his master. That is why a survey of Armstrong's leading educational principles may help toward appraising the influence of Hampton upon the student who later became the leader of his race.

*
* *

By the time Washington entered Hampton, four years after its opening, Samuel Chapman Armstrong had worked out an organic educational philosophy which reconciled his personal beliefs and the pressures of outward necessities. The initial assignment he had received from the Freedmen's Bureau when appointed agent for ten counties in Virginia was vague and challenging :

> We've got a lot of contrabands down on the Virginia Peninsula and can't manage them ; no one has succeeded in keeping them straight. General Howard thinks you might try. [15]

When he realized that educating the masses of starving illiterate Negroes was as vital as feeding them, Armstrong faced the problem of setting up a normal school for the Freedmen in an ex-Confederate state under military occupation. Hence his compromise, which he formulated just before Washington came to Hampton.

Armstrong was an earnest Christian. Born into a missionary family in the Hawaian Islands, he held that the goal of all human activity was «the rounded, perfect Christian life.» [16] The true educator, therefore, should not be content merely to train the mind of his student. Such an education, which relied on books, was incomplete ; it produced men and women out of touch with the realities of life. Samuel Armstrong's idea was to educate the whole man for life. The best means for this end was to develop character, the superior faculty, by training jointly head, hand and heart. The end product, then, would be men who mastered themselves and their environment.

The archetypal hero that the former Union general had in mind when he set forth his educational principles was the New England pioneer, the man and woman of endurance who had built the lasting civilization of Plymouth Rock. Fundamentally, he believed in the value of labor as the cornerstone to Christian civilization :

> Labor is a great moral and educational force. Next to the grace of God, hard work, in its largest sense, is the most vital thing in Christian civilization. Substract from any neighbourhood, within a radius of ten miles, all industry, and in six months, in spite of churches and schools, what would become of order and decency ? [17]

The faith of the Hampton Principal was rooted in the Yankee Puritan work ethics. He valued labor first and foremost as an antidote to idleness — the mother of all vices. Besides its intrinsic value, when it was the result of character, i.e. the expression of economic and moral virtues, labor was naturally rewarded «by the satisfaction of accomplishment as well as by more tangible benefits.» It followed that no good Christian can be a starving man. Conversely, no starving man can be a good Christian, since idleness begets promiscuity and therefore precludes morality. «A hut with only one room and a race with no fixed habit of industry are not unitable with Christianity.» Accordingly, the Christian educator cannot expect to succeed in his task unless he motivates his student to reach a minimum level of material wealth below which he cannot possibly be a Christian. [18]

Such was the conclusion Armstrong derived from the analysis of his father's missionary experience in the Sandwich Islands. It did much to shape his educational policy toward the American Negro, whom he classified in the same category of «weak tropical races» as the Polynesian. [19]

When it came to appraising the Negro, Armstrong did not fail to use the «character» criterion. Ignorance, he says, is not his worst defect, but

> Low ideas of honor and morality, want of foresight & energy, and vanity, are his chief misfortunes. Deficiencies of character, rather than ignorance, is the leading fact to be considered in his education. [20]

Purporting to rely on facts, the General noticed that the Negro student came to him «too often with the inheritance of a debased nature, with all his wrong tendencies either unchecked by innate moral sense or by good domestic influence.» In this respect, the Negro race differed fundamentally from the white race endowed with innate superior faculties : «Gumption, perception, guiding instincts rather than a capacity to learn are the advantages of our more favored race.» [21]

As regards the Negro's ability to acquire knowledge, it seemed about the same as the white man's. Yet, this impression was misleading, for he lacked the power to assimilate such knowledge, as well as «mental strength». He was deficient in logic, prone to subject reason to feeling, act from impulse and behave erratically. In short, much alike as the capabilities of blacks and whites appeared, appearances were not to be trusted : «The Negro is a child of the tropics, and the differentia of races go deeper than the skin.» 22

True, there were redeeming features to the Negro : docility, politeness, loyalty to tried friends, devotion to study, curiosity and an ear for music. The most encouraging element in the eyes of Armstrong was the «deep religious nature of the African», which expressed itself in the Negro spirituals, those songs of suffering and hope which were the only genuine American music. The African was redeemable mostly because his deep religious nature was «capable of the finest development». 23

In view of the terrible disadvantages of the race, the education of the Negro, Armstrong thought, should aim at his regeneration. The Negro needs to be saved, not from his former masters, not from his new friends from the North, but from *himself*. Armstrong's racist analysis provided a sure basis for the reconciliation of antagonistic sectional interests.

For other factors had to be taken into account in an attempt at establishing an educational system for Negroes in the states of the ex-Confederacy. The General realized the South would not admit the Negro to her white schools for generations. Furthermore, Southerners objected to teaching black people or having them taught by whites that came from the North. The regeneration of the race, therefore, rested within the hands of the Blacks. As the Negro normal school student was unable to support himself, he was to be given a chance to work out his expenses in the printing-office, the carpenter's shop, on the farm, or in the kitchen, dining-room and laundry. At Hampton, one-fifth of the schedule was devoted to this remunerative manual work. 24

The most serious constraint in the Hampton education, however, came from Armstrong's axiom that the normal school was a means to an end. In his own terms, the ultimate end was

to lift the illiterate masses of the South *to a degree of intelligence suited to their needs*, and sufficient to prevent those political combinations of ignorant men that are unquestionably the most threatening danger of our future 25

Thus, when Washington entered Hampton, Samuel Armstrong was aware of the socio-political implications of his educational policy, which he geared to the preservation of the existing power structure. The Negro's place within it was confined to a specific economic sector :

> The race will succeed or fail as it shall devote itself with energy to agriculture and the mechanic arts, or avoid these pursuits... [26]

Accordingly, the Hampton student was trained to perform a lifelong missionary task among the black masses living in the abject poverty of the rural South. In view of this state of things, care should be exercised to avoid giving him a refined education, which would unfit him for his task. The mistake to be avoided has a name, overeducation :

> An elaborate course of study, making them polished scholars, would unfit our graduates for the hog and hominy fare and lowly cabin life that awaits most of the workers in our poor and sparsely settled country. A three or four years' course commencing with the rudiments requiring of the beginners a knowledge of reading and writing and the first rules of arithmetic, and embracing, among other things, the elements of grammar, mathematics, science, and history, is enough. [27]

The racist overtones of Armstrong's doctrine are clear. His ideology bears the stamp of social Darwinism. He saw the Negro as entering American civilization at «the dead level of slavery», lagging a long way behind the Anglo-Saxon, that «embodiment of force» who «throngs the ways that lead to success of every kind.» A different race called for a different kind of education : «There must be a difference in the educational methods for the races in our country that are a thousand years behind the whites in the line of development», he asserted on another occasion. [28]

Understandably, Armstrong's educational philosophy as applied to the Negro race and as formulated in 1872, was agreeable to many enlightened, if not to all, Southern whites. These realized how expedient it was to opt for a middle course between the university and illiteracy, and to follow Armstrong's advice to «mold the *now* plastic material». [29] To the missionary and philanthropic North this ideology was equally acceptable, since it promoted temperance, thrift, literacy, Christian morality and Bible truth together with the destruction of race prejudice. Lastly, shrewd capitalists in both sections were presumably glad at the prospect of having a large semi-skilled labor force at hand in a near future. Yet, within the framework of American

Reconstruction, Armstrong's role as a reformer cannot be overlooked. He was a white man convinced that the Negro was worthy of assistance and capable of progress, an optimist among sceptics. He found evidence of his optimism in the faithfulness of the slave to his master's family even when the latter was fighting against his freedom. He found it in the Negro's heroism at Fort Wagner and his productivity since the close of the war. For these reasons he maintained that the Negro deserved to be given «a fair chance» to help himself and accordingly, he devised a system intended to promote Negro progress. Armstrong lived up to his statement that he would not exchange places with the most favored of his colleagues in the North : he devoted himself body and soul to his self-assigned mission for the rest of his life.

A living example of Christian dedication, Armstrong aroused boundless admiration on the part of his students, especially Booker T. Washington. The master transfused the disciple with his ideology. Washington was gradually converted to it by his student experience at Hampton and eventually, shortly before he settled at Tuskegee, became certain that Armstrong had handed down to him the best possible tool for the salvation of his race, so that he modeled his social philosophy on Armstrong's compromise of 1872.

*
* *

Washington began to espouse Armstrong's ideology as early as 1873. To the young mulatto, Hampton was a constant revelation. The first year he discovered «what is was like to be treated as a man instead of a piece of property.» [30] In the course of the second year he discovered, through the model set by the Institute, a philosophy of happiness through unselfish toil :

> One of the things that impressed itself upon me deeply the second year was the unselfishness of the teachers. It was hard for me to understand how any individuals could bring themselves to the point where they could be so happy in working for others. Before the end of the year, I think I began learning that those who are happiest are those who do the most for others. [31]

A shrewd, cheerful and inspired pedagogue, the Principal exerted upon his students an influence commensurate with his Christian faith and persuasive patience ; «In fact, he was worshipped by his students.» [32] He preached by example and by precept. In his Sunday evening talks, he would often tell them they were neither any better nor any worse than the rest, but Providence had sent them to Hampton in order that they might subsequently serve their race, educate, civilize and christianize it. Would any of them object the task was impossible ? «What are Christians put into the world for but to do the impossible in the strength of God ?», he exclaimed in characteristic optimism. [33] Nothing is impossible to a Christian, be he a black man, provided he evinces the virtues of wisdom, courage and patience. This was his advice :

> Be thrifty and industrious. Command the respect of your neighbours by a good record and a good character. Own your own houses. Educate your own children. Make the best of your difficulties. Live down prejudice. Cultivate peaceful relations with all. As a voter, do as you think and not as you are told. Remember that you have seen marvelous changes in sixteen years. In view of it, be patient, thank God and take courage. [34]

Patience seems indeed the cardinal virtue required of the Negro. For although Armstrong did not ban the use of the ballot overtly, he implicitly detered his black listeners and readers from voting by emphasizing frequently that there *was* a safer way to civil rights than politics : «Patience is better than politics, and industry a shorter road to civil rights, than Congress has in its power to make.» Labor unions were not to be trusted either. He described them as «conspiracies to defy the laws of economics and try to get something for nothing.» [35] Self-help was the only means to depend upon.

Immersed in «an atmosphere of business, Christian influence and spirit of self-help», Washington received the baptism of General Armstrong's spirit while he was a student at Hampton. The fact that he never seriously considered practicing a trade for a livelihood [36] is no sign of escapism. The ambitious boy did toy with the idea of becoming a missionary in Africa or a lawyer, but he soon realized that whatever occupation he chose should be connected with the salvation of his own people :

> I had the feeling that most graduates had of General Armstrong — he wanted me to give my life in a different direction, and I felt it would be disobedience of the highest type to do anything that General Armstrong did not wish, and so very soon after I had been at Hampton I made up my mind to give up my life as far as possible to spreading the doctrines that General Armstrong lived and died for. [37]

Armstrong enabled Washington to reconcile ambition and

vocation, self-fulfilment and self-denial.

If the graduate of 1875 was not fully committed to the Hampton ideology, he was at least sufficiently conditioned by it to act up to its principles as soon as he left the Institute and to construe the intermediate years that preceded his Tuskegee experience as a confirmation in the wake of his baptism.

During those years Washington tested Armstrong's lessons over against the events in which he came to be involved. As a teacher in Malden he realized that unselfishness was a source of profound happiness : he taught night and day, regardless of money considerations. From his observation of a protracted miners' strike he concluded that strikes were manipulated by professional agitators and «the workers were worse off at the end.» This judgment echoed Hampton's lesson that «all strikes, or rather forcible strikes, arise from a misconception of the right of property that is vested in every man as regards his labour.» [38]

In politics Washington proved equally cautious. He stayed away from the Republican Party, with which he had been associated earlier, but readily agreed to do his bit in a non-partisan compaign for the election of the capital of West Virginia. Whenever he addressed an audience, he was not content to speak of the forthcoming referendum only. He broadened his subject and advised the black voters to make all their choices according to where the identity of interest between the races lay. The campaign was successful ; Charleston, the city for which Washington had been campaigning, was chosen for capital. This success could have been the beginning of a political career for the promising black teacher. He decided, however, not to go into politics : «I refused, still believing that I could find other service which would prove of more permanent value to my race.» [39]

The following year, his experience of classical education at Wayland Seminary, a Baptist institution in Washington, D.C., was a failure. In this institution, the Hampton graduate felt he had little in common with his fellow-students, who were upward-mobile urban Negroes. He found they were better off but less self-reliant than he, as they had not been taught to «make effort» through the industries to help themselves :

> The students at the other school seemed to be less self-dependent... They knew more about Latin and Greek when they left school, but they seemed to know less about life as they would meet it at their homes. [40]

Such an observation is as redolent of Armstrongian spirit as is Washington's analysis of the black community in the nation's capital. He thought that political agitation had diverted the race from the fundamental priority of beginning at the beginning, i.e. at the agricultural stage

> upon the solid and never deceptive foundation of Mother Nature, where all the nations and races that have ever succeeded have gotten their start — a start that at first may be slow and toilsome, but that nevertheless is real. [41]

Booker was still in Washington when Armstrong invited him to deliver the post-graduate address at Hampton a few weeks later. The General had discerned in the docile student the promise of a leader ; he was now relying on him to disseminate his ideology. Washington «chose» to speak on one of Armstrong's favorite themes, «The Force That Wins». On the appointed day he exhorted his black hearers «to believe in patient, unostentatious, consecrated labour in their efforts to help the race.» [42]

By the next fall Washington had joined the Hampton faculty as director of the night-school. In 1880 Armstrong appointed him «housefather» to a group of Indian trainees from the West which the Federal government sent to Hampton to learn the rudiments of civilization. Despite their proud contempt of the black race, Washington succeeded, with the aid of the Negro students, in winning them over to the white Anglo-Saxon Protestant ethics. A letter by a young Shawnee to the «Chiefs, Elders & Members» of his nation bears evidence to the instructor's persuasiveness :

> ...we must encourage our fellow-men to labor. We know that this is the only way to get along, and that the red men would have to do like white men ; that is, go to work and raise such things we shall live upon, and raise our families ; raise corn, wheat and stock, &c. Give our children up to be educated in this way, that when they should grow up to be men and women, they would be respected by good white people, and become wise and good. [43]

Such is the Gospel according to Armstrong, dutifully conveyed to the American Indian by his black disciple. Washington's success with the Indian, coming on the heels of his failure at Wayland, was decisively convincing. The efficaciousness of the Negro's unselfish behavior toward the destitute Indian demonstrated that the Blacks were capable of overcoming their own prejudice, and that any race which did the same in an attempt to lift up a less favored one *could* meet success. Washington's victory testified to the validity of Armstrong's teachings ; it bode well for the future of race relations in the nation. Consequently, he allowed Armstrong to appoint him Principal of the Tuskegee Normal School. The General recommended him to the trustees of Tuskegee as «a very competent capable mulatto, clear-headed, modest, sensible, polite and a thorough teacher and superior man» ; and the fittest for the job, too : «I know of no white man who would do better.» [44] When Washington left Hampton for the Deep South, the ties that united master and disciple, far from slackening, were considerably reinforced.

In Alabama Washington faced the very task he had been trained for, under conditions even worse than he had imagined. The black population lived in utter ignorance and dire poverty ; the normal school did not exist and had to be built from scratch. Applying the self-help technique was not enough. The young principal needed the assistance of Hampton. He wrote to Hampton for advice and loans, and received them, together with unsolicited contributions from the staff and students. The first normal school for Blacks in Alabama was patronized by Hampton, which, as parent school, felt committed to its success. Washington acted as Armstrong's vicar in the Deep South. Testimonies of mutual admiration bear evidence to the close relationship of the «Great White Father» and his black spiritual son, which was severed only by Armstrong's death in 1893. Of Washington, the General wrote, two years before he died :

> He is a true Moses. As much as any man, he is securing to the whole country the moral results which the Civil War meant to produce. [45]

And the Tuskegeean equated Armstrong with Christ when he exclaimed before his grave :

> Hampton men, ours is a precious heritage. We have been redeemed and made what we are by the lifeblood and death of the greatest men of modern times [46]

A choice product of Samuel Armstrong's educational philosophy, Booker T. Washington inherited the ideology of one who was both a Yankee Puritan and a Darwinist conservative. Being all of a piece, this ambivalent ideology was at once his strength and his weakness.

*

* *

Washington's dynamic force springs from his Christian faith. Had he not known Armstrong, he would have been a believer all the same, whose faith rested on the Christ-like work which the Church of all denominations has done during the last thirty-five years for the elevation of the black man. [47]

His mature response to the General's demanding appeal was anything but emotional. It was that of the apostle to Christ's injunction «I have given you an example that ye should do as I have done to you». Washington followed his leader and abided by his task with unflinching dedication. He kept harping on the primacy of education because «education is the work of saving men's souls». [48] Like Hampton, Tuskegee was «peculiarly a religious seminary» [49] intended to turn out self-sacrificing lay missionaries. No matter what the Tuskegee students expected from their education at the Institute, they all received a training that was both ideological and industrial.

But, as a Black Puritan, the Principal of Tuskegee also stuck to the other side of the Yankee creed : faith is proved by works, and works do not go unrewarded. Honest service done in the interest of others is bound, sooner or later, to pay, in all senses of the term. To illustrate this point for his students, Washington quoted the example of banker William Taylor, a man of so strong a character that, during the business panic of 1857,

> when other people were failing in all parts of the country, the evidence of this man's character, his regard for truth and his honest dealing, caused money to come into his bank when it was being drawn from others. [50]

Here again, Washington duplicates the teaching of Armstrong and refuses to draw the line between the spiritual and the secular. He urged his people to see the practical side of religion, the link between service and wealth, if only because

> It is one of their hymns that says, «Give me Jesus and you take all the rest,» and the white men are only too ready to take them at their word. [51]

In Washington's eyes, the dollar was an instrument of liberation, a requisite to be a Christian and to wield influence. Material wealth was indissociable from but subservient to spiritual uplift : «It is alright to get money, but the getting of money is not the highest aim in the world.» [52] The ultimate aim is to «live in that atmosphere where God dwells», and let love

> take such complete possession that it may be said of us as it was of Him who was greatest of all, that we did no sin but went about doing good. [53]

The spiritual relationship of Washington and Armstrong is best expressed in a statement of peculiar aloofness and magnanimity :

> It is now long ago that I learned this lesson from General Armstrong that I
> would permit no man, no matter what his color might be, to narrow and
> degrade my soul by making me hate him. [54]

His refusal of hate, especially racial hate, made Washington a
gentleman. And it looks as though he had wanted to breed a whole
race of gentlemen and ladies. But was this ideal of a black
chivalry, however much mitigated by American success
mythology, an adequate means to promote the uplift of the race ?
Apparently, Washington relied to a large extent on those evangelic
virtues of his race that had traditionally been equated with
weaknesses, to secure to it the White Man's respect :

> I made up my mind... that in the end the world must come to respect the Negro
> for just those virtues for which some people say he is despised, namely because
> of his patience, his kindliness, and his lack of resentment toward those who do
> him wrong and injustice. [55]

But could unilateral application of the Golden Rule by the
Negro serve this purpose in the jungle of the Gilded Age ?

«I consider Labor as one of the greatest boons which our Creator
has conferred upon human beings», the Tuskegeean para-
phrased [54]. In this respect, he praised industrial education for the
same reasons as Armstrong, and essentially because it inculcated
the redeeming value of dignified labor. He countenanced the
General's recurrent affirmation that

> the mere effort which the student put forth through the industries at Hampton
> to help himself was of the greatest value, whether the labor itself was of very
> much value or not. In a word, he (Armstrong) meant to use the industries as a
> means for building character — to teach that all forms of labor were honorable
> and all forms of idleness a disgrace [57].

and he followed suit. This is the kind of attitude that, if carried to
its extreme, may lead to estheticism in educational leadership (art
for art's sake in character building) or even sadism (the harder and
the less relevant the manual training, the better the character
building). At any rate, it warrants Washington's persistent
advocacy of the primacy of industrial education, and it is
connected with Armstrong's conservative Darwinist philosophy,
which he shares when he appraises his own people in comparison
with the whites :

> The greatest injury that slavery did my people was to deprive them of that
> sense of self-dependence, habit of economy, and executive power which are the
> glory and distinction of the Anglo-Saxon race and we need not expect what was
> 250 years going into a race to be gotten out in 25 or 30 years ; and General

Armstrong early saw that the only way to help these weaknesses was through the teacher educated in head, hand and heart. [58]

Accepting the «character» criterion led Washington to implicitly recognize the inferiority of the Negro. True enough, he did assert his race pride repeatedly («We are a great race» ; «You may not know it, but we are as proud of our racial integrity as you are of yours» [59]), and he did endeavor to convey his feeling to his black public. He never admitted that his race was innately backward, but called it «degraded» or «disadvantaged», and explained that its inferiority was due to the traumatic experience of slavery. Yet, because of his Hampton training, he could not help feeding the very prejudice he was fighting, as when he insisted that the Negro race was immature in the following terms :

It is with an ignorant race as it is with a child ; it craves at first for the ornamental, the signs of progress rather than the reality. The ignorant race is tempted to jump, at one bound, to the position that it has required years of hard work for others to reach. [60]

By the time he died, Washington had become obsessed with the priority of character acquisition. In his last Sunday evening talk, he was insisting that the blessings of teamwork — his subject — were punctuality, reduction of expenses, elimination of waste, cleanliness and honesty. His talk, which in some respects was an anticipation of Frederick Winslow Taylor, lapsed into a complaint about petty thieving :

We want to have teamwork that shall make it absolutely impossible for an unclean character to be here, unclean in his morals, unclean in his living, unclean in his actions in any direction. [61]

The main consequence of his obsession is that he spoke of Negro progress in terms of duty more than of rights and had little patience with the «moral weaknesses» of his race. Though he at times did not spare his white audiences, he did much, by awkward statements and dubious jokes, to uphold the image of the lazy, shiftless, improvident Negro. By playing down politics he implicitly fostered the whites' belief that the blacks were unworthy of suffrage or indifferent to it. He consistently claimed, from graduation day onwards, that the wisest solution was a suffrage restriction based on property, which would affect blacks and whites alike.

He considered the acquisition of property an even more suitable qualification than an education, for an education more often was given, while to acquire and retain property took character and self-reliance. [62]

There is some truth but little realism in such a statement as Washington's «Until there is industrial independence it is hardly possible to have a pure ballot.» [63] Assuming the phrase makes sense, did all American voters then cast a *pure ballot* ? Washington himself provides the answer to this question when he quotes Frederick Douglass in his biography of his famed predecessor :

> If the Negro knows enough to fight for his country, he knows enough to vote ; if he knows enough to pay for his taxes to support the government, he knows enough to vote ; if he knows as much when sober as an Irishman when he is drunk, he knows enough to vote. [64]

Yet, the same Booker T. Washington, though he never recommended that those Negroes who could vote give up their constitutional rights, chose to advise the others to gain gradual access to the ballot through individual and group self-help *and* through the patronage of the Southern white man, which «will be more potent and more lasting then any our Federal Congress or any outside power can confer.» [65] In spite of his denunciations of racial injustice, he never linked up the notions of Negro suffrage and Negro manhood and clung to his avowed belief that «brains, property and character will settle the question of civil rights.» [66]

Never did the Tuskegeean depart fundamentally from Armstrong's lessons. One explanation for his distrust of politics is that «he lacked faith in the democratic process.» [67] Rather, it seems that, insofar as the democratic process was not consistent with morality and public peace, it was to be by-passed. And it little mattered if it was, for Armstrong's disciple placed his faith well above the level of politics, in a ministry of sectional reconciliation whose outcome would be the dream of true Reconstruction fulfilled.

Extrapolating from Armstrong's theory, Washington posited that the fate of the American Negro was inseparable from that of the white American. The moral example set by the Negro and his efforts to live up to the white man's ethos should normally induce North and South to rise to «the sublime heights of unselfishness and self-forgetfulness», by helping the Negro to help himself. Being both object and agent of his regeneration, the Black man found himself at the core of a process of mutual reconstruction. A glowing picture of this process is sketched at the close of one of Washington's speeches :

Let the Negro, the North and the South do their duty with a new spirit and a new determination and at the end of fifty years a picture will be painted — what is it ? A race dragged from its native land in chains, three hundred years of slavery, years of fratricidal war, thousands of lives laid down, freedom for the slave, reconstruction, blunders, bitterness between North and South. The South staggers under the burden ; the North forgets the past and comes to the rescue ; the Negro, in the midst, teaching North and South patience, forbearance, long-suffering, obedience to law, developing in intellect, skill and habits of industry. The North and South joining hands with the Negro, take him whom they have wronged, help him, encourage him, stimulate him in self-help, give him the rights of man, and, in lifting up the Negro, lift themselves up into that atmosphere where there is a new North, a new South — a new citizen — a new republic. [68]

In the eyes of Washington, there were two possible solutions to the Negro problem : the fair uplift of the race within the pattern of the South's and the nation's progress, or sheer deadlock. The Negro would either be lifted up by the White Man, or he would drag him down. This second alternative was clearly enunciated as an ominous threat in the Atlanta Address : «...we shall prove a veritable body of death, stagnating, depressing, retarding every effort to advance the body politic», but it went rather unnoticed.

Washington laid his stakes on the first alternative and, in terms of statistics, lost. [70] He lived to see the whites fail to fulfill their share of the Atlanta compact. He was painfully aware of this failure when he stated that, with regard to his race, neither Christianity nor education had yet been tried. [71] A few days before his death he was still describing the results of the educational policy of the Southern states he had been unable to prevent : in 1914 the South had spent an average $ 10.23 per capita in educating a white child, while only $ 2.82 was spent per black child. Two million black children of school age were still out of school, and another million could not read and write. [72] The weary leader concluded :

At the present rate it is taking, not a few days or a few years, but a century or more to get Negro education on a plane at all similar to that on which the education of the whites is. [73]

Yet, however pointedly Washington may have exposed racial inequality, he never publicly acknowledged that Negro disfranchisement was largely instrumental in the deterioration of Negro conditions. He preferred to be an occasional secret civil rights militant instead. [74] Though he felt it was not wholly relevant to the protection of his race, he chose not to depart from Armstrong's ideology. Shaped in the Hampton mold, the Tuskegeean wielded his leadership primarily to bring about the true Reconstruction. He acted in such a way that he actually refused to implement or countenance tactics that were alien to the Armstrong strategy. Taking after his white father, he systematically deprecated speculative learning, higher education and manhood suffrage for the Negro masses, all of which could have sped up the progress of the race. Possessed of adaptability and character, the Hampton alumnus combined high-mindedness and narrow-mindedness.

NOTES

1. The page numbers of Booker T. Washington's early autobiographical writings (**Up from Slavery**, **The Story of My Life and Work**) refer to Louis R. Harlan, **The Booker T. Washington Papers**, Urbana, U. of Illinois Press.

2. See R.W. Logan, **The Negro in American Life & Thought**, New York, The Dial Press, 1954. pp. 275-313.

3. **Up From Slavery**, 258.

4. ibid. 331.

5. The leit-motiv of his Atlanta Exposition Address ; see **Up From Slavery**, 330-32.

6. ibid. 338-39.

7. Chapters from My Experience, **World's Work**, XXI, Nov. 1910, 1635.

8. E. Davidson Washington, ed. **Selected Speeches of Booker T. Washington**, New York, Doubleday, Doran & Co, 1932, (4-5, 7-8).

9. ibid, 7-8.

10. **Up From Slavery**, 332.

11. W.E.B. Dubois, **The Dial**, July 16, 1901 and **The Soul of Black Folks**, Chicago, 1903, 47.

12. **Up From Slavery**, 234.

13. ibid, 241.

14. B.T.W. **The Story of My Life and Work**, 21.

15. E. Talbot, **Samuel Chapman Armstrong, A Biographical Study**, New York, Doubleday & Page, 1904, 137.

16. Schwab, **Samuel Chapman Armstrong of Hampton, 1839-1893**, London, The Sheldon Press, 1898, 10.

17. S.C. Armstrong, in **Proceedings of the First Lake Mohonk Conference on the Negro, 1890**, Boston, 1890, 12-13.

18. J. Denison, Samuel Chapman Armstrong, **Atlantic Monthly**, Jan. 1894, 92.

19. S.C. Armstrong, Lessons from the Hawaian Experience, **Journal of Christian Philosphy**, III, 1884, p. 213.

20. S.C. Armstrong, Normal School among the Freedmen, in **Proceedings of the Annual Meeting of the National Education Association, 1872**, Boston, 1872, p. 176.

21. Talbot, op. cit., 151.

22. **Proceedings...**, ibid.

23. ibid.

24. Ibid., 179.

25. ibid. emphasis added.

26. ibid.

27. ibid. 180.

28. quoted by Talbot, op. cit. 213.

29. **Proceedings...**, 181. Emphasis added.

30. **The Future of the American Negro**, Boston, Small, Maynard & Co, 1899, p. 107.

31. **Up From Slavery**, 248-49.

32. ibid. 243.

33. Talbot, op. cit., 195.

34. **Southern Workman**, V, Feb. 1877.

35. ibid, Dec. 1874.

36. A. Meier, **Negro Thought in America, Racial Ideologies in the Age of Booker T. Washington**, U. Of Michigan Press, 1965, p. 102.

37. **Southern Workman**, Nov. 24, 1895, p. 182.

38. **Up From Slavery**, 253-54 ; **Southern Workman**, Oct. 1878, p.76.

39. L. Harlan, **Booker T. Washington, The Making of a Black Leader,** vol. I, O.U.P., 1972, pp. 84-5 ; **Up from Slavery**, 263.

40. ibid. 260.

41. ibid. 261.

42. Schwab, op. cit., 12 ; **The Congregationalist**, 31, 169, quoted by Harlan, **B.T.W. Papers**, II, 75-6.

43. Quoted by Washington in **Southern Workman**, 9, Dec. 1880, 125.

44. Samuel C. Armstrong to G.W. Campbell, May 31, 1881.

45. A Recommendation from S.C. Armstrong, Oct. 26, 1891.

46. Memorial Address on General Armstrong, **Selected Speeches**, 29.

47. Up From Slavery, 317.

48. **Up From Slavery**, 317. ; **My larger education,** New York, Garden City, 1911, 146-47.

49. **New York Times,** June 15, 1875, 5.

50. **Character Building**, New York, Doubleday, 1902, 90-91.

51. **Boston Transcript**, July 11, 1896.

52. Self-denial, a Sunday Evening Talk, Feb. 8, 1891, Harlan, ed., **B.T.W. Papers**, III, 130.

53. **Selected Speeches,** 15.

54. **Up From Slavery**, 303.

55. **The Story of the Negro**, New York, Doubleday, 1907, vol. 1, 12.

56. **The Negro in the South,** Philadelphia, Jacobs, 1907, 62.

57. B.T. Washington, quoted by Talbot, op. cit., 208.

58. **Selected Speeches**, 27-8.

59. ibid., 146.

60. ibid., 77, 65.

61. ibid, 276.

62. Harlan, **B.T.W., The Making of a Black Leader**, 302.

63. **Selected Speeches,** 69.

64. Booker T. Washington, **Frederick Douglass,** Philadelphia, Jacobs, 1907, 258-59.

65. **Selected Speeches,** 82.

66. Ibid., 3.

67. Harlan, op. cit., 303.

68. **Selected Speeches**, 50.

60. **Up From Slavery**, 333.

70. See Bullock, **A History of Negro Education in the South,** Harvard U.P., 1967, and Franklin Frazier, **Black Bourgeoisie,** Colliers, 1957, especially ch. III.

71. **My Larger Education Education**, 291 ; **Selected Speeches**, 130.

72. **Selected Speeches,** 282.

73. ibid., 283.

74. See Meier, Toward a Reinterpretation of Booker T. Washington, **JSH**, XXIII, May 1957 ; Meier, op. cit., passim ; Harlan, The Secret Life of Booker T. Washington, **JSH**, XXXVII, Aug. 1971.

Alain SOLARD

The impossible Unity :

Jean Toomer's «Kabnis»

At the turn of the twentieth century, social movements, leading up to a better organization of trade-unionism and to the political emergence of feminism, were followed by a definite renewal in arts and letters, as painters, novelists, poets attempted to break former patterns and to discover new forms of expression. The Black minority was soon to follow suit : with W.E.B. DuBois, intellectuals claimed their rights in courts ; with Garvey, a charismatic leader, the great bulk of Black people, who had been scattered in the rural South, after having recently settled in the large industrial cities in the North as a consequence of the Great Migration, were to dream of a return to their ancestors' native land and draw renewed pride in the concept of Afro-American unity. The city of Harlem was the forum where musicians, writers and reformers made themselves heard.

As a result, the conditions conducive to the spiritual awakening of a new generation of Black Americans were created : Harlem's young intellectuals attempted to find a medium that might fittingly define the 'New Negro', which was to be the title of Alain Locke's anthology and manifesto in 1925. In the artistic, literary and social fields, a need was felt to stop imitating the white pattern present everywhere, and to give to the reader a reflection of his true self by painting him with his exuberance, his supreme indifference, his beauty ; by expressing the essential tragedy of this race and its solitude. The surge of interest caused by jazz musicians opened the door of a few publishing-houses and during the twenties the Americans discovered the originality of a people they had misjudged.

Jean Toomer, one of the writers of the young generation, aimed at creating new forms, likely to express an authentic picture of contemporary man. He proved to be most able to give an authentic outline of Black society, appearing gradually as we read the novellas and poems of *Cane* (1923) [1]. Incidentally the poet was inspired by a stay in Georgia, the cradle of his race, in 1921 [2]. As he witnessed the way of life of the Sparta sharecroppers, the buried image of their ancestral past, which was miraculously preserved, struck his imagination ; then he mastered a literary medium able to give rise, in the reader's mind, to the vision of a newly-framed society — women and farmers in the South, a schoolmistress and a student in the north, those elements of a minority invisible to America.

Beyond a kaleidoscopic vision of society, this work reveals the

Black man's interiorization of racial conflicts : more maimed spiritually as he gets nearer the North, in the South, he exhibits the pre-adamic image of a man in harmony with nature, prompted by instinct, and consequently — according to Toomer — free.

By means of a fable, a new myth arises, liable to counterbalance what Toomer called «the Tyranny of the Anglo-Saxon Ideal» [3], and that could be summed up with the modern slogan «Black is beautiful». But the poet's intention was very far from militancy : indeed the literary medium devised by him — a blend of prose and poetry cast in a dramatic mould — excluded any attempt at a committed expression, prone to reverse the racial prejudices. The hero of the novella we intend to study, a projection of the conflicts of man and the artist in a given situation, is not Lewis, the militant already saved, but Kabnis, the revolted poet. Therefore the road travelled by the latter — a pilgrimage to the sources of his being — is both a narrative and a line of action, inasmuch as it mapped out a new way — the stage of primitivism — to the black men of cities seeking an identity.

Any real work of art represents an interplay of tensions calling for their own solution. By showing a description of this narrative, I shall try to ascertain Toomer's own ideology within the American context of the twenties.

Before mapping out the main character's journey, let us first evoke the atmosphere in which the narrative unfolds. One of the basic themes of «Kabnis» (a theme which underlies the whole of the collection) appears to be that of the «split». This theme is in evidence right from the beginning of the story : «Cracks between the boards are black. These cracks are the lips the night winds use for whispering» (p. 157) . The shack with its lime-washed walls cannot prevent the night wind (symbolising inspiration) from roaring through the black «lips» formed by the gaps between the boards, and into the soul of the poet-narrator. He, in turn, cannot suppress the profound emotion that wells up in him at the sight of the Georgia landscape, the home of his racial kindred, his «brothers». For the gap picked out by the white light of his lamp is at one and the same time symbolic of the distance between two irreconcilable worlds, those of the two races, one of which dominates and exploits the other. Finally, it also signifies the division which exists within Kabnis himself ; Kabnis, the mulatto in search of his own identity, the impossible harmony within him.

This, then, is the debate, be it internal monologue or dramatic dialogue for several voices, with which the narrator's conflict confronts us : the poet grappling with his material — words, the poetic form — and the man, divided against himself, powerless, tortured by the struggle which ranges his «brothers» against the White oppressors, unable to give himself up to the regenerating influence of Lewis, the Northern militant, a man without self-doubt, who tries to rescue him by leading him towards a higher level of consciousness. This preliminary scene is played out against the background of the unchangingly beautiful hills of Georgia, where the songs of the Black peasants starkly encompass the tragedy of their race :

White man's land
Niggers, sing.
Burn, bear black children
Till poor rivers bring
Rest, and sweet glory
In Camp Ground. (p. 157)

Let us, then, briefly review the pilgrimage of the central character, Kabnis, a young teacher who has come from the North to work in a Black school. Already in the first scene we see his awareness of that South whose echo is borne on the night wind — he wants to make his dream real, to give expression to the world by which he is possessed («Give what I know a bull-neck and a heaving body» p. 158), that world whose perspective is the racial ambivalence that divides him against himself («The half-moon is a white child that sleeps upon the tree-tops of the forest»), and which is predestined to tragedy («cradle will fall.../ Teat moon-children at your breasts,/ down will come baby», p. 160).

Indeed the gap which for the poet opens on to the beauties of nature also acts as a channel for everything that represents the South at its most hideous and horrible. The fears that haunt him take shape, through that same allegorical crack that gave access to his dream, in the forms of repulsive animals, such as rats, cackling hens and other denizens of the farmyard, amplified by the night into shapes both ghostly and grotesque.

This double polarity persists throughout the three episodes which make up the first section of the story, centred around the figure of Kabnis working under the orders of Hanby, the head of the school. The second leaf of this literary triptych shows Kabnis as the apprentice of Halsey, the joiner, while the action in the third leaf takes place in Halsey's cellar.

Kabnis's awareness of beauty soon gives way to the feeling of terror that gradually takes possession of him when, during a conversation between Halsey, Layman (the local teacher-cum-preacher) and himself, the problem of the Southern Blacks and the question of lynching crop up. As Layman discreetly refers to the martyrdom of Mame Lamkins (the name is clearly symbolic), the tragic crescendo of a solo voice rises up from the basso continuo of choral singing in a nearby church :

> A shriek pierces the room. The bronze pieces on the mantel hum. The sister cries frantically : «Jesus, Jesus, I've found Jesus. O Lord, glory t God, one mo sister is acomin home !» At the height of this, a stone, wrapped round with paper, crashes through the window. (p. 179).

Kabnis, wild with fear, believes that the burden of the message — «you northern nigger, its time fer y t leave» — is intended for him, and takes panic-stricken flight across the fields of sugar-cane to the refuge of his shack.

So the poet becomes a nightmare creature, «a scarecrow replica of Kabnis, awkwardly animate. Fantastically plastered with red Georgia mud. (...) It skirts the big house...» (pp. 180-1), a grotesque who imagines himself surrounded by howling dogs, and whose hallucinations concretize the imaginary presence of the lynchers hot on his heels : «Their clammy hands were like the love of death playing up and down my spine» (p. 181). Only the arrival of his two companions can finally reassure him ; and Lewis, to whom Halsey has previously referred with admiration, and who is presented as the epitome of the Northern intellectual come to campaign for the rights of the Blacks and to regenerate his brothers, brings him the truth of the matter : the note had in fact been written by Hanby, the Black head of the school, to urge him to leave — him, Lewis, the subversive element, and not Kabnis. Thus, the first leaf of the triptych depicts the degradation of the protagonist, whose poetic vein has been supressed by terror.

As is the case in the stories with a linear plot, it will be convenient to trace the protagonist's journey throughout the three episodes of the novella. We have already noticed that the setting of the young teacher's ordeal first took place on a hillside. At the start of the novel, from his vantage point, he could behold the vision of a world set apart from the civilized North. From now on, the maimed Kabnis will experience a downfall, and the different stages of his degradation will make him follow the Black people's journey backwards. This descent to the bottom of the abysm is in fact an ascent during which the pilgrim will get away from the world of the black Bourgeoisie illustrated by Hanby and reach the world of the rural craftsman ; he will finally gather in the forgotten pit the liberating message from the old slave's lips : «O the sin th white folks 'mitted when they made the Bible lie» (p. 237). So at the end of his journey, the rebellious hero will hear the regenerating words condemning the lies of the Puritan ideology that had justified slavery, and implicitly launching the new gospel of primitivism.

Then, the imagery organic to the poem takes on its full meaning : the top of the hill where the college stands may indeed represent the culminating point of a dominant society having given allegiance to the Whites, embodied by Hanby ; but Kabnis's nearby shack is actually a hole «still as a grave» (p. 164). That is why the revolted man raises his fist at heaven and cries : «Earth's child. The earth my mother. God is a profligate red-nosed man about town». He rebels against the false white God, the better to venerate the gorgeous landscape, with its hills and pine-forests, a mother «heaving with folk songs», the cradle of a happy pastoral people : «They farm. They sing. They love. They sleep». So if Layman's account concerning the death of Mame Lamkins's child, ripped out of his mother's womb, stabbed and fixed to a tree, makes him tremble, it is because he identifies himself with that image of the crucified Christ, for he is «an atom of dust in agony on a hillside» (p. 162). The harmonious rhythms of the poems that came to his mind no longer haunt him, and he is nothing now but the progeny of a bastard race shouting his rebellion :«A bastard son has a right to curse his maker» (p. 161).

The dramatic setting echoes the symbolic framework of the first scenes : the dialogues elicit Kabnis's position : that of a sensitive Northener imbued with modern liberal ideas and averse to the

Washingtonian ideology prevailing in the South : Hanby's avowed desire to «lift up» the Black race to white-ordained, puritanical standards of respectability — temperance, cleanliness, work — was the thin disguise enabling him the better to fasten his rule over the black community. An unholy alliance between the school, the court and the church maintained the people in slavery : «This preacher-ridden race. Pray and shout. Theyre in the preacher's hands. Thats what it is. And the preacher's hands are in the white man's pockets» (p. 174).

The next stage of Kabnis's journey — his stay in Halsey's workshop — represents a transition between an initiation into the ideology of the Black Bourgeoisie and an initiation into the ancestral wisdom. The description of this experience corroborates Toomer's thesis, by picturing, through a *reductio ad absurdum*, the importance of defining a counter-ideology. As a matter of fact the means to salvation proposed to the teacher by the joiner after his dismissal from the school — working with his hands — was none other than the ideal recommended to the young Blacks by Booker T. Washington during the previous decades. Their skill in a specialized handicraft (together with political neutrality) was supposed to earn them the White man's esteem. But if the puritanical virtues of hard work secured the success of the average American, such was not the case for the Black American, not competitive in the labour-market.

Therefore we shall not be surprised to note that Halsey's promise — «He's goin t work with me. Shapin shafts and buildin wagons'll make a man of him what nobody, y get me ? what nobody can take advantage of» (p. 188) — cannot be fulfilled : Kabnis, a misfit, remains ill at ease («he is awkward and ludicrous», p. 196), clumsy in his work, and takes his lack of skill at handling a plane as a bitter insult. At any rate, the joiner's limited number of orders reveals the fact that prosperity was not the lot of the Southern segregated schools' graduates.

To be sure, Kabnis's new guide, Halsey, represents a level of thought superior to that of Hanby. He is part of the Black rural middle-class. Although he is opposed to Hanby, the 'collaborator', and is anxious to listen to Lewis's message, he has to conform to the Southern code of behaviour in his relationship with white customers. This honest craftsman is completely committed to his condition and, as distinct from Kabnis, he «fits» perfectly well in the South. And although he is «an artist in (his) way» (p. 200), he cannot experience the love of beauty that inspires the poet.

So Kabnis is still 'the rebel' in his new role as an apprentice, and his attempt at regaining a sense of balance ends in failure. Actually he seeks something else than what Halsey has to offer : an anwer to his quest — how to give — through words — a shape to his poetic vision. His role is not that of the joiner. Instead, he must tailor the poetical language to his dream. In fact Halsey mistakes the true relationship between him and the poet : *He* is not the mentor, but the reverse might be true, for though both characters are artists in their separate provinces, Kabnis is receptive to a beauty superior to that conferred by finely shaped tools : «Kabnis : That song, Halsey, do you hear it ? (...) Halsey : Hear it, Hear what ? Course I hear it. Listen t what I'm telling you» (p. 193).

As a matter of fact, neither the headmaster nor the craftsman's philosophy will be suitable to the poet come to find an answer to his quest. The final act of the short story, in which the last phase of Kabnis's evolution will unfold — showing a night party gathering the main actors of the drama — will take place in Halsey's cellar which shelters the family ancestor, the hidden slave. Only by associating with this past buried in the unconscious should Kabnis find the roots of his being — for this man who, like his brothers, denies a hybrid kinship, with its fake culture and its fake values, seeks a spiritual relationship that might be substituted to the other. The old man really embodies the father of the true race :

Slave boy whom some Christian mistress taught to read the Bible. Black man who saw Jesus in the ricefields, and began preaching to his people. Moses-and-Christ-words used for songs. Dead blind father of a muted folk who feel their way upward to a life that crushes or absorbs them. (Speak, Father !) suppose your eyes could see, old man. (The years hold hands. O sing !) Suppose your lips... Halsey, does he never talk ? (p. 212).

Hence the continuity of the inverted pattern of images in the story : the church spire soaring skywards is an ambiguous symbol, for «Above (the) squat tower, a great spiral of buzzards reaches far into the heavens. An ironic comment upon the path that leads into the Christian land» (p. 169). This subterranean way, dimly sought by Kabnis — who is depicted as «a promise of soil-soaked beauty ; uprooted, thinning out. Suspended a few feet above the soil whose touch would resurrect him» (p. 191) — indeed leads to the true kingdom, underground, invisible, where the slave, a witness of the past, sits in king-like fashion «in a high-backed chair which stands upon a low platform (...) Gray-haired. Prophetic. Immobile» (p. 211) ; and if Kabnis, the poet in the making, discerns in him a black Vulcan, ruling over «Th smoke an fire of th forge», Lewis, the militant, sees in this blind witness «a mute John the Baptist of a new religion, or a tongue-tied shadow of an old». (p. 211).

So, for Kabnis the intellectual who seeks in the South the truth about himself, the descent into the depths undoubtedly represents a desire for self-identification with his Black forbears. In terms of Toomer's own symbolism, the sky is equated with White supremacy and with the God whom the Whites have invented, whilst the earth is equated with the origin of the Blacks [4]. So the gradual descent underlines the hero's desire to tie again the bond that links him to the Black race, with that part of his origin which he seeks confusedly to comprehend. Furthermore, the restorative properties of the pastoral South, destined to cure the town dweller from the destructive effects of a stultifying civilisation, are persistently referred to in *Cane*. This linking up with the past is a liberation from a civilisation which has scarcely cast off the shackles of Victorian puritanism, and a rejection of repressive taboos. We should not forget that the Black man at this time supplied the Western world with a ready-made image of the natural man, giving rise to a new myth of emancipation, the corner-stone of modern Romanticism.

Another interpretation of this downward movement may be drawn from the obvious psycho-analytical parallels : the cellar represents the mother's womb into which the character descends in order to short-circuit time and return once more to prenatal tranquillity. This cellar is huge and warm, with the warmth of inner recesses. In fact, this exploratory movement towards the life-source marks a phase which foreshadows a possible reascent towards the world of light, a genuine re-birth which should allow the hero, after his circular journey, once again to confront the world of men, fortified by the integration into his own personality of the truth he has learned at this new stage of his experience.

This last enhances Kabnis's revolt : during the night scene — in which the main characters and several women are gathered, with the Black slave in the background — he seems to enjoy reviling the old man and the militant, those two mediators pointing the way towards redemption. He rejects the renewal offered by Lewis — Lewis, his «double» [5], who possesses the courage and faith that he lacks [6]. Rather than seeing the old slave as a link with the past, and getting absorbed in the old man's gaze (like Lewis), he spurns the proferred bond. Indeed his refusal to accept his identity of origin with the Black slave explains his hostility to him, and may represent a typical attitude in Black youths at that time, all too eager to forget a past which they wanted to deny. This explains the dialogue that takes place between Lewis and Kabnis :

> ... he ain't my past. My ancestors were Southern blue-bloods. Lewis : And black.
> Kabnis : Aint much difference between blue and black.
> Lewis : Enough to draw a denial from you. Cant hold them, can you ? Master ; slave. Soil ; and the overarching heavens. Dusk ; dawn. They fight and bastardize you. (pp. 217-8).

Another reason for Kabnis's outbursts of verbal violence has been stated by John M. Reilly, who wrote : «Violence (in black America) has always been present as the chief instrument of social control, so that an expedition into the zones of black identity inevitably describes the effects that violence must have upon personality» [7]. Kabnis is the victim of racial oppression whose spirit has been maimed and whose return to the world (or to the surface) cannot be achieved without a long struggle with himself. The way in which he expresses his condition is clearly stated when he first hears the old man mumbling «sin». He misunderstands the old slave, thinking that the latter is using the puritanical phraseology, and answers :

> It was only a preacher's sin they knew in those old days, an that wasn't sin at all. Mind me, the only sin is whats done against th soul. Th whole world is a conspiracy t sin, especially in America, an against me. I'm a victim of their sin. I am what sin is». (p. 236).

Indeed, the mulatto is the living embodiment of the sin of the Whites against the Blacks, and of the guilt of America. And just as he condemns the «preacher's» philosophy, so does he reject the limited assistance that Halsey can offer him («twont do t lift me bodily (...) But its th soul of me that needs the risin». p. 234). Moreover, this revolted anti-hero cannot share in the epiphany which Lewis achieves when he absorbs himself into the being of the old slave, as it were in his gaze :

> Lewis, seated now that his eyes rest upon the old man, merges with his source and lets the pain and beauty of the South meet him then. White faces, pain-pollen, settle downward through a cane-sweet mist and touch the ovaries of yellow flowers. Cotton-balls bloom, droop. Black roots twist in a parched red soil beneath a blazing sky. Magnolias, fragrant, a trifle futile, lovely, far off... His eyelids close. A force begins to heave and rise... (pp. 214-5)

For the author's solution to his protagonist's search is no less than a fusion of beings and races which would lift the curse that weighs upon them. The phallic image of the White man's knife transfixing the child dissolves in this fusion — here sexual connotations are explicit — and the nightmare is transformed into a dream of fulfilment. Here lies the significance of the story's circular structure, whose narrative design and poetical imagery imply a reconciliation of opposite poles. Let us note, too, that if on the one hand, in the context of the geographical symbolism, the man of the North needs the South (i.e., the sense of his past) in order to find his true life, a link with his origins and a contact with nature, on the other hand the South needs the current of thought which emanates from the North to exorcise the spell under which it lies : «From the back yard, mules tethered to odd trees and posts blink dumbly at (Lewis). They too seem burdened with impotent pain» (p. 205).

Lewis's call to arms against the oppressive thrall in which his «brothers» are held is added to the fascination which this Northern militant intellectual exercises over each and every individual, shaking him out of his lethargy and, by virtue of the «fusion» mentioned above, raising those who are ready to a higher level of consciousness. To live life to the fullest, man must neither sever his links with the past, nor become enslaved to any ideology. In this imagery of fusion, symbolising a basic unity between men and nature, we recognize one of the themes of a group of young writers, Hart Crane, Waldo Frank, Gorham Munson and Kenneth Burke, of which Toomer was a member. Their circle called itself «Art as vision». They followed the mystic, scientifically based philosophy of Ouspensky, whose opus *Tertium Organum* had first appeared in the English translation of 1920 [8].

If, however, Kabnis's search for regeneration is inconclusive, not the same can be said of his vocation as a writer. For the protagonist is also, and above all, the poet, he who works with words as his raw material, trying to confer on the land of Georgia the shape of his dreams :

> The body of the world is bull-necked. A dream is a soft face that fits uncertainly upon it... God, if I could develop that in words (...) If I, the dream (not what is weak and afraid in me) could become the face of the South. How my lips would sing for it, my songs being the lips of its soul (p. 158).

Kabnis's search for regeneration is played out in a carpenter's workshop, and the carpenter fashions his raw materials in the same way as an artist. Halsey as creator considers practice superior to theory : «there aint no books whats got th feel t them of them there tools» (p. 201). This evaluation of art as building with and working on the raw material of words constitutes throughout the story nothing less than Toomer's artistic manifesto, his writer's confession of faith. One senses the presence of theories of imagism and that search for the *mot juste*, for perfection of form which he evokes in his «Outline of Autobiography», when he recounts his literary experiments prior to writing *Cane* :

> Literature, and particularly the craftsman's aspect of it, again became my entire world, and I lived in it as never before (...). This was the period when I was so strongly influenced, first, by the Americans who were dealing with local materials in a poetic way (...) ; and, second, the poems and program of the Imagists. Their insistence on fresh vision and on the perfect clean economical line was just what I was looking for [9].

Hence Halsey's reflection as he offers Kabnis a drink : «Th boys what made this stuff — are y listenin t me, Kabnis ? Th boys what made this stuff have got the art down like I heard you say youd like t be with words» (p. 184).

Whereas the joiner's bench evokes the work of the writer, the forge (in the new phase of experience constituted by the time spent in the cellar) also possesses a symbolic significance. The poet works on his material like a skilled craftsman, an expert :«I've been shapin words t fit m soul (...) ; ah, but sometimes theyre beautiful an golden an have a taste that makes them fine t roll over with y tongue» (p. 223). He feels an obligation to work and by his writing to endue with life the world as he sees it. This world is not tailor-made to his requirements : it is reality, at once sublime and repugnant :

> Th form thats burned int my soul is some twisted awful thing that crept in from a dream, a godam nightmare, an wont stay still unless I feed it. An it lives on words. Not beautiful words. God Almighty no. Misshapen, split-gut, tortured, twisted words. Layman was feedin it back there that day you thought I ran out fearin things. White folks feed it cause their looks are words. Niggers, black niggers feed it cause theyre evil an their looks are words. Yallar niggers feed it. This whole damn bloated purple country feeds it cause its goin down t hell in a holy avalanche of words. I want t feed th soul — I know what that is ; th preachers dont — but I've got t feed it (p. 224) [10].

One may say that, seen on the plane of literary creation, the protagonist becomes progressively more assured as the *dénouement* — the character's emergence into the light — gets nearer. Indeed, the closing pages of the story, whilst underlining the failure of Kabnis's attempt at a recreation of the self, prefigure the ultimate posthumous success of the writer in his work on form and poetic diction. On this point, I agree with William Goede when he says that the conclusion of the story allows us to anticipate the success of the hero on the literary plane, a success which will in turn enable him to communicate his commitment to his people. As Ralph Ellison suggests in the conclusion of *Invisible Man*, the orator's message is none other than the work itself, the sum total of his experience [11].

In this story, one of Toomer's most notable successes, we may discern pointers to the subsequent path the author was to take. Although we may decline to see in the work a mere mirror-image of Toomer himself, the author's lyrical *penchant*, his own allusions on this point, and the numerous autobiographical references that permeate *Cane* induce us to stress the links between the one and the other [12]. As Toomer shares his hero's aesthetic standpoint, so too he experiences his tortures. He tells of the difficulties of that time in his various autobiographies. As Fullenwider wrote, he was unable to achieve the unity of his personality, and the characters of Lewis and Kabnis enshrine to perfection the dichotomy between emotions and intellect from which he suffered [13].

So Kabnis, the main character is partly a projection of Toomer's internal struggles as an artist and as a man. In that respect, Waldo Frank gave Toomer personal directions at the close of a critical appraisal of «Kabnis» :

> O if there is one thing I have learned, living in America, knowing my own life and knowing the lives of so many about me, it is that the artist must have the greater wisdom of fighting for himself, of knowing that only so can the time come when the American world will be a place in which he can live. Today, every rhythm, every will sent through the weave of America is fatal to creation... and so often not alone economic pressure but the subtly insidious Myth of «the duties of manhood, the need of making one's own way» plunges the delicate artist tissues into a corrodent poisonous bath of American «reality» which eats them up. Dont think that you will be helping yourself or America in a newspaper office or an advertising agency. If you can keep away, do ! Keep to the streets, keep to the quiet of your room... let that flame burn clear.

And he added, further on :

> Keep yourself underneath, in the soil, where the throb is... and use every decent means in your reach to protect yourself from a too early pushing to the surface [14].

Here, Waldo Frank raises an interesting question : should the artist «keep away» in order to avoid being crushed, like Kabnis ? Most of the American writers of the twenties, who were expatriates, «kept away», and so did Sherwood Anderson when he broke away from the business world. Toomer's original way of «keeping away» in order to fulfil his mission as an artist was conditioned by the circumstances of his life, and may be accounted for in «Kabnis». The fact that he employs the same metaphor of the forge or the joiner's workshop to symbolize both the act of reconstruction and that of literary creation seems to indicate that he did not dissociate one from the other. Perhaps he felt, like Kabnis, that he had something to say ; but that, like Kabnis, he was too weak to say it. Looking back over the phase of his life when he was writing *Cane*, he stated :

> Life had tied me in a knot, hard and fast. Even in Georgia I was horribly conflicted, strained and tense — more so here. The deep releases caused by my experiences there, could not liberate and harmonize the sum of me,

adding in the same letter that *Cane* «was born in an agony of internal tightness, conflict and chaos» and that, although «the feelings were in me deep and mobile enough (...) the creations of the forms were very difficult».

No wonder if, in 1923, Jean Toomer became so fascinated by Gurjieff's teachings, «Unitism», with its system of self-reconstruction by way of physical, psychological and spiritual exercises. His intense interest in literature had lasted three years but he never gave up writing. He said :

> ...I had failed writing. In my present condition I simply wasn't up to writing. Writing, real writing, it now seemed to me, presupposed the possession of the very thing I knew I lacked, namely self-purity, self-unification, self-development (...). I felt and felt strongly that one ought to *be* something before one essayed to say something. I felt and felt deeply that a man ought to be a Man before he elected to write [15].

The superficial observer might reply, in Gide's words : «Ce n'est pas avec de bons sentiments qu'on fait de la bonne littérature». But Toomer had dismissed «literature» as such. In 1925, Toomer's friend, Gorham Munson, accounted for this viewpoint by saying that as the Western world was in a state of chaos, with Christians having missed the essential message of Christianity and scientists becoming uncertain and groping, it was now the duty of the artist to work «either toward integration or toward disintegration» ; through their magic, artists were, according to Nietzsche, «casters of glamor over progression and retrogression», and could choose to become either «saviors or betrayers» [16]. In 1923, Toomer had found a «scientific» method of improvement and thought that, if his work were the better for it, he could thus be, in his own individual way, one of the «saviors».

Such was the form his commitment was to take : from 1924 on, Jean Toomer came over to France on several occasions to take training periods at the Fontainebleau «Institute for the Harmonious Development of Man» in order to become acquainted with Gurdjieff's theory and practice. Many critics said that his work suffered from this influence, and from the fact that he had cut himself away from a purely Negro source of inspiration. Indeed. although he wrote extensively during his lifetime, only a few short stories, essays and poems of his were published. He tried to write the long novels that were in demand in the thirties, but failed. As a matter of fact, he was not a novelist ; he was a lyricist and a thinker who wrote essays and tried to put his ideas in practice by conducting seminars and one brief psychological experiment somewhat reminiscent of Brook Farm. But he was not sufficiently versed in philosophical matters to produce the ambitious work he had in mind.

Whatever the apparent causes of Toomer's failure as a writer, we must not forget that even before writing *Cane* in 1921-22, he had in him the seeds of his further development : his literary circle insisted on «Art as Vision» and emphasized a necessity to achieve, through literary means, «a universal Meeting of men and the world in a recaptured Wholeness» [17] — a creed which may have been instrumental in leading him away from the concrete experience which is the essential material of the writer. The general trend of this movement was in keeping with a specifically American view of life, with its fundamental dynamism and optimism stemming from Whitman and Emerson. This fundamental faith in life was expressed by the writers of the Black Renaissance, too : in 1924, Countee Cullen's poem «I have a rendez-vous with Life», published by the Black newspaper *Opportunity*, was a fitting answer to the English war poet's line : «I have a rendez-vous with Death».

Toomer's subsequent writings seem to echo those ideas [18]. Even the last image of «Kabnis», showing the revolted protagonist standing out, as he goes upstairs, against a halo of light, concludes with a glimmer of hope. Therefore we shall not be surprised to read, in one of Toomer's autobiographies, this account of his own rebirth, shortly after the publication of *Cane* :

And I, united in myself, found myself thereby joined to people and the whole of life, and I lived in life, in love. And I was made to realize that separateness is unholy, not real, (...) but a tragic mistake that men perpetuate...
In my soul I found my life. There I discovered what I had sought elsewhere, without finding. In their souls I found their life. And there we met. My life and their life became our life. Life was revealed as One [19].

Toomer's imagery of epiphanies in «Kabnis» corresponds to this description : the picture of fusion was his own way of solving his inner contradictions — one that was expressed in a different way when he asserted, at an early age : «I am an American» — meaning : «I am of no particular race. I am of the human race, a man at large in the human world preparing a new race» [20].

FOOTNOTES.

1. Jean Toomer, **Cane**. Harper and Row, New York, 1969. All subsequent references are to this edition.

2. Jean Toomer was a mulatto ; his father was from Georgia, his grandfather on his mother's side had once been a politician from Louisiana.

3. See his letter to Mae (Augst, 1922) ; Fisk University Archives.

4. See William J. Goede's explanation of this point in «Jean Toomer's Ralph Kabnis : Portrait of the Negro Artist as a Young Man», **Phylon**, vol. XXX, n° 1, Spring 1969, p. 80.

5. Jean Wagner sees in Kabnis and Lewis two complementary characters who symbolically represent the author's own divisions. (Cf. **Les Poètes Nègres des Etats-Unis**, Istra, 1963, p. 289). This judgment is confirmed by a letter written in 1922 by Toomer to Lola Ridge : «Lewis, in point of origin, is as authentic as Kabnis. For I myself am frankly the source of both of them». (Correspondence. Jean Toomer Collection, Fisk University Archives).

6. «Lewis has the sense of direction and the intelligent grip of things that Kabnis lacks. Whereas Kabnis has the emotion which I could not possibly give to Lewis without bringing Lewis into the foregroung more than I care to do in this instance». Letter from Toomer to Lola Ridge, 1922. Correspondence. Jean Toomer Collection, Fisk University Archives.

7. See John M. Reilly, «The search for Black Redemption : Jean Toomer's **Cane» Studies in the Novel**, II (1970). pp. 322-323.

8. **Tertium Organum — A key to the enigmas of the world.** Manas Press, 1920. Hart Crane, in a letter of 1922 to Gorham Munson, Waldo Frank in his notebooks, Toomer in his autobiographies, all evoke their experience of moments of illumination and «epiphany». What, however, is of overriding importance to them, and especially to Toomer and Waldo Frank, is the idea of a reconciliation or fusion of human beings ; of a «rencontre universelle des hommes et du monde dans une Totalité retrouvée». (Rougé, **L'Inquiétude Religieuse dans le Roman Américain Moderne,** Klincksieck, 1974).

9. «Outline of Autobiography», p. 55. Jean Toomer Collection, Fisk University Archives.

10. Toomer wrote of **Cane** : «... the book as a whole was somehow distilled from the most terrible strain I have ever known. I had to use my very blood and nerves to project it». Jean Toomer Collection, Fisk University Archives.

11. On this point there is an unmistakable parallelism between «Kabnis» and **Invisible Man**. In both works the hero (or, more precisely, the anti-hero) is in search of his own identity — a problem that besets twentieth-century man in general and the American Black in particular. He evolves from a collaboration with White power inspired by Booker T. Washigton's gradualism, to a more authentic vision of what sets the Blacks apart ; finally, he undergoes a period of regeneration in a cellar which, paradoxically, gives its inhabitant, freed from persecution, an impression of comfort and liberty ; cf. «Kabnis» : «(The Hole) seems huge, limitless, in the candle light. The walls are of stone, wonderfully fitted (...) They are dry and warm» (p. 210). Moreover, the character of the dying patriarch plays an important part in both works. The conclusion, in both cases ambiguous, can give rise to either an optimistic or a pessimistic interpretation.

12. ««Kabnis» is really the story of my own real or imaginary experiences in Georgia». Letter from Toomer to MacGowan, Fisk University Archives.

13. See Fullenwider : «Jean Toomer : lost Generation, or Negro Renaissance ?»,**Phylon**, Winter, 1966, p. p.398.

14. From a letter by Waldo Frank to Jean Toomer, April, 1922, Fisk University Archives.

15. Autobiography : «Unease (in the first river) continued», p. 48. Fisk U.Archives.

16. Gorham Munson, «The Significance of Jean Toomer»,**Opportunity,** September, 1925.

17.   See Footnote n° 8.

18. See «Blue Meridian», **The Poetry of the Negro**, ed. by Langston Hughes and Arna Bontemps, Doubleday, 1970.

19. Autobiography : «Unease Continued», p. 32.

20. **Essentials**. Private Printing. Chicago, 1931.

Michel FABRE

Aesthetics and ideology in Banjo

When *Banjo*, Claude McKay's novel of black life in Marseilles was published in 1929, the leading Afro-American intellectual, Willian E.B. DuBois, stressed its importance as a critical vision, not only of white prejudice towards Blacks, but also of the attitudes of colored people in the United States and in the different European colonial empires towards one other :

> It is in no sense a novel, either in the nature of its story or in the development of character. It is, on one hand, the description of a series of episodes on the docks of Marseilles ; and on the other hand a sort of international philosophy of the Negro race. The first aspect of the book is negligible... The race philosophy, on the other hand, is of great interest. Mc Kay has become an international Negro. He is a direct descendant from Africa. He knows the West Indies ; he knows Europe ; and he philosophizes about the whole thing [1].

DuBois' approval springs from the fact that, in *Banjo* he found, expressed in literary terms, many of the ideas and conceptions he himself had propounded or examined in his pan-african essays or *Crisis* editorials. Historically, DuBois was right, yet in the July, 1929 issue of *Opportunity*, Gwendolyn Bennett better captured McKay's literary perspectives. Not only had she lived in France during those years, but she had been the novelist's close friend in Paris and she could knowledgeably stress his impressionistic technique, the authenticity of his depiction of Marseilles, the realism of scenes in which, «with unsullied curiosity (he) looks about him for the little earmarks that make Negroes outstanding in a world where all men are abandoned» [2].

It is, however, in light of the genesis of *Banjo*, recorded in his unpublished correspondence with his Paris agent and friend William Aspenwell Bradley, that we can best retrace McKay's literary choices due, in part, to his ideological preoccupations and how they became reflected in the structure of the novel as well as in the views propounded by the characters. Such examination not only helps to account for problems of aesthetics posed in general terms, it may also help in reconsidering the evolution of McKay's thinking at the end of the 1920s and show him to be more distant from the major concerns of the Harlem Renaissance group, more original in his outlook, and definitely more cosmopolitan and internationally-minded, than has been hitherto admitted.

*
* *

I spent the better part of 1926 here in Marseille, existing in any way I could, doing a day's work on the docks or sometimes touching a small cheque for a poem. I lived most of the time in the Quartier Réservé with Negroes from America, British, French and Portuguese Africa, the West Indies. *It was then that I got the idea of doing a novel around them with the Vieux Port as a background* [3].

This statement of McKay to his publisher stresses two important points in the genesis of *Banjo* : first, the date of its inception ; second, the fact that Marseilles was meant to remain a backdrop, the group of black beach boys and dockers being the collective hero of the story. In April 1927, the novelist took a room at the Hotel Nautique, Quai des Belges, with the intention of becoming steeped in the life of the Harbor he wanted to recreate and of sharing the adventures of these picturesque characters [4]. When he returned, a year later, the group had disbanded : two of them had died in the hospital ; a couple of Afro-americans had been repatriated ; the banjo players were touring with a band ; and those remaining longed to leave Marseilles. But McKay had seen and shared their life ; once he set to writing, it took him only eighteen months to complete a 370-page manuscript.

Friendship and solidarity, fights with the police, happy carousing, love intrigues, quarrels with the racist shopkeepers and greedy prostitutes, illegal ways of keeping alive or of sailing one day for another fabulous harbor — such were the incidents in the existence of McKay's new heroes, which many a critic judged too close to the happy-go-lucky Jakes and Felices of *Home to Harlem*. As a result McKay was reproached for trying to duplicate the commercial success he had achieved with his novel of low life in the Black Metropolis, which somewhat capitalized on the stereotype of the ingenious, likeable but rather indolent, unreliable, and exceedingly lustful Negro which had made the notoriety of Van Vechten's *Nigger Heaven* [5]. Such charges were completely unfounded. For one thing, *Banjo* was begun months before *Home to Harlem* was published. Moreover, McKay started it out of sheer enthusiasm for his material, whereas he had expanded a short story, «Home to Harlem», into the novel of the same title upon the advice of his agent for commercial purposes.

Although he had early been recognized as a poet and was hailed as the author of *Harlem Shadows*, McKay had encountered much difficulty in getting his fiction in print. He had already burnt a first novel, «Color Scheme», for which he could not find a publisher in

1925 and, that same year, in Marseilles, he had given up an autobiograpical novel which was nearly completed. In spite of the advice of his socialist friend Max Eastman who considered verse more «aristocratic», McKay wanted to turn to prose because he saw it as the means for reaching less sophisticated readers. He had early been confronted with the wants and limitations of his potential audience : in December, 1927, he confessed that, when he wrote his first short stories, he was «trying to reach the Negro magazines with propaganda pieces while also pot-boiling for the New York magazines with cabaret and speakeasy stories» and he knew he could not get those stories into print without «the sop of sentimentality to offset the bawdiness» [6].

Accordingly, in 1927, he contemplated rewriting these stories in a more genuine vein and regretted his attempt to appeal to a wide American audience. There is no doubt that his concern had grown with depicting the kind of social reality he thought most significant in the way he saw it, and the way he saw social and racial issues had itself developed with his cosmopolitan experience.

This in no way means that McKay considered himself as an iconoclast or a challenger of established tastes and literary taboos. His keen sense of what his audience could willingly allow him to represent, of the exact point to which he might go in the depiction of racial relations, is surprising. While writing *Banjo* he kept the prejudices of his white audience in mind, and this reaction to their ideological perspectives certainly influenced his presentation of the characters and their relationships.

He did not want to spoil his chances of being heard by «insisting on situations that might be left out or inferred without any material harm to the book,» like «the indiscriminate throwing together of white and black characters» [7]. Therefore, as far as the love story was concerned, he refrained from making it a «real triangle thing», as Bradley had suggested ; he refused to stress the sexual relations of Banjo with his white girl. In spite of the fad of the «New Negro», which allowed black writers to deviate somewhat from accepted norms of taste, he knew how subtly racism worked in Puritan America and he was persuaded that «much of the success of *Home to Harlem* and what saved it from censorship in spite of the undressed passages is Jake's genuine feeling for the little brown of his race» [8]. Accordingly, he left the sexual relations between the beach-boys and the girls of the Ditch implicit throughout *Banjo* because the literate American public did not want to see «too much of the naked reality». The choice, and structural importance of Latnah, a North African woman, as the female protagonist partly resulted from that : being only half-white, she came in as a handy counterpoint without offending established conventions. On the other hand, a triangle love story between Whites and Blacks would have had to be highly intellectualized in order to win the sympathy of the European-American audience and this in turn might destroy verisimilitude since McKay was primarily interested in depicting a set of characters whose major appeal was, precisely, their healthy lower-class Black reactions to life and their environment.

In McKay's eyes, the originality and interest of the beach-boys came from their lack of sentimentality and from their amorality. He could not and would not, therefore, make much of a love rivalry with a type like Banjo, whom he sometimes characterizes as «heterosexual», meaning somewhat promiscuous and polygamous. And the two women are obviously «unmoral» in the tough unsentimental atmosphere of the Ditch. The sexual and emotional (one might even say «pagan-like») freedom of his protagonists prevented McKay from writing a conventional love-story because he considered their relationship more real than the standard, conventional sentimentality of the bourgeoisie. And he saw his protagonists as morally superior, too : in Latnah, for instance, he praised a lack of jealousy, due to her North African upbringing, which enabled her to accept male polygamy. Banjo is good-natured, sensual, drawn to people and the Ditch, although vacillating from scene to scene. Of course, no single beach-boy is a hero, but collectively they function as such, representing a definite set of values which can be defined for the most part as non-occidental.

Returning to the matter of McKay's awareness of his audiences, we should also note his fear of duplicating *Home to Harlem*, which dictated his choice of an outline. Anxious not to repeat the Jake and Felice story, he preferred to begin rather grimly and end happily by sending Banjo to the United States, instead of having Banjo lose everything and fall in with Latnah before putting him through a series of adventures in Marseilles. This would have made a closely-knit story, he thought, but it would have compelled him to rush Banjo to his death. The outline he retained forced him to keep all his characters concentrated in one place and make them act and talk within the limits of the Vieux Port, whereas Jake had been allowed the entire range of experiences and sights of the

Harlem scene in McKay's previous novel.

Both this structural choice and the depiction of an unso-phisticated relationship between, on the whole, unsophisticated characters, brought about a major difficulty which Eugene Saxton, McKay's editor at Harper's, was quick to point out. In a long letter of critical remarks sent on May 18, 1928, he deplored the absence of a plot as a well-defined story element : the story did not seem to move forward and he feared the reader would lose interest because of the episodic character of the narrative. He accordingly advised McKay to start with Chapter Six, introducing Ray, the intellectual in the group and the only well-rounded character.

McKay's reaction shows not only his conception of the novel as a genre but also what constituted in his eyes the real attraction of people like Banjo. He was aware that this was not a novel in the conventional form, but he felt the thread of the story ran through the episodes and united them :

> Banjo coming to Marseille, finding Latnah after losing the other girl ; his neglect of Latnah ; her yearning for him, her jealousy when she learns that he has spent so much money, and continues to spend, whenever he has some, on the white girl ; the fight between the two women followed by the breaking-up of the beach-boys' group ; Banjo being ill in the hospital, getting better and obtaining by ruse a sum of money to leave Marseille. It is a plot alright, but not a complicated one that thickens as the story progresses, but a slight one carried along by the episodes. (*Ibid*).

McKay added, and this may have prompted Harper's to use «A novel without a plot» as a subtitle :

> After all my book can be called anything else beside a novel : Marseille scenes or episodes of a novel without a plot. My feeling is that the episodes are all so real that reading one will carry the reader through them all to the end. (*Ibid*).

Thus he justified the lack of classical unity in his plot in terms of the intrinsic interest in the incidents or vignettes, in suspense and also in terms of recreating an atmosphere. He concentrated his creative power not on the characters, but on the various scenes in order to make them «vital and absorbing enough to carry the characters and his readers forward with sheer interest». (*Ibid*.) This technique is close to that of popular fiction in the style of Alexandre Dumas. It is also, and this may be more important, very much in line with Hemingway's attempts at recreating the flavor and the mood of a scene. McKay always strived after this atmospheric quality. In fact, it is the atmosphere of the Vieux Port during a brief, hectic summer which holds the group together ;

they cannot be visualized outside of this setting nor as single individuals :

> The characters are sometimes lost in the vivid, crowded scenes. The low life of the port going around in the same vicious circle of cruelty and pleasure. This is the impression I want to convey, and if haven't, then the book is a failure. (*Ibid.*)

From such perspective, the tempo of the narrative becomes secondary and it may even be better if the story moves forward rather slowly and in blocks.

The writing of *Banjo* was made difficult by what we may call McKay's ideological choice — depicting a lower-class section of society in a favorable light — and by the technical problems created because of his viewing the novel in terms that conflicted with established aesthetics. Since McKay could not restrict himself to a purely behavioral approach, the interpretation of his characters' reactions along ideological lines also posed a number of practical problems : while partaking freely of the beach-boys' sensual existence, could the author analyze it and make a judgment about it ? The major question was that of achieving a balance between the realistic rendering of sensation and the intellectual deciphering of motivation, since McKay allowed what he called the subjective element (meaning «interpretative» or «analytical») to mingle from the outset with the humorous. In the novel, he often intrudes upon the scene, not in the persona of the author who comments upon the story he is telling, but as a somewhat undefined narrator, who, in the very first page, feels it necessary to add, when describing Banjo's slippers, that they are «a kind much used by the poor in Provence» (p.5) and who, a few pages later, summarizes Malty's life in the tone and words of a historian. However, the chief commentator is Ray, one of the best-defined characters in the novel. Although McKay refused Saxton's suggestion to start with Ray in Chapter Six Because this would make Banjo secondary, he gave him an extremely important part, both as the representative of the «intellectual perspective» and as a commentator and spokesman.

Already in *Home to Harlem*, McKay had apparently been unable to resist the intrusion of this character, named after a railway pal whom he had at first introduced only to get his railway material straight. So that Ray's «highbrow ideas» would not retard the flow of the story, he had used him episodically, sending him abruptly off the scene when he had served his purpose. He gave Ray a secondary part in *Home to Harlem* largely because he had already thought of saving him for another novel. In fact, he had already created a protagonist who was a reflection of himself in his two earlier, unsuccessful attempts at long fiction and he had been faced with the problem of such a persona occupying too much of the front stage. With *Banjo*, things were not very different, and McKay wrote Bradley on May 23, 1927 : «The character of Ray also gives me a chance to let me go a little». Certainly, the contrast between Ray and Banjo was efficient for structural reasons, because it allowed a balancing of outlooks, not merely because it was based upon factual experience. At the same time, the internalization of character which allowed personal views, could, if properly achieved and accurately limited, leave the novel a nearly picaresque narration of striking episodes. However, McKay apparently could not restrain his lyrical double and Ray's role became prevalent, at times detracting from the action. «May be I was more interested in his ideas than in his life», McKay acknowledged, afraid he might get away from the story and indulge in «philosophizing or propaganda» [9]. He saw Ray as a strong, sophisticated character that might make the story too interpretative, thus spoiling the humor of the book and depriving the scenes of gusto. But, by holding Ray back he thought he could «give just enough of the modern touch of sophistication to the writing and achieve a kind of subjective-objective fusion — a mosaic that puzzles and yet intrigues and holds the reader» [10].

This was no mere technicality. McKay wanted to balance Ray's «intellectual» point of view and Banjo's sensual and natural stance in order to confront two philosophies of existence which might prove more complementary than opposed. To hold the reader, it was sufficient to plan the order of scenes carefully enough to preserve suspense in the parade they formed. Yet McKay chose to retain a mosaic of outlooks mostly for ideological reasons, because in dealing with in-group or inter-group black and white relationships his aim was largely didactic and critical.

At the time, McKay had lived in Europe for a number of years and he was no longer taken in by the claim, often made and upheld by Afro-Americans to shame their white countrymen, that Europeans, especially the French, were unprejudiced. He was not only aware of the «divide and rule» tactics of colonial oppression, he also knew where each person of color — from the Antilles,

Senegal, Jamaica, the Congo or America, or each North African national stood in the scale of white contempt or tolerance. What is more, he had gauged how a Martiniquan served the system by thinking himself superior to a Senegalese, or how secure in his own culture an African was when compared to an Afro-American. His major desire was to stress these nuances of feeling and differences in attitudes among his colored protagonists, nuances which the white reader was unlikely to notice (blinded as he was by racism to differences within what seemed to him the same group), nuances which the black bourgeoisie in the United States affected not to consider.

Writing about a subsequent story, «Romance in Marseilles», which he never completed McKay once declared :

> After all, we read about Americans and Europeans, Russians, Mongolians and Indians for the human interest but we also look for the little things that mark each out as a different division of the human species. To me the most interesting thing is that people are fundamentally human under the apparent differences. That will not prevent individuals from thinking and trying to act along tribal, national and racial lines. The fact is that the majority of the people do so quite unconsciously and the non-conformists are very few [11].

This could easily apply to the conception of *Banjo* and, although in McKay's humanism the most important point is that people are fundamentally human, he is strongly interested in specifics and differences, aesthetically if not ideologically. True, he underplays the exotic element, but this is because the exotic rests upon differences which are too gross, because it capitalizes upon obvious and already stereotyped specificities. McKay preferred to explore more subtle distinctions and to examine modes and roots of racial differences and conflicts in terms of individual, not political or group, reactions ; and the lines along which he pursued his inquiry were free from the implications of bourgeois aesthetics. Thus, in Latnah, for instance he could find several levels of consciousness which he used in shaping the character :

> She is oriental and sympathizes with a man being polygamous. What stirs her and finally makes her hate Banjo is when she discovers that he prefers chair blanche to chair noire. I think this is a much more important point to bring out in the book, don't you ? I mean the kind of instinctive, animal feeling that is so different from the sentimental home and social and pseudoracial conflicts that motivate color problem stories [12].

American reviewers have sometimes argued that McKay had been influenced, not only by the success of *Home to Harlem* as a «bawdy story» but also by the supposedly French outlook upon sex, to the point of replacing what they saw as «true love» relationships by more sexual ones. As already noted, McKay soft-pedalled sex scenes and did not mistake feeling for sentimentality. Besides, his opinion of his characters' free amorality provided an adequate answer to such criticism. But one should note in addition that he took sex seriously enough to berate the French precisely for not doing so. From Spain, he wrote Bradley on July 5, 1929, after a trip to Morocco :

> The sex life in Spain and Morocco has a close resemblance although, because of the differences in religion and the right of divorce, the Arabs are freer. I can't imagine any Frenchman understanding the Spaniards and their attitude towards sex. The French *pretend* to take sex lightly and that pretension has become part of the national consciousness. The Spaniards don't pretend ; They know that sex is a serious affair... I'm sorry I hadn't been able to go to Spain to write *Banjo*. It might have been a better book.

McKay regretted he had not insisted enough upon the earnestness of sexual motivation among the beach-boys as opposed to the shallow sentimentality of the European and American middle-class tradition, for he was convinced of the moral superiority of the beach-boys over the inhabitants of Marseilles : it stemmed from their closeness to nature and instinct, from the spontaneous humanity and idealism they retained :

> The Ditch people are not real heroes because every drop of idealism has been drained out of them by the hard, cruel existence that is theirs... The black boys must be better because they are romantics ; they are playing, while the Ditch is grabbing for a living [13].

McKay would probably never have made this comment, had he not been incensed at the insensitive and chauvinistic review published by André Levinson in the September 1929 issue of *Les Nouvelles Littéraires*. Even before the French translation of *Banjo* appeared, Levinson labeled it as anti-French and anti-white — a reproach that even Dixie newspapers themselves had never made while deploring that McKay had made his Negro characters better than the Whites.

McKay claimed he had made his black heroes better than the Whites in Marseilles because indeed they were, being careless and romantic, «on a holiday, while the white inhabitants were just rats waiting to do them out of whatever they had» [14]. This meant no bias on his part ; he was conscious of the sometimes irresponsible attitude of the Blacks, of their ignorance of economic values and he

had tried to provide a full picture of them, «using Ray as an intelligent, philosophical background» (*Ibid.*) On one hand, such reviewers as Levinson thought he was deliberately stressing the finer values
of the Blacks because they failed to see that it was that environment
and business of the Ditch that made its dwellers what they
were ; McKay insisted he was not taking sides along racial lines
but explaining social differences more in the perspective of
marxism. Moreover, he stated that he had provided enough varied
and dissimilar responses to that situation to achieve a balanced
view of it. A large number of white and black characters reacted
individually, irrespective of systems of thinking, and they did not
react consistently : for example, the white taxi-driver who lived off
girls of all colors did not charge Ray for taking Banjo to the
hospital because he was his friend ; conversely, when one Negro
girl robbed race-conscious Taloufa to supply the needs of her white
pimp, this was not a racial reaction, ironical as it might seem. The
black boys all reacted individually to France :

> Goosey loves France and wants to stay. Banjo is not in the least disturbed
> about loving or hating any country. The Senegalese opts for America. Ray is
> cynical about it all. He is intelligent enough to know that all human beings
> suffer and enjoy life in varying degrees in every country under the sun, although
> he is not unaware that the colored man has especial handicaps to meet with
> under the world-wide domination of occidental civilization. (*Ibid.*)

The titles of chapters like «White Terror», to which Levinson
objected, had largely been used with a fine sense of humor. Yet,
McKay also contended that the terror was all too real to the
beach-boys, up against the exploitation of the Ditch, the discrimination of officers who resented their presence in cafés, the fists
of the police.

Interestingly, he confessed to an anti-French feeling in *Banjo*.
Despite his love of French literature, especially the wry satire of
Voltaire or Anatole France, he did not like the French as «social
animals» because of their blatant chauvinism. He noted that their
outlook on life seemed «the narrowest of any people. They don't
know the outside world and they don't care for it because it is not
French» [15]. This was his reaction to an ideological provincialism
which had been officially built up into a theory of cultural
imperialism in the French colonies and which amounted to
intellectual arrogance vis à vis the rest of the world.

Finally, McKay's deep response to Levinson's criticism also
indicated his position in relationship to the Harlem Renaissance

and the ideology of race solidarity implied by the new brand of black nationalism. He wrote Bradley on October 2nd, 1929 :

I have never been in on the Aframerican fad that he [Levinson] mentions. I was never pushed and whenever I was quoted (the Aframerican critics have never liked my independent spirit neither in poetry nor in prose), it was because I was there and they couldn't get around me.

And he added on November lst. :

I feel very whistlerish about smart European scribblers and I am proud that my grievance is intellectual. My colored brothers don't understand it. They are very angry in America that I should stress in a book an unfavorable attitude toward the colored brother because, they say, the Crackers will use it to parrot the old phrase : «America, mainly the South, understands the Negro better». But I'm interested in facts for the truth and not for one-sided propaganda.

In fact, McKay was just as critical of the Afro-american press which believed it did someone a favor by simply mentioning him, as he was of the self-complacent attitude of the French literary reviews. He wanted to enjoy what he believed he had won after many years of struggling on his own — the right to express himself without attempting to please either Americans or Europeans. Here we see how individual freedom for the writer is asserted against the theory that race-conscious writers must unite and present a positive image of the black race and their friends. Of course, McKay was no utopist and he knew he had to pay «the penalty of being a Negro and therefore even aesthetically prejudiced against the whites» (Ibid.) He acknowledged a strong distaste for the general «white» attitude towards life (meaning materialism, a lack of humane values, racism, economic and cultural oppression), a distaste he proudly shared with many a white intellectual ; he claimed at the same time :

I am not soft-headed about the non-whites, for haven't they also all the faults of humanity in general with some of its virtues ? My attitude is one of perpetual wonderment that the minority peoples can be as human (in the finer sense) as they are tumbling over one another like a gang of crabs in a barrel and struggling against the majority-imposed idea that they are inferior [16].

*
* *

McKay's vision of the Western world and of the black man's situation within it thus appears to have been more perceptive and more nuanced than is commonly thought. Although a few knew him mostly through the exotic vignettes of *Home to Harlem*, for decades he remained in the eyes of many the proud author of «If We Must Die», the black poet who speaks out for the oppressed. These images were but two aspects of the black nationalistic trends which informed the Harlem Renaissance. Others remembered him as the erstwhile member of the *Masses* editorial board, the close friend of Max Eastman, the admirer of Soviet Russia, who strangely turned into a Catholic in search of the absolute towards the end of his life. In the late twenties, when he was writing *Banjo*, Claude McKay put into his novel some of his new convictions as well as many of his doubts : his belief that the sensual enjoyment of life must temper the intellectual approach to it, the fear that no working social system could reconcile basic human drives with the aims of exploitative materialism. The novel thus illuminates the stage in his career when he was attempting to steer clear of the dogmas of the New Negro movement as well as of the near-Marxist political views he had espoused earlier, not in order to wholly reject them but to bend and shape these ideological categories to account more accurately for his experience, instead of dividing up reality into neat conceptual compartments.

Within the cultural and racial context of the times, the novel also illuminates some of the aesthetic choices a novelist like McKay had to make in order to retain his personal integrety vis à vis the prevalent stereotypes and how he felt it necessary to make allowance for the limitations and prejudices of his potential audience. This posed in turn a number of literary problems which McKay's conceptions of the plot and of the hero, different as they were from the European middle-class standards of fiction, did not really enable him to solve in terms acceptable to the critics. McKay's failure to achieve aesthetic harmony in recognized terms in a novel which, ideologically, was a full decade ahead of its contemporaries, probably accounts for the neglect which *Banjo* suffered in the United States until the Black Power movement, even though the founders of Negritude never questioned the importance of the novel. The growing American awareness of its merits since its 1968 paperback publication is a sign that it is at last achieving fuller recognition.

NOTES

1. **The Crisis**, July 1929, p. 234.

2. **Opportunity**, July 1929, p. 254.

3. Letter to a publisher, June 4, 1927. Yale University Library. Emphasis mine. McKay consistently spelt Marseille in the French way.

4. They can still be seen, surrounding a guitar player, in front of a Vieux Port café in one of the photographs preserved in the McKay papers at the Yale University Library.

5. The reaction of such a sophisticated novelist as Francis Scott Fitzgerald to **Home to Harlem** is significant ; he saw in it «one of the two most worthy American Negro novels of the Spring», liking it «with special emphasis on the current key of Harlem motif of dissipation or Pullman scenes» (Paris letter to McKay, May 25, 1928. Yale University library). Note the restrictive use of «Negro» and the emphasis on exoticism.

6. Letter to Bradley, Dec. 19, 1927.

7. Letter to Bradley, October 24, 1927.

8. **Ibid.**, June 3, 1928.

9. **Ibid.**, June 4, 1927.

10. **Ibid.**, June 3, 1928.

11. **Ibid.**, December (?), 1929.

12. **Ibid.**, October 2, 1929.

13. **Ibid.**, November 1, 1929.

14. **Ibid.**, October 2, 1929.

15. **Ibid.**, November 1. 1929.

16. **Ibid.**, November 1, 1929.

This article is part of a study of the relationships between Afro-American writers and the French-speaking world in the twentieth century. The research was made possible in part by the American Philosophical Society and the American Council of Learned Societies. Special thanks are due to the Yale University Library and to Mrs. Jenny Bradley.

Liliane BLARY

Claude Mc Kay and

Black nationalist ideologies

(1934-1948)

I have never aligned myself with any political party because I believe that the approach of the writer and artist to social problems is radically different from the approach of the politician [1].

This quotation reflects McKay's conviction that allegiance to any political party was bound to conflict with the necessity for the writer to retain a spirit of free intellectual enquiry and an unfettered right to dissent. This political declaration of independence was only one facet of his opposition to single-minded, indiscriminate identification with a cause or a group, a hostility which also accounted for his refusal to make alignments solely on a racial basis. During and just after the first World War, McKay had been introduced to American readers by the publication of his poems and essays in white radical left-wing magazines : *Seven Arts*, Frank Harris's *Pearson's Magazine*, and Max Eastman's *The Liberator*. His friendship with this editor was one of the very few that stood the test of time, weathering McKay's temperamental personality. At the time of his death in 1948, he had been sharing the life of a Chicago Catholic community headed by the social-minded Bishop Sheil.

Constant association with the larger world did not conflict with race loyalty : recurringly and proudly, McKay asserted his blackness and expressed his feeling of solidarity with the more deprived elements of his ethnic community. Hailed as a forerunner of the Harlem Renaissance after the publicaton of his book of poems *Harlem Shadows* in spring 1922, he was branded a racialist and a separatist by Negro intellectuals in the late 1930's.

The 1920's had witnessed the blossoming of a wide variety of black nationalist ideologies in all fields, and some form of cultural nationalism had been common to most of them. It had pervaded McKay's poems, filtered into his essays where he celebrated «his warm wonderful race», racial attributes such as «humor, a gift for ripe laughter, a particular rhythm of life» which spelled its superiority to «many a white wretch, baffled and lost in his civilized jungles» [2]. Four-fifths of these essays — written between 1919 and 1923 — had been contributions to the organ of the English Socialist left-wing : Sylvia Pankhurst's *The Workers' Dreadnought*, and, in the United States, to the resolutely Socialist Negro *Messenger* or *The Liberator*, «that spectacular organ of socialism, anarchism, paganism and rebellion» [3]. His determination to have this revolutionary magazine «handle the Negro problem in the class struggle in proportion to the Negro population and its position in the labor world» [4], had given rise to a heated controversy with Max Eastman who contended that «overloading» the periodical with racial material might destroy an instrument which circulated almost exclusively among whites. Yet, despite this resolution to stress the specificity of the Negroes' plight, McKay, in agreement with the basic policies of those magazines, held that the black man's struggle was part of a revolutionary, much larger fight, whose scope far exceeded the boundaries of any particular country, and which aimed at the overthrow of capitalism and imperialism. The negro problem could only be solved through an alliance between the toilers of both races :

> the yearning of the American Negro (...) can only find expression and realization in the class struggle. It has no sense of its unity as a class — as a part rather of the American working-class and so it is powerless [5].

Landing on Ellis Island in January 1934 after eleven years of wandering in Russia, Western Europe and North Africa, McKay was plunged into a country where the havoc wrought by the Depression had caused a shift away from strictly literary and cultural concerns ; the main ideological debate now centered on seemingly more pressing economical issues. It reached a climatic point that very year when James Weldon Johnson published his pamphlet *Negro Americans, What Now* ? [6] in which he pressed for unstinted support of the interracial National Association for the Advancement of Coloured People, and for a continued drive towards making the Negro race an integral part of the nation as quickly as possible, while another of the most influent Negro leaders, W.E. Burghardt Du Bois, resigned from his position within the same organization. Du Bois held that Negroes, faced with the white Americans' determination not to treat them as men, should organize their economic and social power, even though the process compelled them «to increase by voluntary action their separation from their fellow-men» [7].

The clash of such antinomic positions could but intensify the passionate character of the discussions in the black community, and soon McKay got involved into the current controversies. Indeed, from then on, his more distinguished contributions were those of a polemicist rather than of a creative writer. If we except his autobiography *A Long Way From Home* (1937) [8] and a dozen religious sonnets which appeared in Catholic periodicals after 1944, he brought himself to public attention through some 50 essays and columns written between 1935 and 1943. He revised a few of them which he included in a book of eleven chapters, *Harlem : Negro Metropolis*, published in the autumn of 1940. [9] In a score of articles and some longer essays [10], McKay focussed on the growing debate between the interracialists and the separatists.He fully agreed with neither side, and his discussions of various black nationalist movements [11] reveal an ambivalence which Harold Cruse pinpointed when he wrote that McKay remained «intellectually stranded at some undefinable point on the interracial spectrum between integration and group identity» [12].

McKay argued that race was a basic reality, and that latent primitive antagonisms, illogical prejudices, pitted one group of people against the other. In keeping with a new accent on the colour line, he contended that the blacks had sound reasons to assert themselves as a distinct group and that they should cultivate their talents intensively in the cultural, economical, and political fields in order to ward off extinction. Simultaneously, however, he urged cooperation with other American groups whose problems he tended to identify with those of the Negro community. He pressed the Negro writer to explore Negro life, to be his own ultimate judge, but also to compete with other American artists on a national scale. McKay himself could not resist being a spokesman for blacks, while he struggled to have a universal appeal, and accepted the help and advice of white literary agents and friends. He professed his faith in a new democratic order based on the dignity of Labour, exposed the racial roots of capitalism and imperialism ; but he spared no effort to keep his insights from being interpreted as Communist, and maintained that the Negro group should try to work out its salvation within the framework of the competitive system.

Underlying these puzzling contradictions there was the Afro-American's double-consciousness to which McKay never reconciled himself completely. Even though McKay did not allow the nationalistic overtones of his views to challenge his commitment to America during that period, he set himself up as the advocate of cultural pluralism which, he insisted, was the one, truly American ideology.

*
* *

In the 1920's, McKay had taken the position that the American Negro should acquire class-consciousness. He now thought that the colour line determined the nature of one's allegiance more than the class line did. Race had brought about the «aggregation» of Negroes faced with the «intricate problem of minority adjustment and survival under highly centralized systems» [13]. McKay wanted blacks to strive for their promotion not as individuals but as a race-group, and argued that the one serious ground on which their plea for recognition could rest was that of a common culture :

> Wherever I traveled I observed that the people who were getting anywhere were those who could realize the strength of their cultural groups ; their political demands were determined by the force of their cultural grouping : it was the same underlying principle in Communist Russia as in Fascist Spain and Democratic France and England and in Protected Africa. [14]

Long-standing disparagement had, however, sadly battered the Negro's self-image to the point where the black community lacked a group soul and was running away from itself, having lost any awareness of «the beauty and wonder and glory, the warmth and color, rhythm and passion inherent» in its race [15]. It was incumbent upon the Negro artist, gifted with a finer and more discriminating sensibility, to reveal this heritage, but he depended on the members of his ethnic group to fulfill his mission satisfactorily. So far, owing to white cultural imperialism and its attendant patronage and pernicious double standards, the Negro artist had deferred to white criteria. Estranged from the vital sources of folk experience, he had not been able to write truthfully about his own people. To gain his emancipation, he needed encouragement from his peers and intensive commerce with the members of his racial group who, alone, could «generate (the energy) which produces real creative expression» [16]. McKay attempted to forge those instruments of inspirational contact between Negro writers, considering that an all-Negro magazine or organization would be a social force that would foster self-reliance and group unity.

Hardly had he taken time to familiarize himself again with the Harlem scene when he tried to launch a Negro magazine of national scope in the summer of 1934. This magazine would have effected a racial grouping beyond differences of class and creed, and could have been a channel of expression for Negro authors and artists. The name selected for a title, *Bambara*, after a Sudanese tribe «noted for its well-planned community life and art work» [17], reflected the underlying motivations : ethnocentricity and a belief in the primacy of artistic pursuits and in their wider social significance. Unfortunately, this magazine never materialized : the appalling precariousness of McKay's financial situation compelled him to leave the town for a relief camp in upstate New York where he spent several months.

Three years later, he tried to create a purely cultural organization of Negro writers and journalists. At some time or other during the nine-month span of sustained efforts on McKay's part, Countee Cullen, Jessie Fauset, Bruce Nugent, the Haitian poet Maurice Casseus, on the creative side, and journalists such as Henry L. Moon, Theodore Poston, Earl Brown — editor of the *Amsterdam News* — were connected with the venture. He also received the backing of influential personalities : the bibliophile Arthur Schomburg, and James W.Johnson, whose premature death in June 1918 destroyed any remaining hope. McKay's dogged determination to keep the short-lived Negro Writers'Guild — rechristened the League of Negro Writers in early 1938 — an exclusively Negro one, largely accounts for his failure. As he himself put it :

Anathema to (the Negro intellectuals) was any idea of an exclusively Negro organization. It was not merely segregationist : a new label was made «isolationist» [18]

It irked him that the bugaboo of segregation should play the Negro intelligentsia into the hands of the Communists, who had used the candidacies of white liberals to disrupt the guilds which the Harlem artists or the Negro writers employed on the New York Federal Writers' Project had previously set up.

At a time when economic issues were uppermost in people's minds, McKay lay stress on the importance of culture which could work as a potent unifying force by moving the Negroes to a higher pitch of racial awareness and pride. He contended that cultural warfare was an essential part of their overall struggle. True to his conception of himself as an artist first, he believed that his special function was a cultural one, and this was the field in which he tried to exercise leadership.

The conditions of life in Harlem, as well as his own experience and his unrelievedly bleak financial situation, however, served as sharp reminders of the close connection between culture and economics. Any viable and genuine group cultural life depended on the achievement of a measure of economic self-sufficiency, and the Harlem Renaissance of the Twenties had offered ample illustration of this dependency. McKay always disclaimed any attempts to associate him too closely with the literati of the Harlem Renaissance school, on the grounds that such classification not only shortened the span of his literary career unduly, but overlooked the definite reservations he entertained about several aspects of the «New Negro» era. His comments were seldom commendatory : the flowering of Negro talent which had taken place during that period had been ephemeral ; it had sent no roots into the soil of Negro life because the black community could not support its creative intellectuals. In view of the very limited economical possibilities of the Harlemian «Smart Set», and of its failure to play any significant role as sponsor or patron of Negro art, the building up of Harlem as an artistic center could be only an artificial contrivance «inspired and kept alive by the interest and presence of white bohemians» [19]. With its whole apparatus in the hands of whites, there could have been no possibility of its being of any real benefit to the Negro community as a distinctive ethnic entity.

Cultural nationalism and economic nationalism were therefore two interrelated forms of the aggressive group organization which McKay advocated, and he observed the manifestations indicative of a trend towards greater economic control of Harlem by the black minority with interest.

He was convinced that community enterprises run by Negroes themselves would not only alleviate the dreadful lot of the hard-pressed masses but pave the way for the advancement of the whole group as well. The strong feeling of kinship with the masses which had run through his essays of the earlier period had not abated. Nevertheless, though McKay still cast in his lot with that of the labouring classes, his sympathy no longer reached beyond those of his ethnic community :

Even in Harlem, the largest Negro city in the world, the symbol of the black and white handclasp is ideal ; the real thing in Negro experience is the strong white hand against the black. [20]

The same situation prevailed in the world of labour, and it was vain hope on the part of the Negro worker to expect any bounty from his white counterpart engaged in a grim enough fight of his own to secure a living.

As a result, McKay expressed definite misgivings regarding interracial organizations sponsored by the Negro intelligentsia. These lacked force and drive, criticisms which he levelled against the N.A.A.C.P. — equated with a Civil Liberties Union — and the National Urban League which remained essentially a «social service agency» [21] whose help extended to individual Negroes only.

He used a more bitter pen against the National Negro Congress whose creation in 1936 had been sponsored by more than half a thousand Negro organizations of various types. It was known that, during the organizing conference, the delegates had acknowledged that the rank-and-file of the Negro group would be reached only in terms of its own traditions and background ; they had accordingly endorsed a resolution which asked for the support and development of Negro business and of the Negro Church. But the Congress had come to that decision reluctantly, because Communists considered both black business and the black church as reactionary forces which would tend to cut off the Negro worker more completely from his natural allies : the working class. McKay assailed the National Negro Congress as a Communist front built up by the Marxists who — since their 1935 adoption of the united front policy — had devoted all their energies to gaining control over Negro organizations and manipulating them for ends alien to the real interests of the black community. [22]

Commenting on the Harlem scene which was his main focus, he insisted on the inadequacies of the Negro Trade Union Committee created after the Harlem riots of 1935. That Committee grouped thirteen black and twelve white trade-unionists, with the Socialist Frank Crosswaith as chairman. Its aims were to educate Negroes in trade-union consciousness and to bring these workers within the fold of the A.F.L.-C.I.O., while «shunning the Communist party drive to profit from minority exploitation» [23].

McKay claimed — and this was one of the two points over which he stood in disagreement with James Weldon Johnson — that

> So long as the white unions remain selfish and chauvinistic, coloured workers should organize in separate unions to fight for greater economic advantages, even if they have to pass through the scabbing phase to obtain them [24].

Hence, his appreciation of the crude efforts of such lesser popular leaders as Sufi Abdul Hamid, Arthur Reid and Ira Kemp who responded to the inarticulate Negro worker's craving for some kind of group organization. The charges of Negro journalists and trade-unionists that McKay was «utterly fascinated by the so-called racial appeal (of those) racketeers» [25], or that he uncritically exalted them, cannot be fully substantiated. As social analyst McKay did not condone their ignorance of the labour movement or their lack of organizational ability ; nor did he wink at the Sufi's dubious character. But McKay criticized the Negro intelligentsia and white liberals for their neglect of the common Negro prior to the «Black Ides» of March 1935, and he remarked that Hamid should be commended for taking practical steps towards the economic organization of the depressed masses of Negro workers in Harlem, at a time when very little was being undertaken to that effect.

In «Harlem Runs Wild» and «Labor Steps Out In Harlem», carried by the *Nation* in April 1935 and October 1937, and in «Sufi Abdul Hamid and Organized Labor» which concludes *Harlem : Negro Metropolis*, McKay retraces the ups and downs of the «Don't Buy Where You Can't Work» campaign with which the names of Hamid, Reid and Kemp remain associated. He hailed that movement, which aimed at getting more employment for Negroes within the Harlem area, as a step towards greater self-development and community autonomy. The Sufi's action had begun in 1933, when he had resorted to aggressive picketing of the stores of Harlem's main shopping thoroughfare — 125th Street — whose owners, Jews for the most part, refused to employ Negro clerks. The Sufi, a powerfully built black man who paraded as an Egyptian in gorgeous oriental arrays, had demanded the recognition as labor agencies of the organizations through which he had been waging his fight : the Negro Industrial and Clerical Association, founded in 1933, and, later, the Afro-American Federation of Labor, which lasted only a few months in 1934 and early 1935. Two other street agitators, Arthur Reid and Ira Kemp, leaders for a while of the Picketing Committee of the more «respectable» Citizens League, organized the Harlem Labor Union in the latter part of 1935, a union which set itself up on rival terms with the interracial Trade Union Committee. Repeatedly, the action of the three men was checked by Court decisions enjoining them from boycotting and picketing because their organizations were not labour agencies... McKay argued that these injunctions were tantamount to denying the Negroes the right to organize as a racial group, and maintained that those three leaders were to be given their share of credit for the 1937 Supreme Court ruling which reversed that well-established trend, when its judges stated that the picketing of firms which refused to employ Negroes was a legal technique of securing relief.

The determination of those picturesque figures to take immediate action, the aggressive lead they gave to the confused, disorganized Harlemian masses whom they had stirred out of apathy, and whom they had set about to convince of the necessity for self-help, beckoned seductively to McKay who saw an affiliation between them and the Garvey movement.

The allusions to the Back-to-Africa movement scattered throughout McKay's fiction, and two fuller assessments of Garvey's action, testify to McKay's sustained interest in the Universal Negro Improvement Association. This association had known its heyday in the last two years of the 1910's and in the first half of the following decade, but it had planted the seeds of Negro nationalism so deep that the flood of critical appraisal had not subsided.

Harold Cruse's contention that : «like other Negro intellectuals of the period Claude McKay steered away from any association with (the Garvey movement)» [26] accurately sums up McKay's position in the early Twenties. Though he had been a contributing editor to Garvey's *Negro World* before sailing to England late in 1919, almost three years later he had written an article which had been a downright condemnation of Garvey's ignorance and intolerance of modern social ideas, of his «curiously bourgeois-obsolete and fantastically utopian political ideas» [27]. But the forty-page-long chapter in *Harlem : Negro Metropolis* points to an evolution towards a rather more positive view of Garvey's achievement.

In this matter, McKay apparently shared James W. Johnson's opinion, since he concluded his essay with a long quotation from Johnson's «penetrating estimate» of the Garvey movement in *Black Manhattan* (1930), which, according to a scholarly critic of Garvey «had helped to establish the dominant view of the (Universal Negro Improvement Association) for the next generation» [28] :

> Garvey failed : yet he might have succeeded with more than moderate success. He had energy and daring... He stirred the imagination of the Negro masses as no Negro ever had. He raised more money in a few years than any other Negro organization ever dreamed of. He had great power and great possibilities within his grasp. But his deficiencies as a leader outweighed his abilities... Garvey made several vital blunders, which, with any intelligent advice, he might have avoided... He made the mistake of ignoring or looking with disdain upon the technique of the American Negro in dealing with his problems of race... To this man came an opportunity such as comes to few men, and he clutched greedily at the glitter and let the substance slip from his fingers. [29]

Yet, James W. Johnson had laid even more emphasis on Garvey's shortcomings than this quotation might induce the reader to think. Accordingly, McKay's contention that, since the Depression, intellectual hostility had given way to the opinion that «Garvey's ideas were sounder than his methods» [30], was somewhat too sweeping an extrapolation from his personal feelings on the matter.

McKay's criticism of the majority of Negro leaders as members of a Talented Tenth that failed to identify its interests with those of the Negro masses was, indeed, akin to Garvey's castigation of the Negro intelligentsia as «selfish, self-appointed and not elected by the people» [31]. In a period when McKay sympathized with the Negro masses, he could but commend Garvey's espousal of their cause and feel impressed by his spectacular, unmatched popular appeal. He saw Garvey as a leader whose spirit had been fundamentally attuned to that of the common Negro, and even celebrated the indestructible link woven between the two in a sonnet which remained unpublished :

> And nothing that the professors do can sever
> You from the people to whom you belong forever [32].

Garvey's «excessive» group and racial pride, closely related to his fierce cultural nationalism, had «germinated the idea of responsible leadership» [33] in the Negro masses ; it had been a contributing factor to the flowering of Harlem's creative life. The President of the Universal Negro Improvement Association's high-flown addresses to the blacks, in which he had told then that theirs was a mighty race, and his launching of Negro-operated businesses had been attempts to lead the race a few steps along the road to autonomy. Besides, at the root of his action there had stood a question which every Aframerican had to face some day :

«Can Africa be of any practical interest (to me) ?» [34]

Though McKay considered that Garvey's positive legacy was significant enough not to be disregarded, he still dismissed Garvey's central scheme of Liberian colonization as a romantic mirage which had deflected the Negroes' minds from the acute social problems that confronted them in America. It was a project which rested on the assumption that the United States was a white man's country «in which the Negro had no place, no right, no chance, no future» [35]. And, however pessimistic McKay may have felt about the possibility of reaching satisfactory solution of the Negro question, he did not think of Africa as an alternative. For one thing, Americans of whatever hue were not wanted on the African continent where they would meet problems similar to those Europeans had to cope with ; then, as children of Western civilization, they were an integral part of the United States for better and for worse. McKay did occasionally hypothesize some special ties between the blacks of the two continents [36] ; he expressed more indignation over the Fascists in Ethiopia than in Spain [37]. But the remarks which might reveal an emotional commitment to Africa remained very few, as compared to his declarations to the effect that the Aframerican should contribute to the development of America, and that such contribution would be very different from anything that might come out of a purely African community.

*
* *

Rejecting any ideology which would result in the Negro's permanent severance from the rest of America, McKay reacted against being labelled a nationalist. In a retort to Adam Clayton Powell — then pastor of the Abyssinian Baptist church in New York City and elected Congressman in 1945 — who had charged that McKay's «nationalistic bent was bending the facts» reported in «Labor Steps Out in Harlem» [38], he contended that the real Negro nationalists were the Communists who had advocated the right of the Negroes to self-determination in the Black Belt. [39]

McKay's ethnocentric declarations, his insistence that ethnic identity should be the impulse behind group aggregation, his criticisms of white Socialists and Liberals as well as of the Negro intelligentsia, further alienated the greater part of the Negro leadership from him. Middle-class «educated» Negroes argued that he was advocating segregation, voluntary or enforćed, as essential to the economic, social and political promotion of the race in America, and opposed his rejection of interracial collaboration. His alleged separatism was construed as the confession of defeat of a sensitive Negro who had «ghettoized» himself out of disappointment with the slowness of reforms. His name was ·coupled with those of Booker T.Washington and W.E.B. Du Bois.

Well before the dawn of this century, Booker T. Washington had pressed the Negro to concentrate on economic self-sufficiency rather than on political equality. For over three decades, Du Bois had upheld. the opposite idea : that millions of men could not make effective progress if they were deprived of political rights [40] ; but he was now recommending a course of action similar to Washington's.

In several of his essays, McKay expressed his admiration for Washington's constructive, pragmatic mind, and his high esteem for Du Bois, «the eminent Negro leader». In essential agreement with the program of «this great teacher» [41], McKay, however, would not concede the point which Du Bois had made in his 1934 *Crisis* article when he had written :

> this voluntary association for great social and economic ends is segregation (...) It is the separation of human beings and separation despite the will to humanity (...) Such separation is evil ; (...) and yet it is today and in this world inevitable. [42]

On the contrary, McKay defended the idea that the word «segregationist» was an improper term to characterize work which had ushered in an era of cooperation with the elite of the United States in the education of its youth, as was the case both at Tuskegee where Booker T. Washington had founded an institute, and in Atlanta where Du Bois was chairman of the Department of Sociology. The Negro intellectuals' failure — or unwillingness — to make this distinction drove them to maintain that all schemes of racial organization implied segregation, and to imperil the very existence of the Negro group.

Unequivocally, McKay declared himself opposed to enforced segregation :

> No sane Negro believes in or desires legal segregation, in which his racial group will be confined by laws to ghettoes [43]

a system which could only breed the major social evils of congestion, criminality, disease and filth. But that unpleasant aura made the word «segregation» a very «unfortunate» one. It was too often used to refer to, and defeat, any effort of the Negro community to organize its assets. The outcome was a «passive Uncle-Tom-Do-Nothing policy of integration» [44], doomed to remain an empty slogan, because it did not face realistically the facts of virtual discrimination and of continuing white supremacy. To McKay's mind, it was no use agitating for civil rights for the time being, because political equality, even guaranteed by law, would remain a Pyrrhic victory as long as the black masses lacked the economic power to take advantage of such equality.

In May 1935, commenting on Du Bois's new policy and on James W. Johnson's *Negro Americans, What Now* ?, McKay already wondered whether both views could not be reconciled to promote Negro unity and to elaborate a working program. Four years later, he had become convinced that the Tuskegee school of thought and the Northern school were interdependent. The former rightly encouraged blacks to «launch out», to build their economy and culture, while the Northern leaders emphasized the legal and political aspects of civil rights. But the Negro group should lay an economic foundation first. Economic strength would buttress group pressure, and help force the good will and respect of the majority, on which any lasting abolition of the Negroes' unfair status ultimately depended. Only when the two races were on more equal bargaining terms, would meaningful cooperation have a chance to replace charitable patronage.

McKay refused to condone the annihilation of the Negro group which a policy of outright integration would spell. But he thought that isolation, the opposite alternative, was an anachronic concept and defeated man's wholesome instinct for happiness which led most Negroes to try and find some way of compromise and adjustment to white society. McKay advocated group aggregation which, he claimed, was a force universally at work :

It is one of the most natural phenomena of human life everywhere that people possessing special and similar traits will agglomerate in groups [45].

Race had been the catalyst of a distinctive Negro experience just as a common religion or nationality had cemented white minority groups. In these groups, Europeans, Jews, had cultivated their particular ways of life. Selecting the Jewish minority for special attention, McKay urged the Negroes to duplicate its achievement of breaking down «100 % barriers of American prejudice by building up institutions (...) which (were) a credit to the entire American nation» [46].

Thus, while accenting the reality of the colour line and the specificity of Negro experience, McKay stressed simultaneously that it was by no means unique but eminently American. In fact, the tribal phenomenon stood at the very core of the American nation which he defined as a «commonwealth», «preeminently a nation of diverse minorities» [47]. Therefore, the Negro's struggle could be waged within the framework of existing institutions. Indeed, his fight would be directed not so much against a government, which on the whole had deserved his trust and respect, but against the people whose active or even passive will was enough to nullify any legal guarantee. Furthermore,

> if Negroes as a group are ever going to break down what is loosely called segregation, they must first demonstrate to the other minorities that their community can also be like other communities [48].

In the Twenties, McKay had considered that the interests of the Negro were completely at variance with those of Western capitalist countries. He now granted that, in a nation whose other groups were apt to join against the black minority, it was the responsibility of the latter to prove its worth, to win the respect and consideration of its fellow-countrymen. The black minority should defend America first and lift itself up to American standards of living. If American standards were genuinely those of a pluralistic society, then, blacks could agitate for recognition of their rightful place in the nation without lynching the Negro soul. McKay must have been aware, however, that, in the process, the Negro would have to follow — at least to some extent — in the footsteps of an acquisitive society. He would become a cog in a competitive system, which McKay no longer wanted to subvert, if all minorities «that are capable» [49] could be given their chance. In keeping with this more conciliatory view, McKay's very militant type of cultural nationalism which had extolled the superiority of the black man over the de-vitalized inhabitants of the Western world, had gradually faded to be replaced by a milder form, which presented Afro-American culture as one among several subcultures which made up the American mosaic.

*

* *

As an Afro-American, McKay had been painfully confronted with two irreducible realities : his Negro-ness and the indelible imprint of American civilization. Recurringly, the two forces had antagonized each other. McKay believed that race-consciousness was bound to exist in a long-suppressed community, but that it easily assumed disproportionate importance. He admitted to having, himself, floundered in an excessive race-consciousness which had unbalanced his reactions as an individual. Besides, the prevalence of race-consciousness in America had proved detrimental to him as an artist whose responsibility was to no particular ethnic group but to the whole of mankind:McKay felt that his own deep-seated compulsion to write of the «problem of the Negro» had «clogged up» [50] his fiction on the one hand, while a race-conscious public had been bent on denying him full artistic freedom on the other hand.

McKay's craving for psychic wholeness precluded both the solution of black nationalism and that of outright assimilation. He conceived of cultural pluralism as a larger ideology which would not mutilate the Negro but satisfy his urge towards unity. Cultural pluralism also provided McKay with a rationalization both of his own ambivalent status in society and of his association with a predominantly white intellectual world which he often found less parochial and more stimulating than the restricted literary Negro coterie :

I am certain that I could not keep the respect of the whites who have honoured me with their friendship if I were the artificial image of a white man. [51]

He hoped that what had been a functional acceptance for him —intellectually at least — might offer a possibility for his ethnic group, since its members, through the cultivation of their particular identity, would compel their fellow-Americans to acknowledge the full humanity of blacks.

McKay was of the opinion that a community-centered life would improve the lot of the black masses, give them drive and direction, and provide more congenial surroundings,which would, in turn, allow for a full and harmonious development of Afro-Americans. As McKay made it clear, however, he was not «thinking in terms of narrow sectarianism, but rather in universal aspects of group culture.» 52 The exploration of Negro life opened out on the realization of some fundamental sameness. At this final stage, race-consciousness, which had been championed in a transitional period, was ultimately obliterated, or, more accurately, transmuted into the finer sense of belonging to the human race.

NOTES

Much of the material discussed was published a few years ago in a book edited by Wayne COOPER : **The Passion of Claude McKay : Selected Prose and Poetry (1912-1948)**, New-York, Schocken Books, 1973. In the following notes these articles and letters are marked out by +. Page references in brackets are to the same volume.

1. Claude McKAY : + «McKay Says Schuyler Is Writing 'Nonsense'», **New York Amsterdam News,** (November 20, 1937), 12 ; (253-257).

2. Claude McKAY : + «He Who Gets Slapped», **The Liberator,** V, (May 1922), 24-25 ; (69-73).

3. Daniel AARON : **Writers On The Left : Episodes in American Literary Communism**, New York, Harcourt, Brace and World, 1961, 18.

4.   + Max Eastman-Claude McKay Correspondence, Eastman Papers, Indiana University Library ; (79-89).

5. Claude McKAY : + «How Black Sees Green and Red», **The Liberator,** IV, (June 1921), 17-20-21 ; (57-62).

6. James Weldon JOHNSON : **Negro Americans, What Now ?**, New York, The Viking Press, 1934.

7. W.E. Burghardt DU BOIS : «Segregation In The North», **The Crisis**, XLI, (April 1934), 115-117.

8. Claude McKAY : **A Long Way From Home**, New York, Lee Furman, 1937.
See the last chapter : «On Belonging to a Minority Group» for a summary of McKay's ideas on the Negro question in the late Thirties.

9. Claude McKAY : **Harlem : Negro Metropolis**, New York, Dutton, 1940.

10.   The articles particularly relevant to our topic were published in **Jewish Frontier, Nation, The New Leader, New York Amsterdam News**, and **New York Post**. The four chapters in **Harlem : Negro Metropolis** are titled : «Harlem Businessman», «Harlem Politician», «Marcus Aurelius Garvey», and «Sufi Abdul Hamid and Organized Labor».

11. The following definition of «black nationalism» is borrowed from an anthology on the subject : John H. BRACEY, JR., August MEIER and Elliott RUDWICK, **Black Nationalism in America,** Indianapolis and New York, Bobbs-Merrill Company, 1970 :

a body of social thought, attitudes, and actions ranging from the simplest expressions of ethnocentricity and racial solidarity to the comprehensive and sophisticated ideologies of Pan-Negroism or Pan-Africanism. (XXVI).

12. Harold CRUSE : **The Crisis of the Negro Intellectual**, New York, Morrow and Company, 1967, 117.

13. Claude McKAY : «Author Assails Negro Congress for Message Sent to Washington on Jews : Calls Body Organization of Leaders ; No Followers», **New York Amsterdam News**, (November 26, 1938), 11.

14. Letter from Claude McKAY to James W. JOHNSON, (April 15, 1935) ; Johnson Papers, James W. Johnson Collection, Yale University Library. With kind permission of Mrs. James Weldon Johnson.

15. Letter from Claude McKAY to Harold JACKMAN, (May 10, 1928) ; McKay Papers, James W. Johnson Collection, Yale University Library. With kind permission of the Estate of Claude McKay.

16.   + Claude McKAY : «Circular Letter for the Creation of a Negro Writers' Guild», (October 23, 1937) ; (233-234).

17.   + Letter from Claude McKAY to Max EASTMAN, (September 11, 1934), Eastman Papers, Indiana University Library ; (200-201).

18. **Harlem : Negro Metropolis**, 248-249.

19. **Id.**, 248.

20. Claude McKAY : + «Labor Steps Out in Harlem», **Nation**, vol. 145, (October 16, 1937), 399-402 ; (243-252).

21. Claude McKAY : **New York Amsterdam News**, (November 26, 1938), n. 13.

22. Historians widely agree that Communist influence, strong from the inception of the National Negro Congress, grew as the years went by. This control, and the presence of too many white delegates at the 1940 convention, prompted Philip Randolph to resign from the presidency to which he had been elected in 1936.

23. Frank CROSSWAITH, **The New Leader**, (February 24, 1940), 5.

24. Letter from Claude McKAY to James W. JOHNSON, (May 31, 1935) ; Johnson Papers, James W. Johnson Collection, Yale University Library. With kind permission of Mrs. James Weldon Johnson.

25. Frank CROSSWAITH, **op. cit.**

26. Harold CRUSE, **op. cit.**, 58.

27. + Claude McKAY : «Garvey as a Negro Moses», **The Liberator**, V, (May 1922), 8-9 ; (65-69).

28. E. David CRONON, ed. : **Great Lives Observed : Marcus Garvey,** New Jersey, Prentice Hall, 1973, 124.

29. **Harlem : Negro Metropolis**, 179-180.

30. **Ibid.**, 179.

31. E. David CRONON : **Op. cit.**, 55.

32. Claude McKay Papers, James W. Johnson Collection, Yale University Library.

33. **Harlem : Negro Metropolis**, 177.

34. Claude McKay : «Looking Forward», **New York Amsterdam News**, (April 22, 1939), 11.

35. James W. JOHNSON : **Black Manhattan**, in E. David CRONON ed., **op. cit.**, 125.

36. Claude McKAY : «Looking Forward», **New York Amsterdam News**, (April 22, 1939), 11.

37. Claude McKAY : «Looking Forward», **New York Amsterdam News**, (May 20, 1939), 13.

38. Adam Clayton POWELL, Jr., «Soap-Box», **New York Amsterdam News**, (October 30, 1937), 13.

39. This demand which had constituted a central plank of the Communist platform between 1928 and 1935, had been soft-pedalled for two years as a result of the Seventh World Congress of the Communist International and of its adoption of the «united front policy». The doctrine of Negro self-determination was somewhat revived under the Russio-German pact, but was not to be seriously advocated again until the Duclos letter of April 1945.
See Wilson RECORD : **The Negro and the Communist Party**, Chapel Hill, The University of North Carolina Press, 1951, 56 :

> Negroes in the United States (...) met all the requirements of a nation as defined by Stalin, being a historically evolved, stable entity, defined by language, territory, economic life, and psychological make-up, and manifested in a community of culture.

40. W.E. Burghardt DU BOIS : **The Souls of Black Folk**, 1903. Reprint, New York, Washington Square Press, 1970, 42.

41. Claude McKAY : «A Communication», **Jewish Frontier, The Crisis**, XLI, (April 1934), 115-117.

42. W.E. Burghardt DU BOIS : «Segregation in the North», **The Crisis**, XLI, (April 1934), 115-117.

43. + Claude McKAY : «For Group Survival», **Jewish Frontier**, IV, (October 1937), 19-26 ; (234-239).

44. **Ibid.**, (234).

45. **Ibid.**, (234).

46. **Ibid.**, (236).
McKay's interpretation of the Jews' way of dealing with problems of adjustment in America, elicited mixed feelings from the Jews themselves who did not agree that considerations of race should be allowed to interfere with labor issues : «The Jewish organizers rarely appealed to race-pride, nor ever visualized the (labor) union as an agency of developing Jewish cultural unity. They did not describe their struggle as even in the slightest sense, a Jew-Gentile issue. The religious, cultural and national issues, they most assiduously left to the Zionists.»
(Jacob J. WEINSTEIN : «Harlem : Negro Metropolis», **Jewish Frontier**, X, (February 1941), 23-24.)

47. Claude McKAY : «Lest We Forget», **Jewish Frontier,** VIII, (January 1940), 9-10.

48. Claude McKAY : «Harlem's 'Chinese Wall' : Fear of 'Segregation' Furthers Negro Disunity», **The New Leader**, (November 15, 1941), 4.

49. Claude McKAY : «A Communication», **Jewish Frontier**, X, (April 1941), 25.

50. + Letter from Claude McKAY to Harold JACKMAN, (September 20, 1929) ; James W. Johnson Collection, Yale University Library ; (147-148).

51. «A Communication», see n. 49.

52. + Claude McKAY : «Circular Letter For the Creation of a Negro Writers' Guild», (October 23, 1937) ; (233-234).

Bernard JACQUIN

The ideological dimension

of American Black music

A survey of the contemporary musical scene shows that American Black music is following three directions.

First one comes across the established celebrities who fashioned their style, say, any time before 1960, and have been spending the last fifteen years refining upon it, or more simply repeating themselves. And if one may wonder whether the music of their younger imitators is quite valid, hardly anybody would question the right of Thelonious Monk, or Milt Jackson, or Count Basie — or any authentic dixielander for that matter — to keep to the idiom they evolved during their formative years or early in their careers.

Then there is the pervading world of Rhythm and Blues and its by-products, which since the late '50s has been forcibly reasserting the traditional values, with its heavy, compulsive beat, simple harmonies and unsophisticated melodies. From Ray Charles to James Brown or the late Jimi Hendrix, from Aretha Franklin or Nina Simone to Tina Turner, a number of black artists preserve an unbroken tradition feeding on the spirit of the blues, the field-hollers and the work-songs, and the spirituals that took shape in the camp-meetings of the early nineteenth century. Their financial success simply confirms the vitality of a common musical fund that has gone happily through successive alterations without running the risk of becoming a dead form.

But alongside these two predictable currents, the world of American black music in the '60s and early '70s has been shattered by forces raising a series of questions about its nature and significance. Not only has the music proper been subjected to spectacular changes, but some of the prominent musicians responsible for this dramatic disruption have commented on their practice and their aims, and assumed the artistic, but also political, attitude implied in their sayings. Besides, the adepts of this new idiom have claimed that the critical tools used so far to describe jazz were totally obsolete. The recent emergence of several black writers setting themselves the task of studying the music of their own community practically for the first time in the history of the American Negro, did much to pose the problem in more general terms. In their writings, questions about how to approach American black music are linked to — or rather derive from — questions about its very nature and its situation in the total experience of the racial minority that gave birth to it. Reflections have followed ; bitter arguments have been exchanged, recalling the days when the music of Charlie Parker played havoc in the ranks of hostile or fascinated jazz amateurs ; attempts have been made to define and apply a new critical approach, to elaborate a methodology, and jointly to propose a definition of the music concerned and analyse its nature, preferably in the light of some established ideological system.

In fact the first problem that faces anyone wishing to generalize about this musical object rests in its extreme diversity. It is true that jazz grew polymorphous at an early stage. After all, Louis Armstrong was its contemporary, and John Coltrane recorded *Flamenco Sketches* the year when Bechet died [1], and *Giant Steps* only a few months later. But the fact that in the '50s, for instance, the artists one could listen to ranged from New Orleans musicians, or soloists or big bands from the Swing Era, to neo-boppers exploiting — or systematizing — the discoveries of Charlie Parker, has never prevented historians of jazz from dividing it into fairly definite periods, named after the prevalent styles that followed one another : New Orleans, Chicago and Dixieland, Swing, Be-bop, Cool, Neo-bop or Funky were as many convenient landmarks and met with common assent. Whereas the contemporary scene displays such a variety of aspects that it may seem hard at first to discuss it as if it formed a more or less compact unit. Clearly, there is a vast difference between the music of Sun Ra and that of Albert Ayler, or Cecil Taylor, or Archie Shepp. Besides, the pronouncements of some leading musicians only confirm the impression that the world of jazz has split off in a number of directions. Ayler harping on his dreams of spiritual unity, and Shepp making explicit allusions to Marxism, stand poles apart. Sonny Sharrock and others wave aside the insistent references to Islam and to Africa of the majority of their colleagues, and proclaim unambiguously that jazz is American. As for Charles Mingus, in spite of the fact that he did much to bring about what is currently referred to as Free Jazz, he does not spare those of his fellow-artists who apparently fail to meet the musical requirements that in fact they may have deliberately ignored, and this precisely in the name of freedom. Be it as it may, according to him Ornette Coleman and Cecil Taylor are unable to read music or to follow a harmonic structure ; consequently they usurp the title of jazzmen.
But in spite of the contradictory views and of the divergent styles

which have been flourishing since 1959 (the year when Ornette Coleman recorded several albums whose titles — *Tomorrow is the question, The shape of Jazz to come, Change of the Century* — explicitly stated that a «new thing» was coming to life) [2], the American black music of the last fifteen years as a whole differs radically from what it was before, both in its form and in the place it occupies — or at least claims to occupy — in the culture of American Negroes.

Significantly, a question of terminology appeared at the outset : the very word «jazz» got to be questioned, and has been since discarded by many. Yet generations of musicians, from King Oliver to Miles Davis inclusively, had been quite happy with it. It is true that Charlie Parker is reported to have declared that what he played was not jazz, but then he presumably referred to the commercial music that was churned out in the late '30s to meet the demands of a large public feasting on cheap exoticism. In any case his statement had no implications outside the domain of music proper. Whereas what the contemporary musicians object to is that the term is associated with a series of connotations which they claim have been greatly harmful to the statute of their art. «Jazz» calls up at once its early circumstances, its infancy in the red-light district of New Orleans and adolescence in the speakeasies of Chicago, and more generally the clichés of drug-addiction, sex and violence. Besides the stigma of immorality, it implies economic dispossession. Since the days when record companies realized black music was marketable, «jazz» has proved a handy label to promote sales, helping to boost a variety of more or less emasculated imitations, and to maintain white supremacy all along. Accordingly, the first group to be recorded and to enjoy notoriety was the all-white Original Dixieland Jazz Band ; in the '20s the ambitious music of Paul Whiteman performing Gershwin's *Rhapsody in Blue* was acclaimed by music-lovers for refining the crude music of New Orleans into «Symphonic Jazz», thus conferring upon it the status of art ; and during the «Swing Craze», it was the white clarinet-player Benny Goodman who was sacred King of Swing, and who had the honour of bringing jazz into the temple of classical music : Carnegie Hall. As for the black performers, they were required to be cooperative, that is to say play according to the taste of the public rather than to to their own taste, and rub out all the elements that might have puzzled or antagonized customers who were prepared to venture outside their own cultural sphere and pay for the excitement of listening to illicit sounds provided their quest remained perfectly safe. Fighting against the recuperation of their idiom by cultural smugness and the forces of show-business first implies that the word «jazz» should be discarded altogether, and replaced by the uncompromising words «black music». Both terms are assigned a specific function. «Music» is intended to put an end to the implicit discrimination existing between real music on the one hand, and the oddity named jazz on the other hand, whose peculiar idiosyncrasy is at its best a thrilling derivative from serious music — or more simply from music properly speaking — and at its worst an outrageous onslaught on good taste. «Black» of course is pregnant with meaning : ethnic alterity is part and parcel of the cultural object the word helps define.

The issue is obvious, yet one point should be made clear. Those who contend today that jazz is inseperable from negritude no longer ground their claim on the so-called nature of the Negro. Indeed the belief that his physical constitution and his mental disposition enable him to apprehend primeval rhythms, and to express them through the medium of art, long served to account for the supremacy of Negro jazz-men. But this theory, reminiscent of the myth of the Noble Savage, has been replaced by more valid references to culture. Extravagant eulogy has given way to critical discrimination, and unquestioning enthusiasm to rational investigation. Now this passage from the dogma of innateness to sociological and historical examination — in other words from nature to culture — finds its linguistic counterpart in the passage from «jazz» to «black music». Or better still : «Afro-American music». Drummer Max Roach's favoring of the latter wording only emphasizes the point : his semantic strictures on «black music» are passed in the name of accuracy. Not only must the appellation bring out the racial identity of the music concerned, it must also refer to its dual geographical location, its insertion in a cultural continuum which roots it in Africa, and brings it through slavery, emancipation and the struggles of the twentieth century, to its most recent developments.

Clearly, the urge to inscribe jazz in the history of the Negro community in the United States is but a particular aspect of cultural nationalism. This is best exemplified in LeRoi Jones's *Blues People*, a book which gained immediate notoriety, if only because it was the first critical work of any length written by a Negro on Negro music. LeRoi Jones's assumption is that the evolution of black music in the United States helps focus the evolution of the African slave into a second-rate American citizen. He contends that in a transplanted community where very soon oral literature withered away under all sorts of pressures, where written literature was until fairly recently out of the question, music long remained the only common medium, the only consistent vehicle of a cultural tradition reduced to a subculture.

Incidentally, this accounts for its frequent assimilation to a language. No doubt, the notion that music, or art in general, conveys a message, and therefore is a means of communication — a language — is not original. But what may sound as an empty cliché, or at best a rash formulation, in the context of Western civilization, should be viewed quite differently here. For the musical production of the slaves imported from Africa had specific motivations. For one thing, they came from a land where music presided over numerous aspects of tribal life : daily work, war, propitiatory rites... Besides, on a very concrete level, they brought along the use of drums as a way to transmit information. On the other hand, many found themselves unable to communicate orally because they were isolated among Africans speaking other dialects, or simply because white slave-owners forbade all African dialects, together with African cults and traditional literatures. So that they naturally resorted to music as the only way out of their cultural void ; through it, they could somehow get round their linguistic handicap : music was for them, if not a language proper, at least a substitute for it. And the deep sense of community linking a preacher and his congregation, or a blues singer and his audience, continues to bear witness to this reality.

Of course LeRoi Jones's approach is that of a sociologist rather than that of a musicologist : when he undertakes to trace the history of the American Negro in his music, music is only subservient. It remains that he paved the way for a conspicuous renovation of jazz criticism, at a time when the first disturbing manifestations of free jazz raised unanswered questions. The essential novelty of his venture was to centre his study on the historical determinism of jazz, to offer in his book a body of theoretical reflections on its modes of production, its function in American society, its situation in American experience as a whole, its insertion in a cultural, sociological, economic milieu, in a network of external forces to which it is strictly submitted.

The ultimate outcome of LeRoi Jones's work is nothing less than a new history of jazz. Gone are the days when, not so long ago, its future seemed to lie in the happy blending of two idioms, when John Lewis's mannered arrangements on Renaissance or Baroque melodies, or the ambitious scores of Gunther Schuller, attempted to infuse its pulse or spicy sounds into Western music, which in its turn was expected to lend its elaborate form. Free Jazz came along, and upset perspectives. Instead of merging two musical streams (as the ambitious «third stream» had set out to do), it seemed that its chief aim was to wipe out references to white music, or to treat them as an element of derision. And this deliberate rejection has been viewed as the last and most drastic of a whole series of reactions which in the course of time have all striven to rid black music of white elements, to stress its essential otherness. The logical conclusion of this interpretation is that far from being the history of a progressive assimilation of foreign elements, the history of American Negro music is that of its resilience in a white environment, of its resistance to amalgamation, of its successive response to a cultural rape, of its assertion of a black culture right in the midst of a dominant white culture. More precisely, it is made up of the dialectical succession of periods when its cultural identity tends to dissolve, and periods when it gains new vigour, when it is revitalized thanks to fresh borrowings from its great tradition. In the light of this theory, the blues for instance was a positive departure from the influence of the Protestant hymns that produced the spiritual. Jazz in New Orleans, although it started as an imitation of light music from Europe, bore little resemblance to its model, thanks to the peculiar instrumental technique of its performers and the practice of collective improvisation. Be-bop was an astounding break-away from the music of the late '30s, and its revolutionary rhythmic conceptions were regarded as the direct outcome of a return to the rhythmic complexity of African tribal music. As for free jazz, some of its leading musicians give it such a thorough cleaning that it seems to exclude all risks of further contamination, and it is tempting to look upon it as the last phase in the cultural struggle waged by black people in white America, as the decisive step towards negritude, as the ultimate process of cultural decolonization.

Before going into details about free jazz, a word should be said about a particular aspect of this quest of cultural identity : education. Confronted with the well-known fact that the Negro elite seeking integration tends to cross out references to a traumatic past and consequently ignore its own culture, a growing number of those whose mission it is to promote negritude have become aware of the urgency to bring the blacks, and more particularly the young, to a better knowledge and undertanding of the music of their community. Accordingly, several higher educational institutions include it in their programmes, and entrust the teaching to prominent jazz musicians. Thus Bill Dixon at Bennington College, Cecil Taylor at the University of Wisconsin, then at Antioch College, Bill Hassan at the Institute for Pan-African Culture, Archie Shepp at the University of Massachusetts, find the opportunity to lecture on Negro music and to train young musicians. In this respect, Shepp's comments on his teaching activities help one to undestand the significance of this new form of cultural proselytism. The task he assigns himself goes much beyond the scope of «jazz» proper : his ambition is to embrace the whole of the black diaspora, and to trace, not only in the United States, but also in the West Indies and Latin America, the essential continuity of African music. A central figure in the most recent developments of jazz, he is in fact steeped in tradition, and his inspiration feeds on a thorough knowledge of the past ; he pays reverence to the whole of black music, from John Coltrane to boogie-woogie pianist Pinetop Smith, from the latest experiments to the most primitive forms of the blues.

But Shepp's eclecticism does not proceed from the serene open-mindedness of the art-lover. Far from it. The sense of urgency informing his comments on his teaching and his music is that of a man committed to the safeguard of a cultural heritage. For according to his tragic vision of race relations, Negro culture in white America is submitted to a permanent aggression exerted by a society fated to absorb or to destroy. Hence the function he assigns to the pedagogue and the artist : to resist assimilation, to bear witness to a cultural past, to ensure the survival of a tradition, to proclaim the historical reality of Negro otherness.

The question arising at this stage is precisely to know if and how the avant-garde jazz movement fulfils its mission. Shepp's manichean outlook provides a convenient starting-point : what he suggests in terms of aggression and resistance is the same notion as that expressed unambiguously by Stokely Carmichael telling the students of Howard University that when they fight for a black culture, they fight against America, since America is against the blacks. In other words, the primary task of free jazz should be to get rid of the standards of Western music, and the implication is that this departure cannot fail to become aggressive in its turn. Indeed, the most striking feature of the «new thing» lies in its subversive qualities. To say that European musical standards cease to serve as a system of reference is an understatement. It is true that the music of Cecil Taylor has sometimes been compared to that of Stockhausen, and that French composer André Hodeir relates that as early as 1957 Varese held a workshop in New-York to experiment with black musicians on the possibilities of free improvisation. But if such instances show a superficial convergence in certain directions, they are of little significance beside the destructive spirit animating most of free jazz. The notions of harmony, melody, theme, form, instrumental technique, often seem irrelevant. Or rather, they are held in derision, they are flouted by musicians who pursue iconoclastic aims through frustration. Against the idea that the role of the artist is to produce a definite object, answering certain norms, they refuse to create a form of beauty that would conform to accepted canons, to satisfy the aesthetic expectations of listeners conditioned by their cultural habits. Instead, they purposely violate the «normal» use of their medium, they decondition it through so-called technical mistakes and squeaks, illicit sounds, all sorts of «musical graffiti» which blur the frontier between music and non-music.

But their comment also extends to their own cultural past. Through quotations and stylistic devices, they undertake a sort of reassessment of the basic ingredients of jazz and of its vocal origins. Only, this comment is often ambiguous. There is probably an element of parody in the literal use of clichés or standard themes ; conversely, references to such traditional forms as the blues or church music, or the revival of collective improvisation which fell into disuse with the emergence of Louis Armstrong, may be looked upon as a tribute paid to authenticity. So that one function of free jazz would be to mete out derision and reverence, according as the style or the musician referred to fell sinfully into the traps of show-business, or managed to preserve the essence of black music.

The situation of free jazz in American Negro experience and its relations to the whole of its music, is perhaps better apprehended through the time-sequence of a typical performance and its effect on the listener.

Most of the time, the spontaneous improvisations of the musicians take place in a haphazard fashion, whether simultaneously or successively, with periods of intense accumulation alternating with periods of abatement. The notion of form, of a structure made up of well-defined parts arranged according to a strict order, is conspicuously absent. Whereas from nineteenth century vocal music down to the late '50s the twelve-bar blues, the sixteen-bar or thirty-two-bar songs had imposed their rigid frame to the standard succession theme-chorus, here destructuration is radical. No doubt the purpose of it is similar to that pursued in the domain of sound : the disruption of form is another facet of the same destructive mood. But beyond the subversive intent, there is also an attempt to recapture the spirit of the past. What is at stake is a process of creation calling up the conditions of musical production in tribal societies, where no definite preliminary structure presides over the act of playing or singing, where the organization of the time-sequence is left to the musician himself.

This search for a lost tradition also accounts for the nature and purpose of certain free jazz performances. According to Western concepts, the aim of the artist is to produce an object that will be a source of aesthetic enjoyment : what matters, for the producer as well as for the consumer, is the artefact, not the creative act. And the function of museums, picture-galleries, or records, is precisely to preserve the artefact from destruction. But it seems that a number of jazz musicians today feel much less concerned by the product — a record, that is a musical fragment forming an identifiable aesthetic object and surviving the moment of creation — than by this moment itself : what matters for them is the musical event proper, the act of playing, the physical reality of the spontaneous experience, the «movement with existence» [3].

It is not only the status of music which is brought in question, but also the nature of the relationship between the musician and the listener. Through obsessive reiteration, Albert Ayler, John Coltrane, or Pharoah Sanders, build up a climate that upsets our habitual mode of perception, and whose hypnotic quality recalls the ritual function of African music helping to bring about a state of tension resolving itself into religious transe. The declarations of certain musicians about the mystical significance of their art confirm the view that they mean to abolish the usual distinction between the role of the artist and that of the public, and to propose instead to the consumer to share with the producer a common experience. So that playing music is reinstated in a social context, becomes a gesture assuming a definite function within a community.

References in free jazz are not only temporal, but spatial. If it borrows from jazz, from the blues and the spiritual and the field-hollers, as well as from African music, it takes an equal interest in musics from India, Islamic countries, Asia, the third world in general. It is as if it had inherited the syncretist faculty of African religions and paradoxically freed itself from its ethnic roots to become a universal idiom.

And this raises the controversial question of its political dimension.

It is tempting to establish a parallel between the widening of its source of inspiration and the itinerary of Malcolm X for instance, from a mythology extolling the merits of the black race to an enlarged vision replacing the problems of his people in a worldwide context. As the Negro poet Ted Joans aptly puts it : «Malcolm X did wail/what John Coltrane did yell». And to show that in his view the convergence between music and politics outgrows the scope of avant-garde jazz, he adds this caustic comment : «M.L. King did tell/what Louis Armstrong does sell» [4]. More broadly, this passage from the musical idioms of black peoples to musical idioms borrowed from all types of cultures might be said to reflect the evolution of the political ideology of American Negroes in general from the slogan «Black is beautiful» to international solidarity.

There is no doubt that the «new thing» emerged at the time when black Americans asserted their political maturity, rejected integration, and questioned the validity of non-violence. Hence the view that «Freedom now» is echoed in «Free Jazz», street riots in musical aggressivity, that its disruptive power expresses in its own way the revolt and protest of the Black Panther Party (which incidentally includes the study of jazz in its educational programme).

But unless words are allowed to slip into vagueness, it is hazardous to assimilate a cultural phenomenon to a political gesture. In this respect, the grossly exaggerated importance attached to titles warps perspective. *Malcom Semper Malcolm* may well signal an intention, confirmed by the short poem recited by Shepp [5], but does the music proper contain any extra-musical message ? Similarly, the fact that *On this Night* claims to be «a tribute to W.E.B. Du Bois» is of little help to «understand» the music, that is to look upon it as an evocation of a people fighting for its emancipation. This we learn only through Shepp's comments on the significance he attributes to his composition. And if the talking sections of *Faubus Fables* were removed, would the music carry out the precise, vindictive intention of Charles Mingus ? Speech is the vehicle of his attack against the racist governor of Arkansas, not music. It is also rather facile to explain that the many free jazz musicians who protest that their music has no political implication whatsoever unconsciously transfer into mysticism, esoteric philosophies, or other substitutes, the political positions expressed by Max Roach or Archie Shepp.

The latter fell a victim to his own whishes when he declared in 1965 that jazz was against war in general, and against that in Viet-Nam in particular, that it was for Cuba (« ... Fidel is black ... Ho Chi Minh is black» [6]), for the liberation of all oppressed communities, of all colonized peoples.

Again, if words are to remain at all precise, the only instances when black music assumes unambiguously a political dimension occur when it finds itself associated with a political event ; and even then its political dimension is granted from outside, from its circumstancial commitment. Such is the case for instance each time a musician plays for the benefit of a Negro organization. Such was perhaps also the case in 1969 at the Algiers Panafrican Cultural Festival, when Shepp as a black musician, Ted Joans and Don Lee as black poets, Eldridge Cleaver as a black political leader, proclaimed through music and through words the African roots of American Negro culture, but also, through their bodily presence, together on the same stage, the solidarity of their individual enterprise.

The upheaval free jazz brought about could not but have repercussions on jazz criticism as a whole.

The absence of safe landmarks makes the position of critics in front of the new music very uncomfortable indeed. The object of their study presents itself as a foreign body, and their usual tools often prove of little help when they try to apprehend it : they cannot discern in this disturbing phenomenon the coherence, the structure, the basic elements that have always been regarded as the *sine qua non* condition of music. They are all the less prepared to account for it as until fairly recently their praiseworthy ambition to obtain the recognition of jazz led them to show that in spite of appearances it conformed in fact to the accepted norms of white culture. Today they are accused of having given a distorted image of it, and it seems that all their guidelines and knowledge are in reality as many handicaps, that their culture disables them from commenting on an object born of a fundamentally different culture.

This feeling of insecurity is increased by the claim that Negro music is engaged in a revolutionary process, that it is no longer innocent — that in fact it never was. For the notion of music as serving a purpose, as helping in a cause that goes much beyond it, runs counter to the dogma of art for art's sake, of the gratuitous quality of art, which places it by definition above all causes and ideologies.

So that jazz critics are confronted with a methodological dilemma. Can black music in the United States be isolated from the economic, political, sociological, cultural struggle of American Negroes ? Has it got a reality outside the history of a minority fighting for its liberation ? If not, does it follow that all aesthetic considerations will be vain ? And if such is the case, what will be the task of criticism ? Or will there be any left ?

In *Blues People*, LeRoi Jones initiated a sociological approach. Others followed suit, and in France Philippe Carles and Jean-Louis Comolli, in *Free Jazz/Black Power*, tried to widen the scope by linking the cultural conflict to the exploitation by Western capitalism of the underdeveloped countries of the third world. The sum of information collected about the conditions of artistic creation, the attitudes and motivations that determine the emergence and disappearance of successive styles, is far from negligible. But the limitations of the method are cruelly felt when it is applied to individual works. Comments on the proclaimed or supposed intention of a musician do not account for his music. In *Black Music*, LeRoi Jones declares bluntly that formal musicology is useless. Unfortunately, the book as a whole comes as a bitter disappointment. Admittedly, it is made up of a series of articles written over a period of several years, but the rigorous approach of *Blues People* is nowhere to be found ; instead the writer indulges in impressionistic, rambling comments about clubs, records and musicians, which are void of significance. And of course his failure is all the more spectacular as his previous contribution to jazz criticism had opened up such new vistas.

In *Dutchman*, Clay is made to say that Bessie Smith singing the blues or Charlie Parker playing the saxophone, are in fact venting their hatred on the white beotians listening to them [7]. Archie Shepp holds the same view when he declares that today there are two ways for an American Negro to remain himself : take part in urban guerilla, or pick up a musical instrument and play... To say that Shepp and Jones are wrong, that the fact Charlie Parker chose to play the saxophone rather than use a gun makes a lot of difference, does not mean that his social environment had no influence on his art, but that his music is also something specific, which it is legitimate to consider in itself. There is on the one hand a sociological, cultural reality, on the other hand an aesthetic reality, which no doubt includes its own ideological determinations, but also transforms and transcends them.

Paul Oliver has insisted that the blues cannot be reduced to the words of the blues, that it is also, and primarily, music, and that to know what it tells through language in no way accounts for its impact on the listener. Similarly, jazz must be apprehended at two levels. It does not arise from a vacuum, and one of the tasks of criticism is to identify the forces at work that allow it — and compel it — to grow and evolve in a certain direction. But in no case will this knowledge provide the key to the form of jazz, to its aesthetic status.

On the other hand, a fundamental reassessment has been made, and is still under way. Thanks to the vehemence of committed artists, and thanks to the emergence of a new type of criticism, a new dimension has been given to the history and function of black music. The ideological perspective, which roots it in its context, which brings out its various motivations, greatly helps our understanding of its nature and evolution. But this enlightening approach is not without risks. It tends to revive the old myth of the purity of jazz, and to excommunicate in its name the styles and musicians showing too many traces of «foreign» — that is to say European — influences. When dealing with the contemporary production, it considers intentions rather than realizations. In fact, it is the whole question of the nature of art which is at stake here. It is true that its insertion in a social reality is particularly significant in the case of American Negro music. Yet this music cannot be reduced to the ideology of the social group which produces it. It exists on another level. Primarily, it is an aesthetic object, lending itself to an aesthetic approach, as its international vocation clearly shows.

NOTES

1. 1959. Bechet cut his last record on December 12, 1958.

2. Of course the date 1959 and Coleman's recording sessions are mentioned for the sake of convenience. Free jazz requires no official date of birth.

3. Jimmy STEWART : **The Black Aesthethic**, New York, Doubleday and Co., 1972, p. 79.

4. quoted in **Jazz Hot**, July 1969, p. 24.

5. A song is not what is seems
A tune, perhaps.
Bird whistled
while even America listened.
We play
but we aren't always dumb.
We are murdered
in amphitheaters
on the podia of the autobahn — the Earl
Philadelphia 1945 !
Malcolm — My People
Dear God
Malcolm !

6. quoted in **Down Beat**, December 16, 1965, p. II.

7. «(...) Old-headed four-eyed ofays popping their fingers... and don't know yet what they're doing. They say, «I love Bessie Smith». And don't even understand that Bessie Smith is saying, «Kiss my ass, kiss my black unruly ass». Before love, suffering, desire anything you can explain, she's saying, and very plainly, «Kiss my black ass». And if you don't know that, it's you that's doing the kissing.

Charlie Parker ? Charlie Parker. All the hip white boys scream for Bird. And Bird saying, «Up your ass, feeble-minded ofay ! Up your ass». And they sit there talking about the tortured genius of Charlie Parker. Bird would've played not a note of music if he just walked up to East Sixty-seventh Street and killed the first ten white people he saw. Not a note ! (...) If Bessie Smith had killed some white people she wouldn't have needed that music (...)». LeRoi JONES : **Dutchman**, London, Faber and Faber, 1967, pp. 34-35.

SHORT BIBLIOGRAPHY

IN ENGLISH

The Black Aesthetic, edited by Addison GAYLE, Jr, New York, Anchor Books, Doubleday and Co, 1972.

LeRoi JONES : *Blues People,* New York, Apollo Editions, 1963.

Frank KOFSKY : *Black Nationalism and The Revolution in Music*, New York, Pathfinder Press, 1970.

IN FRENCH

Philippe CARLES and Jean-Louis COMOLLI : *Free Jazz/Black Power*, Editions Champ Libre, 1971.

Jean-Louis COMOLLI : «Voyage au bout de la New Thing», *Jazz Magazine*, April 1966, pp. 24-29.

Jean-Louis COMOLLI : «Les conquérants d'un nouveau monde», *Jazz Magazine*, June 1966, pp. 30-35.

Eric PLAISANCE : «Idéologie et esthétique à propos du free jazz», *Les Cahiers du Jazz*, Paris, 1967, pp. 6-23.

Eric PLAISANCE : «Jazz, champ esthétique et idéologique», *La Nouvelle Critique*, Paris, les Editions de la Nouvelle Critique, 1969, pp. 23-27.

«Neuf entretiens sur le jazz neuf», *Les Cahiers du Jazz*, Paris, Nemm, 1968, pp. 8-60.

Monique LECOMTE

The Quota controversy :

a Press study

In his acceptance speech to the 1972 Republican Convention, R.Nixon congratulated his party for proving to the nation that «[one] can have an open convention without dividing Americans into quotas». When he added that «dividing Americans into quotas is totally alien to the American tradition», it became clear that the compliment was in fact intended as a slur on the Democrats' own convention, where the proportion of women and other «minorities» had been fixed in order to make the nominating body more representative of the electorate. A week later, in his Labor Day speech, the President renewed his attack against «the rise of the fixed quota system», aiming this time at employment quotas designed to improve the minorities' opportunities. Once more, Nixon saw in the advocacy of quotas a «challenge» to «the values that built America.» References to the nation's traditional values are of course a staple of campaign speeches, but the volume of the discussion that ensued in the press, the assessment of quotas in relation to the ideal of equal opportunity, the work ethic and the merit system suggest that «quotas» had indeed become something of a national issue, and one moreover that involved a conflict of ideals.

Politically, the alignment of forces on the issue was rather odd : both Nixon and Mc Govern agreed to oppose quotas in employment. Yet Jewish opinion, which usually sides with liberals detected enough of a threat in Mc Govern's adoption of political quotas to consider withdrawing its support to the Democrats. To some extent, the ideological discussion, which outlasted the presidential campaign and actually gathered momentum as the so-called quotas extended to new fields (education) and new «minorities» (women), also created a paradoxical alignment : not only did most of the Jews — until recently a «minority» — join the Anglo-Saxon majority in opposing the measures, but businessmen and labor leaders, conservatives and professed liberals also found themselves united. Meanwhile, moderate black leaders like Vernon Jordan of the National Urban League, small groups within the Jewish community [1], and members of the Administration — some of whom belonged to minority groups — defended the idea of quotas.

In this study, which examines the ideological content of the debate as reflected by the periodical press in 1972 and 1973, we shall be dealing with the views of the majority that opposed quotas in the name of the nation's ideals [2]. An analysis of the minority's views would of course seem to be in order. Yet a close comparison of the two ideological perspectives is hardly possible. The minority press rarely deals with quotas as an isolated topic [3] ; nor does it represent the issue as a conflict of ideals, except in response to the majority's attacks, or in an attempt to revive or strengthen a strategic alliance [4]. Thus it appears from the start that the function assigned to ideological arguments by supporters and opponents of quotas is significantly different. What our study will attempt to explore is the significance of the context in which the majority chose to discuss «quotas», namely the «American tradition». Since the term tradition evokes both an ideological content and a valuation of historical continuity, we have studied these articles with two questions in mind : how and why does one refer to the past ? what ideology is invoked and what function does it serve ? But it may be useful first to trace the origin and development of the measures that came to be considered as «quotas».

If Richard Nixon could attack with such vigor the quotas enforced by his own administration, the reason may be that he had inherited the whole problem from President Johnson. In 1965, the latter had issued Executive Order N° 11246, requiring contractors in federally-assisted construction work to «take affirmative action to ensure that applicants are employed (...) without regard to their race, color, religion, sex, or national origin.» The order was not implemented until June 1969, when contract bidders in the Philadelphia area were called upon to make jobs available to Negroes in accordance with «specific goals of minority manpower utilisation.» Johnson's aim was to establish percentages of minority labor to be hired over a four-year period. He hoped thereby to increase the proportion of black workers in the skilled construction trades, where employers must hire workers exclusively through union hiring halls, and where unions have so far admitted very few blacks into their ranks. In 1970 the concept of «affirmative action» and «result-oriented procedures» was extended by Labor Department Order N° 4 to minorities and women, and the Department of Health, Education and Welfare was granted authority to demand similar plans from universities receiving federal funds. Then, unconnected yet coinciding with, the Philadelphia Plan, came the Democratic Party's revision of its convention rules calling upon state parties to encourage participation of minorities, women and the young «in reasonable relationship to their presence in the state» (NYTM) as a result of which Mayor Daley's delegation was refused seating. Meanwhile, the validity of the Philadelphia Plan was upheld by a Federal Appeals Court decision which the Supreme Court decided to review. HEW's Office for Civil Rights began demanding from universities holding government contracts data on their hiring practices and commitment to specific goals and timetables in recruiting from underutilized groups. With the passage in 1972 of the Equal Employment Opportunity Act, the Equal Employment Opportunity Commission set up in 1964 as an information-gathering agency was given power to sue in Federal Courts and saw its jurisdiction extended to state and local government employees.

When «affirmative action» spread to education — a field in which Jews are numerous — the President of the American Jewish Committee, voicing the anxiety of his community, asked both presidential candidates to state their position on quotas. Both repudiated them ; as a result government agencies hastily revised their directives and issued new guidelines insisting that affirmative action should not result in the imposition of quotas nor in the hiring of unqualified persons. At the same time a white student, Marco de Funis, was being denied admission to the University of Washington Law School despite records slightly superior to those of admitted minority students. The Washington State Supreme Court, reversing a lower court decision, upheld the University's right to operate a two-track admission system. Again, the Federal Supreme Court refused (in April 1974) to review the case, leaving the weakened executive arm of the government to implement a program which neither Congress nor the Judiciary have explicitly sanctioned or rejected.

The semantic debate over the use of the term «quotas» is in itself an index of the ambiguities that characterize references to the past in discussions of the issue. The Government's choice of terms like «affirmative action» and «result-oriented programs» or «goals» emphasized long-term but effective action more than immediate enforcement of rigid percentages. Officials also made it clear that the «goals» were indicative rather than compulsory, that they were to be related to the size of the available work force in a specific trade and area. and were not binding if a contractor who failed to meet them could prove that he had made every good-faith effort to recruit minorities. Despite these precautions, the press, reflecting but also no doubt influencing public opinion, took goals to be euphemisms for «quotas». As a result, while pretending to share the official reluctance to use a term «charged with emotional connotations» (AMER 1) or «implying vast sins against democratic ideals» (T), the majority press often capitalized on these connotations, hailing the «Return of the Quota System» (NYTM) or envisioning «Job Quotas for Minorities ?» (AMER 1) in titles that must have sounded ominous to anyone acquainted with recent history. For during the last fifty years, the United States have twice enforced restrictive quotas : first officially, to keep out undesirable immigrants, by the Quota Laws of 1921-24, then unofficially, to halt the massive influx of Jewish students into the private colleges and medical schools of the East. Under the guise of a policy of «regional balance» ostensibly aimed at encouraging out-of-state recruitment, these quotas were used to limit enrolment of qualified students at a time when both the Jewish students and the best colleges were concentrated in the East. Memories of this are still very much alive in the Jewish press and elsewhere too, which accounts for the general feeling that the quota concept «is not progressive but regressive. It is not reform but recidivism. If it succeeds it will most assuredly push America backward into the failures of a bygone era of narrow-minded prejudices and internecine conflicts». [5]

The simultaneous reference to the past and the future is typical of the perspective of most of the articles : quotas are assessed in view of the models or warnings offered by the past and of a future over which looms the shadow of fear, but they are rarely assessed in view of the present difficulties they are intended to remedy. In that respect, the imagery pertaining to the possible effects of affirmative action is revealing : it conjures up threats of disease («the perils of contagion are manifest», AMER 2) disaster (reverse discrimination «has spread like wildfire to other groups», CY6) or death (minor officials go about «like *Alice in Wonderland*'s Red Queen, issuing threats of decapitation for frivolous purposes», CY3) not to mention the unhealthy motives of those who go «lusting after relevance» (CY3) and recommend that universities devise more accessible curriculums. It is the potentialities of affirmative action rather than its present workings that induce judgment — the fear that «the philosophy of quotas may ultimately be taken to its logical extreme» (NSWK) or that «to-morrow may always bring new demands» (T).

Implementing quotas, then, seemingly amounts to unleashing uncontrollable forces into the future. Perhaps because the future is so full of dangers, the opponents of quotas turn to the past for comfort and guidance. The paradoxical conclusion is that one should remain faithful to this past and yet not «return» to it. To enforce affirmative action plans would signal both «a momentous change» (F) and «a return of vaudeville» (NYTM), «a major alteration in the laws of discrimination» (F) and «a return to past discrimination» (T), a «dangerous departure portending a regressive development» (NYTM). A radical change would be dangerous but so would a mere repetition of the past. What then is the «true» legacy of the past, and why does one refer to it ? First of all, the past is the mainspring and repository of values and doctrines that remain absolutes : the notion of unalienable rights written into the Declaration of Independence, the «American Constitutional system» which «does not recognize group rights» (AMER 2) or Hamilton's warning that a proportional representation of all classes of citizens «will never happen under any arrangement that leaves the people free» (T). But the authority that is most often invoked is that of previous Supreme Court decisions. Indeed, as H.S. Commager pointed out, the Judiciary which has so often been called upon to arbitrate between the demands of majority rule and those of minority rights (and most recently in the De Funis case) has become « [the country's] church, [its] confessional, [its] sanctuary, [its] safety valve, [its] preceptor, [its] palladium» [6]. And yet, because its political composition changes, because successive courts respond differently to the mood of their times, we cannot expect the Supreme Court's decisions to be consistent in the long run. Indeed, much of the recent progress in race relations is due to the Court's ability to reverse some of its decisions. So, when adversaries of the quotas invoke Harlan's dissenting opinion of 1896 in Plessy vs Ferguson to support their view that the Constitution is and should remain «color-blind» (AMER 1), the reference is somewhat ambiguous. It certainly pays tribute to the Court's capacity for producing prophetic dissenters, and thereby strengthens its prestige ; at the same time, it overlooks the fact that the Court's actual decision as formulated by the other judges led to another fifty years of colour-consciousness [7].

So far, the claim that one should preserve the legacy of the past springs from an attitude of reverence for the country's institutions as such ; but it cannot always be substantiated by the actual role these institutions have played. Yet the facts of history are not ignored. They even serve to account for the present. Thus «reasons of history and habit» explain the Jews' over-representation in teaching (NYTM) even though «they had to overcome long-standing quotas restricting their opportunities» (T). The latter remark might well be taken as a proof that to-day's «minorities» could overcome their own handicaps without recurring to reverse discrimination. The recent past, in particular the last decade, lends itself to various interpretations : thus the quota system arises now from «failure to give more than lip service to the ideal of equal opportunity» (NYTM), now as a «distorted result of the civil rights drive of the 1960's» (T). Yet the dominant note, as regards the acquisitions of the sixties, is one of satisfaction — even self-satisfaction for those groups which, like labor, can boast a long record of fighting for civil rights. At the same time, this very record serves to ward off accusations of insensitivity to the fate of minorities, and to give the authority of experience to those who disclaim quotas as «unsound» means of achieving equality (CP). As for the global history of minorities, all commentators admit as a matter of course that it has been one of discrimination : yet they rarely go on to analyze the consequences of this in relation to the proposed quotas. They focus on the dangers of reverse discrimination towards whites, and if an example were needed of the contrast between the guilt-ridden rhetoric of the sixties and the present one, it might be found in the images referring to the history of minorities. Whether one views the sixties as a decade of efforts to open up «avenues of American society long closed to minorities» (NSWK) or «fields previously inhospitable to them» (ibid), or whether one speaks of groups being «introduced into lines of work where they have never traditionally participated» (ibid) or «brought into the mainstream of American life» (CR), the landscape of the past is empty, the actors of history have disappeared. The use of passive forms blurs responsibilities, and euphemisms like «inhospitable» tend to de-dramatize the past and as a result detract from the urgency of remedial action.

What finally emerges is an optimistic conception of history as leading inevitably to progress, provided one remain faithful to the country's best ideals without returning to past «errors». But from consideration of the recent past one also draws sobering lessons that argue against radical change. Here is an example of the advocacy of gradual improvement :

> Our energies ought to go into training the disadvantaged and the excluded, not into compromising and ruining, morally and practically, the society that has wronged them in the past, as it earlier wronged others, and which now recognizes their just complaint. (NR2)

History should be allowed to proceed smoothly, and each group should undergo the same processes that ultimately led to-day's «majority» to its present position. The assumption is that one can and should redress past wrongs without upsetting the status quo. The minorities of course disagree with this optimistic interpretation of the historical process and reject the status quo. Eleanor H. Norton, Chairman of New York City's Commission on Human Rights, holds that

> The majority has for too long enjoyed an advantage of its own, based on the discriminatory exclusion of another group. The special treatment of minorities is not a preference but a remedial measure designed to rectify the present imbalance that has resulted from past discrimination. (NYTM)

Her view that disadvantaged groups should receive compensation beyond a mere recognition of their «rights», and that the «natural» course of history should perhaps be altered or accelerated, is rejected by the majority with a touch of moral disapproval for its «do-unto-others-as-others-have-done-unto-you-line-of- reasoning» (NYTM). Moreover, where E.H. Norton seeks to «rectify imbalance», the A.F.L. — C.I.O. perceives «a quantum jump in the potential for a violent disequilibrium» (AC). Obviously, the use of supposedly neutral terms borrowed from mathematics of physics to describe social relations fails to exorcise tensions and conflicts, since two groups may have contradictory notions of what «equilibrium» is ; another case in point would be the concept of «minority», to which the opponents of quotas have discovered a confusing and dangerous «accordion-like expansibility.» (CY 6)

In fact, «social harmony» (AC) is the predominant concern of the majority. The A.F.L. — C.I.O.'s fear that quotas might «increase social tension» (ibid.) echoes other warnings that the policy might «weaken or shatter a consensus» on doctrinès of equality and social justice (AMER 1). The achievement of harmony and consensus is both the desirable and perhaps the natural end of the historical process ; for the time being at least, the quality of social interaction seems as important as its foundation in right and justice when it comes to evaluating a policy.

* * *

The majority press, then, rejects job quotas as a betrayal of tradition, a sin against history, and a threat to the quality of social life. But the main locus of the debate has been the ideals and values which the enforcement of quotas would jeopardize, and among these equal opportunity, which is often presented as the victim of a Manichean contest [8]. The concept is never defined directly : instead it emerges from the evocation of what threatens it. The danger in the majority's view is threefold : it lies in the possibility that unqualified applicants get jobs to the detriment of qualified ones, in the advantage given to groups, and in the disregard of individual rights.

The adversaries of quotas feel that, as a result of preferential hiring on the basis of ethnicity or historical disadvantage, in arbitrary proportions and without reference to normal tests, «standards of merit and achievement are bound to be eroded» (AMER 2). Government officials have done their best to answer the charge, but the opposition to «the hiring of unqualified persons for irrelevant reasons» (NYTM) persisted, pointing at the importance of merit as a basis for recruitment and as an index of status in a society that from the start vowed to do away with classes and privileges. Not surprisingly, the most articulate discussion of merit, and its warmest apology are to be found in *Commentary*, not only because historically «the merit system has been good to America's Jews» (NYTM), but because it offers a safeguard against arbitrary preference and discrimination. But the ideal of a meritocracy is also revered because it has deep roots in the American past, in Jefferson's celebrated distinction between «an artificial aristocracy founded on wealth and birth» and a «natural aristocracy [characterized by] virtue and talents» [9]. Confident that the people would naturally be able to separate the wheat from the chaff in the electoral process, Jefferson had devoted his greatest efforts to social measures that would guarantee equal opportunity. To this effect, he had abolished the laws of primogeniture and entail, and drafted plans for free, universal education. While his infringements of the estate-owners' right to dispose of their property apparently created no great unrest, the education laws that were to ensure the predominance of achieved over ascribed status failed to be be passed in his own days.

Hardly anyone to-day claims that the merit system is still alive in the political field, or that it ever was completely enforced in the social field. The spoils system, the practice of «apportioning jobs by political clout» (NYTM), the representation of regions and groups on the Supreme Court and on the Cabinet, which is even deemed «right and traditional» (NR 2), the admission of workers into unions on the basis of family connections, have given the lie to the ideal. Yet the recognition that «countervailing tendencies» (CY 6) exist, or even that «[we] have never had a true meritocracy» (AMER) does not preclude the use of the «merit» argument against quotas : the defense of the merit principle sometimes links up with a concern for the actual quality of the work performed by the beneficiaries of job quotas, especially in the field of education, but the reference to «the traditional value of measuring a person on the basis of ability» [10] also functions at times as a mere incantation. If the meritocratic ideal retains such a powerful hold, despite obvious shortcomings in its implementation, the reason may be that, aside from being the best theoretical defence against privilege, it finds reinforcement in the ideology that has guided the economic and social development of the United States, especially in the Puritan work ethic and the darwinistic notion of competition. An undercurrent of this competitive ethos runs through the following comment on the San Francisco case [11] where, according to Earl Raab,

> It was no longer a matter of giving members of a disadvantaged group an edge in the process of competition, here it became a matter of eliminating competition altogether. It was not a matter of affirmative action toward equal opportunity, but a matter of eliminating equal opportunity altogether. (CY 1)

The link that is thus established between equal opportunity and competition, or the warning that

> In a society in which men expect to succeed by hard work and to better themselves by making themselves better, a society in which (...) for some groups the expectation has begun to be fully met, it is no trivial moral wrong to now proceed to defeat it. (NR 2)

bear the stamp of nineteenth-century apologies of individual striving. Here too, hard work is more than a path to economic success ; it is a means of moral improvement as well as a source of gratification. Here too, self-reliance (pulling oneself up by one's own bootstraps ?) appears preferable to compensatory treatment which «denies minority group members who have made it on their own the satisfaction of knowing that» (F), and the argument that a strict quota system amounts to «a social welfare program, pure and simple» (CY 1) carries an implicit condemnation of anything that interferes with the laws of competition.

The strain of individualism that underlies Jefferson's philosophy and the competitive ethos also appears in the refusal to consider people as members of groups, in the argument that «people are not to be judged on the basis of their race, religion, or place of grandfather's origin» (NYTM) — an argument that applies to minorities as well as to whites. To grant minorities preferential treatment on the basis of group membership is «demeaning and paternalistic» (NSWK), a return to «the vice of stereotyping» (AMER 1), it is psychologically hurtful. But it is also a moral crime, an injustice to «the white male applicant who ... is rejected for the sole reason that he is the wrong color or sex» (NR2). The shift from «No discrimination to individuals (...) to fair shares for groups» (CY4) is viewed as a perversion of the concept of equal opportunity and of the American creed which recognizes the primacy of the individual ; and the anxiety that ensues is shared even by unions whose very existence springs from the recognition that the individual is powerless in the economic world. Group definitions appear inadequate because they entail inevitable distortions of reality (not all blacks are disadvantaged, not all whites are privileged), but they are above all dangerous. The assignment of group labels that goes with a quota policy revives an old fear of «group animosities» (NYTM) and «polarization into racial and ethnic blocs» (AMER 1), a danger against which every generation of immigrants has probably been warned with words similar to those used by Woodrow Wilson :

> You cannot become thorough Americans if you think of yourselves in groups. America does not consist of groups. A man who thinks of himself as belonging to a particular national group in America has not yet become an American. (...) The man who seeks to divide man from man, group from group, interest from interest in this great Union is striking at its very heart. [12]

The insistence that «America does not consist of groups», here, is intended to safeguard social harmony, rather than national unity as was the case in Wilson's time. But the implication that American history was made by individuals carries with it the corollary that in strict justice no compensation or retribution is possible :

> Since each individual has basic rights to equality of treatment in the public
> sector (...) the past sins of some other individuals of one's group do not
> outstrip this particular person from his basic rights. Ideally at least, in
> democratic theory, there are no minorities or second class citizens. (AMER 1)

Neither a kind of responsibility for the past, nor a sense of
solidarity with a group can detract from the individual's enjoyment
of his rights. Nor indeed should government's intervention in
social matters interfere with these rights. The vision of «minor
officials issuing ultimata while crocodile tears flow from the gimlet
eyes of HEW investigators who observe [the universities'
sufferings] from distant federal offices» (CY3), and the constant
reviling, throughout the articles, of the equal opportunity
«bureaucracy» remind one of Hoover's somewhat hysterical
strictures against a bureaucracy «ever desirous of spreading its
influence and its power» and whose growth «poisons the very roots
of liberalism — that is political equality, free speech, free press,
and equality of opportunity.» [13]

If one takes individual rights as an absolute — as indeed all the
opponents of quotas do — there is no logical way out of the
impossibility of discriminating in favor of blacks without
discriminating against some whites, except perhaps by questioning
the real nature and validity of the whites' «rights», as does this
paper of the Human Rights Commission of the City of New York :

> The majority has for too long enjoyed an advantage of its own, based on the
> discriminatory exclusion of another group. What is lost therefore, to the
> majority, is not a right but an expectation of benefits flowing from illegal
> practices and systems, to which the majority class was never entitled in the
> first place. (NYTM)

Short of this radical attempt by proponents of the minority
viewpoint to re-interpret history, nothing can provide a suitable
base from which to assail the majority's arguments.

*
* *

In its content, the ideology which the opponents of quotas
invoke is indeed one that has deep roots in the American past : the
ideal of an open society where equality of rights guarantees
equality of opportunity, and where the elite imposes itself by virtue
of its talents dates from the very birth of the country. And no one
to-day, even among the minorities, questions this ideal. Vernon
Jordan, speaking for blacks, makes it clear that «[they] have no

quarrel with the merit system nor with the concept that rigid numerical quotas that overlook individual differences and attributes are wrong» and that «[they] have no commitment to incompetence.» [14] The consensus on the vision of society that underlies much of the discussion is perhaps more surprising : the view that society is primarily a collection of individuals, with the corollaries that «groups» should not be recognized and that government should not intervene in what remains a species of individual interaction, seems to conflict with the existence of trade unions as active lobbyists or as bargaining agents. This may account for the fact that labor's opposition to quotas tends to be pragmatic rather than ideological, and to focus on the soundness and efficiency of the plans. We can easily understand that Jews, who have suffered from discrimination as a group, should object to a return to group labels. Where all liberals, however, depart from a «traditional» position is in their opposition to government intervention. The «laissez-faire» tendency in politics has usually been more characteristic of Republicans and conservatives than of Democrats and Liberals, and in the last forty years at least, the government has often initiated trends that were later to spread to the private sector, and that benefited labor and minorities.

If the ideology is «traditional», the way it is marshalled to the defense of equal opportunity calls for several remarks. To label an ideal as «traditional», in a country where institutions derive their prestige from their stability, can only increase its appeal ; on the other hand, the implicit assumption seems to be that the function of history (or tradition) is not only to account for the past but to offer guidelines for the future, to point at the direction in which society must be moving. But in the debate we have studied, these two functions are divorced. To use the distinction suggested by Warren I. Susman, between myths which «propose fundamental goals» and history which «defines and illuminates basic processes involved in achieving goals» [15], history functions here as a myth, or a Utopian vision. It does not account for actual facts : the claim that American society does not consist of groups, among others, is irreconcilable with the actual processes by which nativist movements between 1880 and 1920 pressed for restrictive immigration laws that dealt with aliens as groups. One of the differences between the minority and majority positions is that minorities are concerned with actual historical processes. They point out, for instance that «black people have been subjected to a quota system» and «reject the suggestion that a merit system is actually in operation to-day.» [16] Again, while the majority trusts that the historical process will eventually lead to a state of harmony and consensus, the minority holds, with the late President Johnson, that «we must overcome unequal history before we overcome unequal opportunity.» [17] Even though labor and the Jews are often less inclined than the rest of the Establishment press to overlook the damaging effects of past policies, all three groups still maintain the primacy of «sacred» or inalienable rights over the claims of «unequal history».

As we noted earlier, the majority also differs from the minority in choosing to stand on ideological ground. Yet the ideological discussion veils but cannot conceal completely the conflict of political or economic interests : labor makes political good of Nixon's attacks on the building trade unions, by turning them back against him and suggesting that he is in fact attempting to cover his own retreat from the fight for civil rights. Economic concerns are even more perceptible, even though anxious references to the shrinking economic pie usually appear only at the end of discussions on quotas, as a mere additional argument against the latter. Yet where no interests are threatened — or where they are determining — no ideological defence is needed : businessmen, who are well-equipped as a group to exert pressure on the government if needed, are shown to enforce quotas with a kind of fatalistic zeal, and hardly any qualms of conscience : «Contractors are encouraged to assume that they are under-utilizing women and minorities, and accordingly they have goals and timetables everywhere.» (F) One might compare this submissiveness with the business leaders' opposition to restrictive immigration quotas in the twenties. Complex discussions over the morality of means and ends also fail to obscure the fact that the majority is trying to preserve a status quo : thus labor favors plans that «do not disrupt the normal procedures and practices of the construction industry.» (CP) Adequate remedies are those which «apply pressure without too much precision» [18], and affirmative action programs «should be pushed as far as the traffic will bear at any given time.» (CY 1) This eminently pragmatic suggestion contrasts with the frequent invocation of ideals, and other signs of strain between professions and practice appear when whites admit to some anxiety at the prospect of increased competition [19] or when Jewish editors advocate a return to thinking in terms of group interests (cf CY 2).

Paradoxically the attempt of those who oppose quotas to do so in the name of tradition and to trace a continuity between past and present brings to light several signs of change. The emphasis, in equal opportunity, has shifted from a removal of discriminatory barriers (Jefferson's attempt) to a preservation of individual rights — a posture which is defensive and static rather than dynamic and affirmative. The liberalism that had united whites, Jews and labor in the sixties now appears as a lost cause or a slightly affected pose [20], and the coalition has collapsed. If it is true that «the great chapters in [American] history have been written by those who tried to improve the lot of other and all Americans» [21] and not by those who fought for themselves, a new chapter is to be started, with blacks fighting to «drive that bus» in which they have just been allowed to ride [22]. Meanwhile, historians like D.J. Boorstin will be there to remind us that «the direction of [our] history was never to give power to minorities.» [23]

NOTES

1. e.g. the National Council of Jewish Women, the Union of American Hebrew Congregations, and the «progressive» magazine **Jewish Currents.**

2. See below the list of articles consulted. In the text, these will be referred to by the initials that follow the date of articles.

3. **Ebony** for instance, mentions affirmative action measures in the course of an historical article on «the Black Worker from 1890 to the present» (July 1972)

4. e.g. «More on Quotas», **Jewish Currents,** Feb. 1973.

5. Spiro AGNEW, acceptance speech for the Vice Presidency, Aug. 23, 1972.

6. H.S. COMMAGER, «Democracy and Judicial Review» in **Freedom and Order,** New York, Braziller, 1966, p. 12.

7. Other frequently mentioned decisions include : Shelley vs Kraemer, Mc Laughlin vs Florida, Griggs vs Duke Power Co, and the due process and fair procedures decisions of the Warren Court.

8. cf Daniel Seligman : «How Equal Opportunity turned into Employment Quotas», **Fortune,** March 1973.

9. Thomas JEFFERSON, Letter to John Adams, 1813.

10. Richard NIXON, Labor Day Address, 1972, quoted in T.

11. E. Raab refers to the stand taken by the San Francisco School Board when it decided to demote 71 persons : the Board planned to demote only white administrators. In fact the plan was never carried through. cf CY 1

12. W. WILSON, speech pronounced at a naturalization ceremony, reprinted in Max J. HERTZBERG (ed), **This America,** New York, Pocket Books, 1950, pp. 78-81.

13. Herbert HOOVER, New York City Speech, in **«The New Day : Campaign Speeches of Herbert Hoover»,** Stanford University Press, 1928.

14. Vernon E. JORDAN : «the Black and Jewish Communities : the Quota System», a speech delivered at Annual Meeting, Atlanta Chapter, American Jewish Committee, Atlanta, Georgia, June 2, 1974.

15. Warren I. SUSMAN : «History and the American Intellectual : Uses of a usable past» in **The American Experience,** ed. by Hennig COHEN, Boston, Houghton Mifflin, 1968, p. 87.

16. Vernon E. JORDAN, **op. cit.**

17. quoted by Vernon E. Jordan, **ibid.**

18. Nathan GLAZER, quoted in NSWK.

19. cf «Quotas at A.T&T», **Time,** Oct 2, 1972.

20. Paul Seabury in CY 6 refers to «us beleaguered liberals», and Milton Himmelfarb, in CY 2 notes that «the current liberal-to-radical thing is to be for quotas».

21. Daniel J. BOORSTIN : **Democracy and its discontents,** Ch VI, p. 59.

22. Vernon E. JORDAN : speech delivered at the AFL . CIO Convention Nov 22, 1971.

23. BOORSTIN, **ibid.,** p. 57.

268

BIBLIOGRAPHY

a) Labor Statements :

«Labor and Equal Rights», Resolution on Civil Rights adopted by the 7th AFL.CIO convention, Dec. 1967. LER.
«Civil Rights», Resolution adopted by the 8th AFL.CIO Convention, Oct 1969. CR 1.
«The Chicago Plan», Jan. 1970. CP.
«The AFL.CIO and Civil Rights», Report of the AFL.CIO executive to the 10th Convention, Nov. 1973, CR 2.
«Brief for the AFL.CIO as Amicus Curiae in De Funis vs Odegaard», Supreme Court of the United States, October Term 1973. AC.

b) articles from Commentary (organ of the American Jewish Committee) : Earl RAAB : «Quotas by any other Name., Jan. 1972. CY 1.
Norman PODHORETZ : «Is is good for the Jew ?», Feb. 1972, CY 2.
Paul SEABURY : «HEW and the Universities», Feb. 1972. CY 3.
Milton HIMMELFARB : «Mc Govern and the Jews», Sept. 1972. CY 4.
Elliott ABRAMS : «The Quota Commission», Oct. 1972. CY 5.
Paul SEABURY : «The Idea of Merit», Dec. 1972. CY 6.

c) articles from other periodicals :

«The Philadelphia Plan is Valid», **Monthly Labor Review,** Sept. 1971, MLR 1.
«Removing Roadblacks to Minority Hiring», **Monthly Labor Review** April 1972, MLR 2.
«Politics May Kill Quotas for Hiring», **Business Week**, Sept. 9, 1972, BW 1.
«The Return of the Quota System», **New York Times Magazine**, Sept. 10, 1972. NYTM.
«Quotas : the Sleeper Issue of 1972 ?», **Newsweek**, Sept. 18. 1972. NSWK.
«Quarrel over Quotas», **Time**, Oct. 9, 1972. T.
«The Quota Controversy», **New Republic**, Oct. 21, 1972. NR 1.
«More on Quotas», **New Republic**, Oct. 28, 1972. NR 2.
«Job Quotas for Minorities», **America,** Dec. 30, 1972. AMER 1.
«How Equal Opportunity turned into Employment Quotas», **Fortune**, March 1973, F.
«Law School Minorities : What Price Admissions ?», **America**, Apr. 28, 1973. AMER 2.
«The Snags in Trying to get Minorities Hired», **Business Week**, Dec. 1. 1973. BW 2.

NOTE ON CONTRIBUTORS

Liliane BLARY, *Assistant* at the University of Lille III is working on a study of Claude McKay.

Rachel BLAU DUPLESSIS has taught at the University of Lille III and is now *Assistant-Professor* at Temple University, Philadelphia. She has written on Pound, W.C. Williams and Albee.

Pierre DENAIN, *Assistant* at the University of Lille III is co-author of *Protest U.S.A.*, Paris : Masson, 1972. He is now at work on a study of Booker T. Washington.

Régis DURAND, *Maître de Conférences* at Lille III has published several articles on 20th century American fiction and drama. He is currently editing *Etudes Canadiennes*, an interdisciplinary bulletin of Canadian studies in France.

Michel FABRE, *Professor* at the University of Paris III (Sorbonne Nouvelle) is the author of *Les Noirs Américains* (1966), *The Unfinished Quest of Richard Wright* (New York : William Morrow, 1973) and numerous articles. He is currently working on relations between Afro-American intellectuals and the French-speaking world.

Kathleen HULLEY, is *Maître de Conférences Associé* at the University of Lille III. Her field is modern American and British literature.

Bernard JACQUIN, *Maître-Assistant* at Lille III works on L.P. Hartley and is an expert in Afro-American music.

Monique LECOMTE *Maître-Assistant* at Lille III is co-author of *Protest U.S.A.* and is currently studying relations between ethnic groups in the U.S.A.

Jean-Philippe LECOURT, *Maître-Assistant* at the University of Lille III, is working on Theodore Roethke.

Jean-Michel RABATE, *Assistant* at the University of Dijon, is working on intertextuality in Joyce, Pound and H. Broch. He has published an article on *Finnegans Wake* in *Poétique 17*, and often translates articles for the same journal.

Catherine RIHOIT, *Assistant* at the University of Paris IV is interested in linguistic criticism. Her essay on James, «Waiting for Isabel» appeared in *Studies in English Grammar,* Presses Universitaires de Lille III, and she is co-author of *Le Commentaire Grammatical des Textes Anglais,* 1976.

Alain SOLARD, *Assistant* at the University of Lille III, is writing a study of Jean Toomer.

Roland TISSOT, *Maître-Assistant* at the University of Lyon III specializes in American art. His book, *Peinture and Sculpture aux Etats-Unis,* was published by A. Colin in 1973.

CENTRE D'ETUDES ET DE RECHERCHES NORD-AMERICAINES ET CANADIENNES

U.E.R. ANGELLIER
UNIVERSITE DE LILLE III
59650 VILLENEUVE D'ASCQ

BUREAU : Régis DURAND (Directeur) ; Monique LECOMTE (Directeur-Adjoint) ; Pierre DENAIN (Trésorier) ; Jean-Philippe LECOURT (Secrétaire)

MEMBRES : L. Blary (Lille III ; A. Bourgois (Lille III) ; J.-F. Egéa (Amiens) ; M. Fabre (Paris III) ; K. Hulley (Lille III) ; B. Jacquin (Lille III) ; A. Kaspi (Lille III) ; A. LeVot (Paris III) ; A. Solard (Lille III) ; P. Spriet (Bordeaux III) ; C. Thomas (Lille III).

ACTIVITES : Le Centre organise des conférences et des rencontres, ainsi qu'un séminaire qui en 1976 et 1977 portera sur la représentation et les discours de la violence dans la culture américaine contemporaine (approche pluridisciplinaire.

PUBLICATIONS : Le Centre publie chaque année, dans toute la mesure du possible, un cahier d'études américaines. Le prochain numéro, à paraître en 1976, portera sur «Le discours de la violence dans la culture américaine contemporaine». Le Centre publie en outre une fois l'an, en association avec l'Université de Bordeaux III, ETUDES CANADIENNES, Bulletin interdisciplinaire des études canadiennes en France. Les articles paraissent en anglais ou en français.
Pour être tenu au courant de nos activités et publications, et recevoir gratuitement ETUDES CANADIENNES, renvoyez-nous la fiche ci-dessous :

_____

NOM : ....

UNIVERSITE : ....

ADRESSE : ....

M. BARUCH, N. CLEMESSY, C. COLONGE, J. COVO, L.F. DIAZ LARIOS, M. FLOURET, M. MEYER C. MINGUET, R. PAGEARD, J. PENOT, E.J. RODGERS, *Nationalisme et Comospolitisme dans les littératures ibériques au XIXe siècle.*

COLLOQUE INTERNATIONAL DE L'UNIVERSITE DE LILLE III — Janvier-Mai 1972, *Les Langages, le Sens et l'Histoire.*

A. LOTTIN, J.R. MACHUELLE, S. MALOLEPSY, K. PASQUIER, G. SAVELON, *La désunion du couple sous l'Ancien Régime – l'Exemple du Nord.*

Ysabel DE ANDIA, *Présence et Eschatologie dans la pensée de Martin Heidegger.*

Communications au Colloque tenu au CIRSH les 30 et 31 mai 1975, *Une région en mutation : Le Nord –Pas-de-Calais.*

Société d'Etudes Romantiques, Centre de Recherche spécialisée, Lettres, Art, Pensée, XIXe siècle, *Intime, Intimité, Intimisme.*

Félix-Paul CODACCIONI, *De l'inégalité sociale dans une grande ville industrielle. Le drame de Lille de 1850 à 1914.*

Centre de Recherches sur le XVIIIe siècle Britannique, P.G. BOUCE, R. COSTA DE BEAUREGARD, P. DENIZOT, J.C. DUPAS, J. GURY, G. LAMOINE, D. LEVIER, M. MONTABRUT, F. MOREUX, C. TOURNEBIZE, Michèle Plaisant, Editor, *L'excentricité en Grande-Bretagne au 18e siècle.*

ACHEVE D'IMPRIMER
SUR LES PRESSES DE L'UNIVERSITE DE LILLE III

Dépôt légal : 1er trimestre 1976   N^O d'édition : 705